The Critical Heritage Series

· SCHOCKEN BOOKS ·

New York

The Wizard of OZ

by L. Frank Baum
with pictures by W. W. Denslow

· Michael Patrick Hearn ·

EDITOR

For Fred M. Meyer

M.P.H.

First published by Schocken Books 1983
10 9 8 7 6 5 4 3 2 1   83 84 85 86
Copyright © 1983 by Michael Patrick Hearn
All rights reserved

Library of Congress Cataloging in Publication Data

Baum, L. Frank (Lyman Frank), 1856–1919.
The wizard of Oz.

(The Critical heritage series)
1. Baum, L. Frank (Lyman Frank), 1856–1919.
Wizard of Oz—Addresses, essays, lectures.
I. Denslow, W. W. (William Wallace), 1856–1915.
II. Hearn, Michael Patrick. III. Title.
IV. Series: Critical heritage series (New York, N.Y.)
PS3503.A923W59 1983   813'.4   82–16953

Designed by Jane Byers Bierhorst
Manufactured in the United States of America
ISBN 0–8052–3812–3

Contents

Librarians and Oz

Current Criticism

· Preface ·

L. Frank Baum would have been surprised by all the controversy his fairy tale *The Wizard of Oz* has inspired since its publication in 1900. Gentle Baum said in his introduction to the book that his sole purpose in writing it was to please the children of his day. Indeed it did, but often to the protests of their elders. Certainly no other American children's book of the twentieth century has been more widely disputed than has the first of the famous Oz books. But one can safely say today that the story has survived beyond being just a classic of juvenile literature to having entered American folklore. No child (not even he or she who has never read the book nor seen the famous motion picture) can grow up in the United States ignorant of Dorothy, the Scarecrow, the Tin Woodman, and the Cowardly Lion.

Nothing Baum had previously done anticipated the originality of *The Wizard of Oz*. Playwright, job printer, chicken farmer, axle grease manufacturer, dry goods store owner, newspaper editor, crockery salesman, Baum succeeded at nothing until he began to place the little stories and verses he had told his own four sons at bedtime. His reputation as a children's book author was not established until he was past forty, in 1897, with the publication of *Mother Goose in Prose*, a collection of fairy-tale elaborations of classic nursery rhymes. Unfortunately the book was an artistic, but not a financial, success; and except that the last story in the volume, "Little Bun Rabbit," introduced another Dorothy as its heroine, *Mother Goose in Prose* is remembered primarily for being the first book illustrated by Maxfield Parrish. However, Baum's second effort, *Father Goose, His Book*, a bright picture book of his nonsense verse boldly illustrated by the newspaper cartoonist W. W. Denslow, was the bestselling juvenile of 1899.

In part to prove that *Father Goose* was not just a freak success, Baum followed that book with several clever new titles for 1900, the most ambitious being his "modernized fairy tale" *The Wonderful Wizard of Oz*. This work, also illustrated by Denslow, became the bestselling children's book of the year. The press was ecstatic. At once seduced by the novelty of a fantasy woven from commonplace American materials, the reviewers also recognized *The Wizard of Oz* as a significant contribution to fairy lore and a worthy successor to *Alice in Wonderland*. Some even realized that in Baum's attempt to eliminate all horrible and blood-curdling incidents from his wonder tale, *The Wizard of Oz* introduced a revolutionary attitude toward literature for American girls and boys.

Because of the great popularity of *The Wizard of Oz*, Baum decided to devote the rest of his life to the writing of children's books. With the large sales of his early efforts came the luxury of his being able to publish whatever caught his unique fancy, and he was determined to test both the novel and the traditional in his subsequent wonder tales. In addition to considerable teenage fiction and several adult novels published pseudonymously, Baum produced "American fairy tales," "old-fashioned fairy tales," "animal fairy tales," "nature fairy tales"—but the children would have none of these. All they wanted was "more about Oz." Only reluctantly, after a hit musical of *The Wizard of Oz* demanded a sequel, did Baum publish *The Marvelous Land of Oz* (1904). He continued to meet the demands of his young readers until the sixth in the series, *The Emerald City of Oz* (1910), in which he cut off the Land of Oz from the rest of the world with a Barrier of Invisibility. He said he had other things to write, not only other kinds of children's books but also other plays; he never did repeat the success of *The Wizard of Oz* musical, and he eventually drifted into the infant motion picture industry with disastrous results. Two of his later works *The Sea Fairies* (1911) and *Sky Island* (1912) are among his finest fairy tales, but they did not gain the sales of the Oz books. Baum could no more destroy Oz than Sir Arthur Conan Doyle could kill Sherlock Holmes, and so, with *The Patchwork Girl of Oz* (1913), Baum returned to his American fairyland and wrote a new volume a year until his death in 1919. The finding of a new Oz book under the Christmas tree became an annual national tradition; and on Baum's death, *The New York Times* published an editorial acknowledging the loss of an American original.

But the Oz series did not end with the death of its "Royal Historian." The publishers, Reilly & Lee, contracted with the author's widow to issue further volumes "founded on and continuing the Oz stories by L. Frank Baum," written by Ruth Plumly Thompson, John R. Neill, and others. A whole generation of boys and girls had grown up since the first of Baum's fourteen Oz books had been published, and in maturity several now acknowledged the pleasure Baum's work had given them in their childhoods. Edward Wagenknecht in his autobiography *As Far As Yesterday* (Norman, Okla.: University of Oklahoma Press, 1968) has explained the significance of *The Wizard of Oz* during his early years: "Not only did it bring me unbounded delight; it also showed me what I wished to do with my life. From the time I encountered it, at the age of six, I knew I must become a writer" (p. 152). Consequently Dr. Wagenknecht wrote *Utopia Americana* (1929), the first critical study of the Oz books. Likewise James Thurber wrote an early appreciation of

Baum, "The Wizard of Chittenango" (*The New Republic*, December 12, 1934).

However, just as the critical recognition of Baum's work was beginning, the books were no longer available in many of the children's libraries across the country. When Anne Carroll Moore removed the Oz series from the Children's Room of the New York Public Library, her colleagues followed her example. No explanation was given for this "ban" of Oz books. Even when Ruth Plumly Thompson confronted Miss Moore at a publishing party in New York, the librarian refused to say in public why she disliked the Oz books; she invited Miss Thompson to lunch to discuss the matter, but she would admit nothing at that press reception.

Similarly, the acknowledged children's literature critics of the time remained silent. What they would not attack, they just ignored. Neither Baum nor *The Wizard of Oz* was even mentioned in first editions of the two standard library school textbooks: *A Critical History of Children's Literature* (1953), edited by Cornelia Meigs; and May Hill Arbuthnot's *Children and Books* (1947). One of the few who did speak out about the Oz books was Edward Eager, author of several contemporary fantasies admired by children's book specialists. Writing in "A Father's Minority Report" (*The Horn Book*, March 1948), Eager admitted that *The Wizard of Oz*, *The Land of Oz*, and *Ozma of Oz* had "a certain homely American charm which in a way compensates for their lack of literary distinction. As L. Frank Baum continued to expand the series, his writing deteriorated, and some of his later books really typify all one doesn't like about the America of the World War One period" (p. 108). This was peculiar criticism from a writer who, lacking in invention, "borrowed" incidents not only from E. Nesbit's stories but also from Baum's in his own undistinguished fantasy tales.

Eager did touch on certain prejudices then current with the library profession. All series are bad. Nevertheless most children's rooms stocked the Peter Rabbit and the Little House Books, but not the Oz series. The Oz books are poorly written. But if quality of literary style were reason to ban books, then certainly most library shelves would have to be stripped. Perhaps the reason was political: In an attempt "to make good-natured fun of those who constantly see Red where no Red is," Stewart Robb suggested in "The Red Wizard of Oz" (*New Masses*, October 4, 1934), "Good heavens! The land of Oz is a fairyland run on Communistic lines, and is perhaps the only Communistic fairyland in all of children's literature" (p. 8). This tongue-in-cheek assertion that Baum was a Marxist subversive persists as in Anne Pellowski's objection, in "Old and New Sexual Messages in Fairy Tales" (*Wilson Library*

Bulletin, October 1971), to telling boys and girls about the author of *The Wizard of Oz* because of "the alleged Communist activities of L. Frank Baum" (p. 164). Oddly, in 1939, when Alexander Volkov was translating *The Wizard of Oz* into Russian, he said he had to rewrite much of the story to remove "the bourgeois morality typical of Anglo-Saxon literature" that he encountered in Baum's original text. But Red is in the eye of the beholder. When the editors of *Collier's*, in "45 Years of *The Wizard*" (February 9, 1946), tried to explain the perennial charm of Baum's book, they defined the point of this children's story as "Don't believe in the big, bad wolf. . . . Don't be overawed by people who talk big. . . . Dig out the facts for yourself. . . . Don't depend on hearsay and propaganda." The editorial continued, "It was that attitude, if you'll pardon a bit of flag-waving, that did much to make this country great. The latest achievement to its credit was that it kept us from being intimidated by Messrs. Hitler and Tojo when they were riding their highest and widest, and inspired us in due time to step up and contribute heavily to the slapping of them down. Let's just hang onto that realistic, inquiring, skeptical and fearless attitude of mind. It's a precious national asset" (p. 86).

The release of the lavish MGM musical film of *The Wizard of Oz* in 1939 did nothing to change the situation with the librarians. Apparently these children's book specialists hated Hollywood as much as Oz; after all, those who damned Walt Disney's *Snow White* could hardly be expected to like the Technicolor *Wizard of Oz*. Nevertheless, despite the librarians, *The Wizard of Oz* continued to sell, and by 1950 it was said to be not only *the* bestselling American *juvenile* of the last fifty years but one of the top-selling books of the twentieth century. The approaching centennial of the birth of the author of *The Wizard of Oz* demanded a reevaluation of Baum's contribution to American literature. In 1956 Roland S. Baughman, head of Special Collections at Columbia University Libraries and one of the pioneers in Baum bibliography, mounted the first retrospective exhibition of the work of L. Frank Baum. The following year Michigan State University Press at East Lansing published *The Wizard of Oz and Who He Was*, with erudite essays by Martin Gardner and the Pulitzer Prize–winning historian Russel B. Nye. While other tributes were published throughout the country, the press was astonished that while several of the country's leading universities were paying homage to Baum, *The Wizard of Oz* was "banned" from many children's libraries.

The increasing pressure from Baum's defenders demanded some clarification of exactly what about *The Wizard of Oz* so offended the librarians. One could no longer merely overlook Baum's work. Ruth Hill

Viguers now revised her chapter "Golden Years and Time of Tumult" in the 1969 edition of *A Critical History of Children's Literature:* "Had L. Frank Baum possessed stylistic genius along with his lively imagination, he might have succeeded in being the first American to write great fantasy for children. But, inventive though it was, *The Wizard of Oz* (1900) was told in such lifeless prose that rereading it in adulthood is a disappointment. Because there is no grace in the style, no subtlety in the storytelling to give conviction to the fantastic people and incidents, it lost nothing in translation to the screen. It is probably one of the few children's books to be successfully filmed" (p. 412). Similarly, Mary F. Thwaite in *From Primer to Pleasure in Reading* (Boston: The Horn Book, 1972) pooh-poohed *The Wizard of Oz* as "a book which has won much fame at home and abroad, more so than it deserves and largely through its stage and screen presentations" (p. 238). And Zena Sutherland in her revision of Arbuthnot's *Children and Books* skirted the issue of the series' worth under "Books That Stir Controversy" by explaining that "many authorities in the field of children's literature feel that the style is flat and dull, and that the inventiveness of the first book was followed by mediocrity and repetition in subsequent volumes." The English critic John Rowe Townsend in *Written for Children* (Philadelphia: J. B. Lippincott, 1974) struggled with these criticisms: He suspected that they expressed some unconscious eastern snobbery against Baum's midwestern fairy tale and concluded, "Yet to an outsider it seems that the unabashed Americanness of the Oz books makes them all the more original and attractive" (pp. 109–110).

Perhaps the most damning criticism came from the director of the Detroit library system, who in 1957 confessed that he kept the Oz books out of the circulating collections and was proud of it. He argued that they are of "no value," possess "a cowardly approach to life," promote "negativism," and when compared to the Grimm and Andersen tales, there is "nothing uplifting or elevating about the Baum series." He said the public preferred how-to books to wonder tales anyway. And these attitudes were then prevalent among most librarians and educators. "Magic has no place in children's books any more," Shirley Jackson explained in "The Lost Kingdom of Oz" (*The Reporter*, December 10, 1959); "*facts* are what children are supposed to be reading. The old favorites are being slowly frozen out, suppressed—and in some cases deliberately—by grave people who believe that reading and learning are inseparable. . . . Ten minutes in the children's department of any bookstore will demonstrate clearly that our children are being brutally cheated" (p. 42). And still the Oz books endured.

In part as an answer to Baum's critics, the International Wizard of Oz

Club, Inc., was founded in 1957 by a group of writers, artists, rare-book collectors, and Oz enthusiasts in general. Their triquarterly *The Baum Bugle* has slowly evolved from a mimeographed newsletter into a reputable semi-scholarly journal, and it and the club have inmeasurably advanced the recognition of L. Frank Baum as a major American children's book author. Their efforts received an added boost with the publication in 1961 of the first full-length biography of Baum, *To Please a Child* by Frank Joslyn Baum and Russell P. MacFall, still the principal study of the author and his work.

Times change, tastes change. During the 1960s popular literature, once scorned, was now ripe for reconsideration, and fantasy in particular, whether science fiction or fairy tales, was worthy of scholarly dissertation. The Oz books were no exception. In 1973 appeared *The Annotated Wizard of Oz*, the first scholarly appraisal of the Oz books which gave current legitimacy to the study of Baum's work as literature. The following year Raylyn Moore in *Wonderful Wizard, Marvelous Land* discussed Baum's contribution to American popular culture. Books written for boys and girls were not just for children anymore: childhood classics were read in university English courses, and the Children's Literature Society had been founded in 1971 to further the study of these works. In 1976 this organization took a poll to determine which were the finest American children's books published since 1776; predictably, *The Wizard of Oz* was among the ten chosen. During the last twenty years *The Wizard of Oz* has been treated like any other influential work of American literature: it has been interpreted and reinterpreted according to nearly every current academic trend. These include the philosophical (S. J. Sackett's "The Utopia of Oz"), the sociopolitical (Henry M. Littlefield's "The Wizard of Oz: Parable of Populism"), the psychosexual (Osmond Beckwith's "The Oddness of Oz"), the feminist (Alix Kates Shulman's "Ozomania Under the Rainbow"). There have also been several perceptive appreciations by such different writers as Ray Bradbury and Gore Vidal. One may not agree with all of these disparate (and sometimes conflicting) opinions of the work, but none can deny that *The Wizard of Oz* and its many sequels have already secured a rich and varied critical heritage.

The WON-DERFUL WIZARD OF OZ

By L. Frank Baum

With Pictures by

W.W. Denslow.

Geo·M·Hill Co.
CHICAGO.
NEW YORK.

1 9 0 0

· Introduction. ·

Folk lore, legends, myths and fairy tales have followed childhood through the ages, for every healthy youngster has a wholesome and instinctive love for stories fantastic, marvelous and manifestly unreal. The winged fairies of Grimm and Andersen have brought more happiness to childish hearts than all other human creations.

Yet the old-time fairy tale, having served for generations, may now be classed as "historical" in the children's library; for the time has come for a series of newer "wonder tales" in which the stereotyped genie, dwarf and fairy are eliminated, together with all the horrible and blood-curdling incident devised by their authors to point a fearsome moral to each tale. Modern education includes morality; therefore the modern child seeks only entertainment in its wonder-tales and gladly dispenses with all disagreeable incident.

Having this thought in mind, the story of "The Wonderful Wizard of Oz" was written solely to pleasure children of today. It aspires to being a modernized fairy tale, in which the wonderment and joy are retained and the heart-aches and nightmares are left out.

L. Frank Baum.

Chicago, April, 1900.

· List of Chapters ·

*This book is dedicated to my
good friend & comrade.
My Wife*

L.F.B.

Chapter I

· The Cyclone ·

Dorothy lived in the midst of the great Kansas prairies, with Uncle Henry, who was a farmer, and Aunt Em, who was the farmer's wife. Their house was small, for the lumber to build it had to be carried by wagon many miles. There were four walls, a floor and a roof, which made one room; and this room contained a rusty looking cooking stove, a cupboard for the dishes, a table, three or four chairs, and the beds. Uncle Henry and Aunt Em had a big bed in one corner, and Dorothy a little bed in another corner. There was no garret at all, and no cellar—except a small hole, dug in the ground, called a cyclone cellar, where the family could go in case one of those great whirlwinds arose, mighty enough to crush any building in its path. It was reached by a trap-door in the middle of the floor, from which a ladder led down into the small, dark hole.

When Dorothy stood in the doorway and looked around, she could see nothing but the great gray prairie on every side. Not a tree nor a house broke the broad sweep of flat country that reached the edge of the sky in all directions. The sun had baked the plowed land into a gray mass, with little cracks running through it. Even the grass was not green, for the sun had burned the tops of the long blades until they were the same gray color to be seen everywhere. Once the house had been painted, but the sun blistered the paint and the rains washed it away, and now the house was as dull and gray as everything else.

When Aunt Em came there to live she was a young, pretty wife. The sun and wind had changed her, too. They had taken the sparkle from her eyes and left them a sober gray; they had taken the red from her cheeks and lips, and they were gray also. She was thin and gaunt, and never smiled, now. When Dorothy, who was an orphan, first came to her, Aunt Em had been so startled by the child's laughter that she would scream and press her hand upon her heart whenever Dorothy's merry voice reached her ears; and she still looked at the little girl with wonder that she could find anything to laugh at.

Uncle Henry never laughed. He worked hard from morning till night and did not know what joy was. He was gray also, from his long beard to his rough boots, and he looked stern and solemn, and rarely spoke.

It was Toto that made Dorothy laugh, and saved her from growing as gray as her other surroundings. Toto was not gray; he was a little black dog, with long, silky hair and small black eyes that twinkled merrily on either side of his funny, wee nose. Toto played all day long, and Dorothy played with him, and loved him dearly.

To-day, however, they were not playing. Uncle Henry sat upon the door-step and looked anxiously at the sky, which was even grayer than usual. Dorothy stood in the door with Toto in her arms, and looked at the sky too. Aunt Em was washing the dishes.

From the far north they heard a low wail of the wind, and Uncle Henry and Dorothy could see where the long grass bowed in waves before the coming storm. There now came a sharp whistling in the air from the south, and as they turned their eyes that way they saw ripples in the grass coming from that direction also.

Suddenly Uncle Henry stood up.

"There's a cyclone coming, Em," he called to his wife; "I'll go look after the stock." Then he ran toward the sheds where the cows and horses were kept.

Aunt Em dropped her work and came to the door. One glance told her of the danger close at hand.

"Quick, Dorothy!" she screamed; "run for the cellar!"

Toto jumped out of Dorothy's arms and hid under the bed, and the girl started to get him. Aunt Em, badly frightened, threw open the trap-door in the floor and climbed down the ladder into the small, dark hole. Dorothy caught Toto at last, and started to follow her aunt. When she was half way across the room there came a great shriek from the wind, and the house shook so hard that she lost her footing and sat down suddenly upon the floor.

A strange thing then happened.

The house whirled around two or three times and rose slowly through the air. Dorothy felt as if she were going up in a balloon.

The north and south winds met where the house stood, and made it the exact center of the cyclone. In the middle of a cyclone the air is generally still, but the great pressure of the wind on every side of the house raised it up higher and higher, until it was at the very top of the cyclone; and there it remained and was carried miles and miles away as easily as you could carry a feather.

It was very dark, and the wind howled horribly around her, but Dorothy found she was riding quite easily. After the first few whirls around, and one other time when the house tipped badly, she felt as if she were being rocked gently, like a baby in a cradle.

Toto did not like it. He ran about the room, now here, now there, barking loudly; but Dorothy sat quite still on the floor and waited to see what would happen.

Once Toto got too near the open trap-door, and fell in; and at first the little girl thought she had lost him. But soon she saw one of his ears sticking up through the hole, for the strong pressure of the air was keeping him up so that he could not fall. She crept to the hole, caught Toto by the ear, and dragged him into the room again; afterward closing the trap-door so that no more accidents could happen.

Hour after hour passed away, and slowly Dorothy got over her fright; but she felt quite lonely, and the wind shrieked so loudly all about her that she nearly became deaf. At first she had wondered if she would be dashed to pieces when the house fell again; but as the hours passed and nothing terrible happened, she stopped worrying and resolved to wait calmly and see what the future would bring. At last she crawled over the swaying floor to her bed, and lay down upon it; and Toto followed and lay down beside her.

In spite of the swaying of the house and the wailing of the wind, Dorothy soon closed her eyes and fell fast asleep.

Chapter II

· The Council with the Munchkins ·

She was awakened by a shock, so sudden and severe that if Dorothy had not been lying on the soft bed she might have been hurt. As it was, the jar made her catch her breath and wonder what had happened; and Toto put his cold little nose into her face and whined dismally. Dorothy sat up and noticed that the house was not moving; nor was it dark, for the bright sunshine came in at the window, flooding the little room. She sprang from her bed and with Toto at her heels ran and opened the door.

The little girl gave a cry of amazement and looked about her, her eyes growing bigger and bigger at the wonderful sights she saw.

The cyclone had set the house down, very gently—for a cyclone—in the midst of a country of marvelous beauty. There were lovely patches of green sward all about, with stately trees bearing rich and luscious fruits. Banks of gorgeous flowers were on every hand, and birds with rare and brilliant plumage sang and fluttered in the trees and bushes. A little way off was a

small brook, rushing and sparkling along between green banks, and murmuring in a voice very grateful to a little girl who had lived so long on the dry, gray prairies.

While she stood looking eagerly at the strange and beautiful sights, she noticed coming toward her a group of the queerest people she had ever seen. They were not as big as the grown folk she had always been used to; but neither were they very small. In fact, they seemed about as tall as Dorothy, who was a well-grown child for her age, although they were, so far as looks go, many years older.

Three were men and one a woman, and all were oddly dressed. They wore round hats that rose to a small point a foot above their heads, with little bells around the brims that tinkled sweetly as they moved. The hats of the men were blue; the little woman's hat was white, and she wore a white gown that hung in plaits from her shoulders; over it were sprinkled little stars that glistened in the sun like diamonds. The men were dressed in blue, of the same shade as their hats, and wore well polished boots with a deep roll of blue at the tops. The men, Dorothy thought, were about as old as Uncle Henry, for two of them had beards. But the little woman was doubtless much older: her face was covered with wrinkles, her hair was nearly white, and she walked rather stiffly.

When these people drew near the house where Dorothy was standing in the doorway, they paused and whispered among themselves, as if afraid to come farther. But the little old woman walked up to Dorothy, made a low bow and said, in a sweet voice,

"You are welcome, most noble Sorceress, to the land of the Munchkins. We are so grateful to you for having killed the wicked Witch of the East, and for setting our people free from bondage."

Dorothy listened to this speech with wonder. What could the little woman possibly mean by calling her a sorceress, and saying she had killed the wicked Witch of the East? Dorothy was an innocent, harmless little girl, who had been carried by a cyclone many miles from home; and she had never killed anything in all her life.

But the little woman evidently expected her to answer; so Dorothy said, with hesitation,

"You are very kind; but there must be some mistake. I have not killed anything."

"Your house did, anyway," replied the little old woman, with a laugh; "and that is the same thing. See!" she continued, pointing to the corner of the house; "there are her two toes, still sticking out from under a block of wood."

Dorothy looked, and gave a little cry of fright. There, indeed, just under the corner of the great beam the house rested on, two feet were sticking out, shod in silver shoes with pointed toes.

"Oh, dear! oh, dear!" cried Dorothy, clasping her hands together in dismay; "the house must have fallen on her. What ever shall we do?"

"There is nothing to be done," said the little woman, calmly.

"But who was she?" asked Dorothy.

"She was the wicked Witch of the East, as I said," answered the little woman. "She has held all the Munchkins in bondage for many years, making them slave for her night and day. Now they are all set free, and are grateful to you for the favour."

"Who are the Munchkins?" enquired Dorothy.

"They are the people who live in this land of the East, where the wicked Witch ruled."

"Are you a Munchkin?" asked Dorothy.

"No; but I am their friend, although I live in the land of the North. When they saw the Witch of the East was dead the Munchkins sent a swift messenger to me, and I came at once. I am the Witch of the North."

"Oh, gracious!" cried Dorothy; "are you a real witch?"

"Yes, indeed;" answered the little woman. "But I am a good witch, and the people love me. I am not as powerful as the wicked Witch was who ruled here, or I should have set the people free myself."

"But I thought all witches were wicked," said the girl, who was half frightened at facing a real witch.

"Oh, no; that is a great mistake. There were only four witches in all the Land of Oz, and two of them, those who live in the North and the South, are good witches. I know this is true, for I

am one of them myself, and cannot be mistaken. Those who dwelt in the East and the West were, indeed, wicked witches; but now that you have killed one of them, there is but one wicked Witch in all the Land of Oz—the one who lives in the West."

"But," said Dorothy, after a moment's thought, "Aunt Em has told me that the witches were all dead—years and years ago."

"Who is Aunt Em?" inquired the little old woman.

"She is my aunt who lives in Kansas, where I came from."

The Witch of the North seemed to think for a time, with her head bowed and her eyes upon the ground. Then she looked up and said,

"I do not know where Kansas is, for I have never heard that country mentioned before. But tell me, is it a civilized country?"

"Oh, yes;" replied Dorothy.

"Then that accounts for it. In the civilized countries I believe there are no witches left; nor wizards, nor sorceresses, nor magicians. But, you see, the Land of Oz has never been civilized, for we are cut off from all the rest of the world. Therefore we still have witches and wizards amongst us."

"Who are the Wizards?" asked Dorothy.

"Oz himself is the Great Wizard," answered the Witch, sinking her voice to a whisper. "He is more powerful than all the rest of us together. He lives in the City of Emeralds."

Dorothy was going to ask another question, but just then the Munchkins, who had been standing silently by, gave a loud shout and pointed to the corner of the house where the wicked Witch had been lying.

"What is it?" asked the little old woman; and looked, and began to laugh. The feet of the dead Witch had disappeared entirely and nothing was left but the silver shoes.

"She was so old," explained the Witch of the North, "that she dried up quickly in the sun. That is the end of her. But the silver shoes are yours, and you shall have them to wear." She reached down and picked up the shoes, and after shaking the dust out of them handed them to Dorothy.

"The Witch of the East was proud of those silver shoes," said one of the Munchkins; "and there is some charm connected with them; but what it is we never knew."

Dorothy carried the shoes into the house and placed them on the table. Then she came out again to the Munchkins and said,

"I am anxious to get back to my Aunt and Uncle, for I am sure they will worry about me. Can you help me find my way?"

The Munchkins and the Witch first looked at one another, and then at Dorothy, and then shook their heads.

"At the East, not far from here," said one, "there is a great desert, and none could live to cross it."

"It is the same at the South," said another, "for I have been there and seen it. The South is the country of the Quadlings."

"I am told," said the third man, "that it is the same at the West. And that country, where the Winkies live, is ruled by the wicked Witch of the West, who would make you her slave if you passed her way."

"The North is my home," said the old lady, "and at its edge is the same great desert that surrounds this land of Oz. I'm afraid, my dear, you will have to live with us."

Dorothy began to sob, at this, for she felt lonely among all these strange people. Her tears seemed to grieve the kind-hearted Munchkins, for they immediately took out their hand-kerchiefs and began to weep also. As for the little old woman, she took off her cap and balanced the point on the end of her nose, while she counted "one, two, three" in a solemn voice. At once the cap changed to a slate, on which was written in big, white chalk marks:

"LET DOROTHY GO TO THE CITY OF EMERALDS."

The little old woman took the slate from her nose, and, having read the words on it, asked,

"Is your name Dorothy, my dear?"

"Yes," answered the child, looking up and drying her tears.

"Then you must go to the City of Emeralds. Perhaps Oz will help you."

"Where is this City?" asked Dorothy.

"It is exactly in the center of the country, and is ruled by Oz, the Great Wizard I told you of."

"Is he a good man?" enquired the girl, anxiously.

"He is a good Wizard. Whether he is a man or not I cannot tell, for I have never seen him."

"How can I get there?" asked Dorothy.

"You must walk. It is a long journey, through a country that is sometimes pleasant and sometimes dark and terrible. However, I will use all the magic arts I know of to keep you from harm."

"Won't you go with me?" pleaded the girl, who had begun to look upon the little old woman as her only friend.

"No, I cannot do that," she replied; "but I will give you my kiss, and no one will dare injure a person who has been kissed by the Witch of the North."

She came close to Dorothy and kissed her gently on the forehead. Where her lips touched the girl they left a round, shining mark, as Dorothy found out soon after.

"The road to the City of Emeralds is paved with yellow brick," said the Witch; "so you cannot miss it. When you get to Oz do not be afraid of him, but tell your story and ask him to help you. Good-bye, my dear."

The three Munchkins bowed low to her and wished her a pleasant journey, after which they walked away through the trees. The Witch gave Dorothy a friendly little nod, whirled around on her left heel three times, and straight-way disappeared, much to the surprise of little Toto, who barked after her loudly enough when she was gone, because he had been afraid even to growl while she stood by.

But Dorothy, knowing her to be a witch, had expected her to disappear in just that way, and was not surprised in the least.

Chapter III

· How Dorothy Saved the Scarecrow ·

When Dorothy was left alone she began to feel hungry. So she went to the cupboard and cut herself some bread, which she spread with butter. She gave some to Toto, and taking a pail from the shelf she carried it down to the little brook and filled it with clear, sparkling water. Toto ran over to the trees and began to bark at the birds sitting there. Dorothy went to get him, and saw such delicious fruit hanging from the branches that she gathered some of it, finding it just what she wanted to help out her breakfast.

Then she went back to the house, and having helped herself and Toto to a good drink of the cool, clear water, she set about making ready for the journey to the City of Emeralds.

Dorothy had only one other dress, but that happened to be clean and was hanging on a peg beside her bed. It was gingham, with checks of white and blue; and although the blue was somewhat faded with many washings, it was still a pretty frock. The girl washed herself carefully, dressed herself in the clean gingham, and tied her pink sunbonnet on her head. She took a little basket and filled it with bread from the cupboard, laying a white cloth over the top. Then she looked down at her feet and noticed how old and worn her shoes were.

"They surely will never do for a long journey, Toto," she said. And Toto looked up into her face with his little black eyes and wagged his tail to show he knew what she meant.

At that moment Dorothy saw lying on the table the silver shoes that had belonged to the Witch of the East.

"I wonder if they will fit me," she said to Toto. "They would be just the thing to take a long walk in, for they could not wear out."

She took off her old leather shoes and tried on the silver ones, which fitted her as well as if they had been made for her.

Finally she picked up her basket.

"Come along, Toto," she said, "we will go to the Emerald City and ask the great Oz how to get back to Kansas again."

She closed the door, locked it, and put the key carefully in the pocket of her dress. And so, with Toto trotting along soberly behind her, she started on her journey.

There were several roads near by, but it did not take her long to find the one paved with yellow brick. Within a short time she was walking briskly toward the Emerald City, her silver shoes tinkling merrily on the hard, yellow roadbed. The sun shone bright and the birds sang sweet and Dorothy did not feel nearly as bad as you might think a little girl would who had been suddenly whisked away from her own country and set down in the midst of a strange land.

She was surprised, as she walked along, to see how pretty the country was about her. There were neat fences at the sides of the road, painted a dainty blue color, and beyond them were fields of grain and vegetables in abundance. Evidently the Munchkins were good farmers and able to raise large crops. Once in a while she would pass a house, and the people came out to look at her and bow low as she went by; for everyone knew she had been the means of destroying the wicked witch and setting them free from bondage. The houses of the Munchkins were odd looking dwellings, for each was round, with a big dome for a roof. All were painted blue, for in this country of the East blue was the favorite color.

Towards evening, when Dorothy was tired with her long walk and began to wonder where she should pass the night, she came to a house rather larger than the rest. On the green lawn before it many men and women were dancing. Five little fiddlers played as loudly as possible and the people were laughing and singing, while a big table near by was loaded with delicious fruits and nuts, pies and cakes, and many other good things to eat.

The people greeted Dorothy kindly, and invited her to supper and to pass the night with them; for this was the home of one of the richest Munchkins in the land, and his friends were gathered with him to celebrate their freedom from the bondage of the wicked witch.

Dorothy ate a hearty supper and was waited upon by the rich Munchkin himself, whose name was Boq. Then she sat down upon a settee and watched the people dance.

When Boq saw her silver shoes he said,

"You must be a great sorceress."

"Why?" asked the girl.

"Because you wear silver shoes and have killed the wicked witch. Besides, you have white in your frock, and only witches and sorceresses wear white."

"My dress is blue and white checked," said Dorothy, smoothing out the wrinkles in it.

"It is kind of you to wear that," said Boq. "Blue is the color of the Munchkins, and white is the witch color; so we know you are a friendly witch."

Dorothy did not know what to say to this, for all the people

seemed to think her a witch, and she knew very well she was only an ordinary little girl who had come by the chance of a cyclone into a strange land.

When she had tired watching the dancing, Boq led her into the house, where he gave her a room with a pretty bed in it. The sheets were made of blue cloth, and Dorothy slept soundly in them till morning, with Toto curled up on the blue rug beside her.

She ate a hearty breakfast, and watched a wee Munchkin baby, who played with Toto and pulled his tail and crowed and laughed in a way that greatly amused Dorothy. Toto was a fine curiosity to all the people, for they had never seen a dog before.

"How far is it to the Emerald City?" the girl asked.

"I do not know," answered Boq, gravely, "for I have never been there. It is better for people to keep away from Oz, unless they have business with him. But it is a long way to the Emerald City, and it will take you many days. The country here is rich and pleasant, but you must pass through rough and dangerous places before you reach the end of your journey."

This worried Dorothy a little, but she knew that only the great Oz could help her get to Kansas again, so she bravely resolved not to turn back.

She bade her friends good-bye, and again started along the road of yellow brick. When she had gone several miles she thought she would stop to rest, and so climbed to the top of the fence beside the road and sat down. There was a great cornfield beyond the fence, and not far away she saw a Scarecrow, placed high on a pole to keep the birds from the ripe corn.

Dorothy leaned her chin upon her hand and gazed thoughtfully at the Scarecrow. Its head was a small sack of stuffed straw, with eyes, nose and mouth painted on it to represent a face. An old, pointed blue hat, that had belonged to some Munchkin, was perched on this head, and the rest of the figure was a blue suit of clothes, worn and faded, which had also been stuffed with straw. On the feet were some old boots with blue tops, such as every man wore in this country, and the figure was raised above the stalks of corn by means of the pole stuck up its back.

While Dorothy was looking earnestly into the queer, painted face of the Scarecrow, she was surprised to see one of the eyes

slowly wink at her. She thought she must have been mistaken, at first, for none of the scarecrows in Kansas ever wink; but presently the figure nodded its head to her in a friendly way. Then she climbed down from the fence and walked up to it, while Toto ran around the pole and barked.

"Good day," said the Scarecrow, in a rather husky voice.

"Did you speak?" asked the girl, in wonder.

"Certainly," answered the Scarecrow; "how do you do?"

"I'm pretty well, thank you," replied Dorothy, politely; "how do you do?"

"I'm not feeling well," said the Scarecrow, with a smile, "for it is very tedious being perched up here night and day to scare away crows."

"Can't you get down?" asked Dorothy.

"No, for this pole is stuck up my back. If you will please take away the pole I shall be greatly obliged to you."

Dorothy reached up both arms and lifted the figure off the pole; for, being stuffed with straw, it was quite light.

"Thank you very much," said the Scarecrow, when he had been set down on the ground. "I feel like a new man."

Dorothy was puzzled at this, for it sounded queer to hear a stuffed man speak, and to see him bow and walk along beside her.

"Who are you?" asked the Scarecrow, when he had stretched himself and yawned, "and where are you going?"

"My name is Dorothy," said the girl, "and I am going to the Emerald City, to ask the great Oz to send me back to Kansas."

"Where is the Emerald City?" he enquired; "and who is Oz?"

"Why, don't you know?" she returned, in surprise.

"No, indeed; I don't know anything. You see, I am stuffed, so I have no brains at all," he answered, sadly.

"Oh," said Dorothy; "I'm awfully sorry for you."

"Do you think," he asked, "If I go to the Emerald City with you, that the great Oz would give me some brains?"

"I cannot tell," she returned; "but you may come with me, if you like. If Oz will not give you any brains you will be no worse off than you are now."

"That is true," said the Scarecrow. "You see," he continued, confidentially, "I don't mind my legs and arms and body being stuffed, because I cannot get hurt. If anyone treads on my toes or sticks a pin into me, it doesn't matter, for I can't feel it. But I do not want people to call me a fool, and if my head stays stuffed with straw instead of with brains, as yours is, how am I ever to know anything?"

"I understand how you feel," said the little girl, who was truly sorry for him. "If you will come with me I'll ask Oz to do all he can for you."

"Thank you," he answered, gratefully.

They walked back to the road, Dorothy helped him over the fence, and they started along the path of yellow brick for the Emerald City.

Toto did not like this addition to the party, at first. He smelled around the stuffed man as if he suspected there might be a nest of rats in the straw, and he often growled in an unfriendly way at the Scarecrow.

"Don't mind Toto," said Dorothy, to her new friend; "he never bites."

"Oh, I'm not afraid," replied the Scarecrow, "he can't hurt the straw. Do let me carry that basket for you. I shall not mind it, for I can't get tired. I'll tell you a secret," he continued, as he walked along; "there is only one thing in the world I am afraid of."

"What is that?" asked Dorothy; "the Munchkin farmer who made you?"

"No," answered the Scarecrow; "it's a lighted match."

Chapter IV

· The Road Through the Forest ·

After a few hours the road began to be rough, and the walking grew so difficult that the Scarecrow often stumbled over the yellow brick, which were here very uneven. Sometimes, indeed, they were broken or missing altogether, leaving holes that Toto jumped across and Dorothy walked around. As for the Scarecrow, having no brains he walked straight ahead, and so stepped into the holes and fell at full length on the hard bricks. It never hurt him, however, and Dorothy would pick him up and set him upon his feet again, while he joined her in laughing merrily at his own mishap.

The farms were not nearly so well cared for here as they were farther back. There were fewer houses and fewer trees, and the farther they went the more dismal and lonesome the country became.

At noon they sat down by the roadside, near a little brook, and Dorothy opened her basket and got out some bread. She offered a piece to the Scarecrow, but he refused.

"I am never hungry," he said; "and it is a lucky thing I am not. For my mouth is only painted, and if I should cut a hole in it so I could eat, the straw I am stuffed with would come out, and that would spoil the shape of my head."

Dorothy saw at once that this was true, so she only nodded and went on eating her bread.

"Tell me something about yourself, and the country you came from," said the Scarecrow, when she had finished her dinner. So she told him all about Kansas, and how gray everything was there, and how the cyclone had carried her to this queer land of Oz. The Scarecrow listened carefully, and said,

"I cannot understand why you should wish to leave this beautiful country and go back to the dry, gray place you call Kansas."

"That is because you have no brains," answered the girl. "No matter how dreary and gray our homes are, we people of flesh and blood would rather live there than in any other country, be it ever so beautiful. There is no place like home."

The Scarecrow sighed.

"Of course I cannot understand it," he said. "If your heads were stuffed with straw, like mine, you would probably all live in the beautiful places, and then Kansas would have no people at all. It is fortunate for Kansas that you have brains."

"Won't you tell me a story, while we are resting?" asked the child.

The Scarecrow looked at her reproachfully, and answered,

"My life has been so short that I really know nothing whatever. I was only made day before yesterday. What happened in the world before that time is all unknown to me. Luckily, when

the farmer made my head, one of the first things he did was to paint my ears, so that I heard what was going on. There was another Munchkin with him, and the first thing I heard was the farmer saying,

" 'How do you like those ears?'

" 'They aren't straight,' answered the other.

" 'Never mind,' said the farmer; 'they are ears just the same,' which was true enough.

" 'Now I'll make the eyes,' said the farmer. So he painted my right eye, and as soon as it was finished I found myself looking at him and at everything around me with a great deal of curiosity, for this was my first glimpse of the world.

" 'That's rather pretty eye,' remarked the Munchkin who was watching the farmer; 'blue paint is just the color for eyes.'

" 'I think I'll make the other a little bigger,' said the farmer; and when the second eye was done I could see much better than before. Then he made my nose and my mouth; but I did not speak, because at that time I didn't know what a mouth was for. I had the fun of watching them make my body and my arms and legs; and when they fastened on my head, at last, I felt very proud, for I thought I was just as good a man as anyone.

" 'This fellow will scare the crows fast enough,' said the farmer; 'he looks just like a man.'

" 'Why, he is a man,' said the other, and I quite agreed with him. The farmer carried me under his arm to the cornfield, and set me up on a tall stick, where you found me. He and his friend soon after walked away and left me alone.

"I did not like to be deserted this way; so I tried to walk after them, but my feet would not touch the ground, and I was forced to stay on that pole. It was a lonely life to lead, for I had nothing to think of, having been made such a little while before. Many crows and other birds flew into the cornfield, but as soon as they saw me they flew away again, thinking I was a Munchkin; and this pleased me and made me feel that I was quite an important person. By and by an old crow flew near me, and after looking at me carefully he perched upon my shoulder and said,

" 'I wonder if that farmer thought to fool me in this clumsy manner. Any crow of sense could see that you are only stuffed with straw.' Then he hopped down at my feet and ate all the corn he wanted. The other birds, seeing he was not harmed by me, came to eat the corn too, so in a short time there was a great flock of them about me.

"I felt sad at this, for it showed I was not such a good Scarecrow after all; but the old crow comforted me, saying: 'If you only had brains in your head you would be as good a man as any of them, and a better man than some of them. Brains are the only things worth having in this world, no matter whether one is a crow or a man.'

"After the crows had gone I thought this over, and decided I would try to get some brains. By good luck, you came along and pulled me off the stake, and from what you say I am sure the great Oz will give me brains as soon as we get to the Emerald City."

"I hope so," said Dorothy, earnestly, "since you seem anxious to have them."

"Oh yes; I am anxious," returned the Scarecrow. "It is such an uncomfortable feeling to know one is a fool."

"Well," said the girl, "let us go." And she handed the basket to the Scarecrow.

There were no fences at all by the road side now, and the land was rough and untilled. Towards evening they came to a great forest, where the trees grew so big and close together that their branches met over the road of yellow brick. It was almost dark under the trees, for the branches shut out the daylight; but the travellers did not stop, and went on into the forest.

"If this road goes in, it must come out," said the Scarecrow, "and as the Emerald City is at the other end of the road, we must go wherever it leads us."

"Anyone would know that," said Dorothy.

"Certainly; that is why I know it," returned the Scarecrow. "If it required brains to figure it out, I never should have said it."

After an hour or so the light faded away, and they found themselves stumbling along in the darkness. Dorothy could not see at all, but Toto could, for some dogs see very well in the dark; and the Scarecrow declared he could see as well as by day. So she took hold of his arm, and managed to get along fairly well.

"If you see any house, or any place where we can pass the

night," she said, "you must tell me; for it is very uncomfortable walking in the dark."

Soon after the Scarecrow stopped.

"I see a little cottage at the right of us," he said, "built of logs and branches. Shall we go there?"

"Yes, indeed;" answered the child. "I am all tired out."

So the Scarecrow led her through the trees until they reached the cottage, and Dorothy entered and found a bed of dried leaves in one corner. She lay down at once, and with Toto beside her soon fell into a sound sleep. The Scarecrow, who was never tired, stood up in another corner and waited patiently until morning came.

Chapter V
· The Rescue of the Tin Woodman ·

When Dorothy awoke the sun was shining through the trees and Toto had long been out chasing birds and squirrels. She sat up and looked around her. There was the Scarecrow, still standing patiently in his corner, waiting for her.

"We must go and search for water," she said to him.

"Why do you want water?" he asked.

"To wash my face clean after the dust of the road, and to drink, so the dry bread will not stick in my throat."

"It must be inconvenient to be made of flesh," said the Scarecrow, thoughtfully; "for you must sleep, and eat and drink. However, you have brains, and it is worth a lot of bother to be able to think properly."

They left the cottage and walked through the trees until they found a little spring of clear water, where Dorothy drank and bathed and ate her breakfast. She saw there was not much bread left in the basket, and the girl was thankful the Scarecrow did not have to eat anything, for there was scarcely enough for herself and Toto for the day.

When she had finished her meal, and was about to go back to

the road of yellow brick, she was startled to hear a deep groan near by.

"What was that?" she asked, timidly.

"I cannot imagine," replied the Scarecrow; "but we can go and see."

Just then another groan reached their ears, and the sound seemed to come from behind them. They turned and walked through the forest a few steps, when Dorothy discovered something shining in a ray of sunshine that fell between the trees. She ran to the place, and then stopped short, with a cry of surprise.

One of the big trees had been partly chopped through, and standing beside it, with an uplifted axe in his hands, was a man made entirely of tin. His head and arms and legs were jointed upon his body, but he stood perfectly motionless, as if he could not stir at all.

Dorothy looked at him in amazement, and so did the Scarecrow, while Toto barked sharply and made a snap at the tin legs, which hurt his teeth.

"Did you groan?" asked Dorothy.

"Yes," answered the tin man; "I did. I've been groaning for more than a year, and no one has ever heard me before or come to help me."

"What can I do for you?" she enquired, softly, for she was moved by the sad voice in which the man spoke.

"Get an oil-can and oil my joints," he answered. "They are rusted so badly that I cannot move them at all; if I am well oiled I shall soon be all right again. You will find an oil-can on a shelf in my cottage."

Dorothy at once ran back to the cottage and found the oil-can, and then she returned and asked, anxiously,

"Where are your joints?"

"Oil my neck, first," replied the Tin Woodman. So she oiled it, and as it was quite badly rusted the Scarecrow took hold of the tin head and moved it gently from side to side until it worked freely, and then the man could turn it himself.

"Now oil the joints in my arms," he said. And Dorothy oiled them and the Scarecrow bent them carefully until they were quite free from rust and as good as new.

The Tin Woodman gave a sigh of satisfaction and lowered his axe, which he leaned against the tree.

"This is a great comfort," he said. "I have been holding that axe in the air ever since I rusted, and I'm glad to be able to put it down at last. Now, if you will oil the joints of my legs, I shall be all right once more."

So they oiled his legs until he could move them freely; and he thanked them again and again for his release, for he seemed a very polite creature, and very grateful.

"I might have stood there always if you had not come along," he said; "so you have certainly saved my life. How did you happen to be here?"

"We are on our way to the Emerald City, to see the great Oz," she answered, "and we stopped at your cottage to pass the night."

"Why do you wish to see Oz?" he asked.

"I want him to send me back to Kansas; and the Scarecrow wants him to put a few brains into his head," she replied.

The Tin Woodman appeared to think deeply for a moment. Then he said:

"Do you suppose Oz could give me a heart?"

'Why, I guess so," Dorothy answered; "it would be as easy as to give the Scarecrow brains."

"True," the Tin Woodman returned. "So, if you will allow me to join your party, I will also go to the Emerald City and ask Oz to help me."

"Come along," said the Scarecrow, heartily; and Dorothy added that she would be pleased to have his company. So the Tin Woodman shouldered his axe and they all passed through the forest until they came to the road that was paved with yellow brick.

The Tin Woodman had asked Dorothy to put the oil-can in her basket. "For," he said, "if I should get caught in the rain, and rust again, I would need the oil-can badly."

It was a bit of good luck to have their new comrade join the party, for soon after they had begun their journey again they came to a place where the trees and branches grew so thick over the road that the travellers could not pass. But the Tin Woodman set to work with his axe and chopped so well that soon he cleared a passage for the entire party.

Dorothy was thinking so earnestly as they walked along that she did not notice when the Scarecrow stumbled into a hole and rolled over to the side of the road. Indeed, he was obliged to call to her to help him up again.

"Why didn't you walk around the hole?" asked the Tin Woodman.

"I don't know enough," replied the Scarecrow, cheerfully. "My head is stuffed with straw, you know, and that is why I am going to Oz to ask him for some brains."

"Oh, I see;" said the Tin Woodman. "But, after all, brains are not the best things in the world."

"Have you any?" enquired the Scarecrow.

"No, my head is quite empty," answered the Woodman; "but once I had brains, and a heart also; so, having tried them both, I should much rather have a heart."

"And why is that?" asked the Scarecrow.

"I will tell you my story, and then you will know."

So, while they were walking through the forest, the Tin Woodman told the following story:

"I was born the son of a woodman who chopped down trees in the forest and sold the wood for a living. When I grew up I too became a wood-chopper, and after my father died I took care of my old mother as long as she lived. Then I made up my mind that instead of living alone I would marry, so that I might not become lonely.

"There was one of the Munchkin girls who was so beautiful that I soon grew to love her with all my heart. She, on her part, promised to marry me as soon as I could earn enough money to build a better house for her; so I set to work harder than ever. But the girl lived with an old woman who did not want her to marry anyone, for she was so lazy she wished the girl to remain with her and do the cooking and the housework. So the old woman went to the wicked Witch of the East, and promised her two sheep and a cow if she would prevent the marriage. Thereupon the wicked Witch enchanted my axe, and when I was chopping away at my best one day, for I was anxious to get the new house and my wife as soon as possible, the axe slipped all at once and cut off my left leg.

"This at first seemed a great misfortune, for I knew a one-legged man could not do very well as a wood-chopper. So I went to a tin-smith and had him make me a new leg out of tin. The leg worked very well, once I was used to it; but my action angered the wicked Witch of the East, for she had promised the old woman I should not marry the pretty Munchkin girl. When I began chopping again my axe slipped and cut off my right leg. Again I went to the tinner, and again he made me a leg out of tin. After this the enchanted axe cut off my arms, one after the other; but, nothing daunted, I had them replaced with tin ones. The wicked Witch then made the axe slip and cut off my head, and at first I thought that was the end of me. But the tinner happened to come along, and he made me a new head out of tin.

"I thought I had beaten the wicked Witch then, and I worked harder than ever; but I little knew how cruel my enemy could be. She thought of a new way to kill my love for the beautiful Munchkin maiden, and made my axe slip again, so that it cut right through my body, splitting me into two halves. Once more the tinner came to my help and made me a body of tin, fastening my tin arms and legs and head to it, by means of joints, so that I could move around as well as ever. But, alas! I had now no heart, so that I lost all my love for the Munchkin girl, and did not care whether I married her or not. I suppose she is still living with the old woman, waiting for me to come after her.

"My body shone so brightly in the sun that I felt very proud of it and it did not matter now if my axe slipped, for it could not cut me. There was only one danger—that my joints would rust; but I kept an oil-can in my cottage and took care to oil myself whenever I needed it. However, there came a day when I forgot to do this, and, being caught in a rainstorm, before I thought of the danger my joints had rusted, and I was left to stand in the woods until you came to help me. It was a terrible thing to undergo, but during the year I stood there I had time to think that the greatest loss I had known was the loss of my heart. While I was in love I was the happiest man on earth; but no one can love who has not a heart, and so I am resolved to ask Oz to give me one. If he does, I will go back to the Munchkin maiden and marry her."

Both Dorothy and the Scarecrow had been greatly interested in the story of the Tin Woodman, and now they knew why he was so anxious to get a new heart.

"All the same," said the Scarecrow, "I shall ask for brains instead of a heart; for a fool would not know what to do with a heart if he had one."

"I shall take the heart," returned the Tin Woodman; "for brains do not make one happy, and happiness is the best thing in the world."

Dorothy did not say anything, for she was puzzled to know which of her two friends was right, and she decided if she could only get back to Kansas and Aunt Em it did not matter so much whether the Woodman had no brains and the Scarecrow no heart, or each got what he wanted.

What worried her most was that the bread was nearly gone, and another meal for herself and Toto would empty the basket. To be sure neither the Woodman nor the Scarecrow ever ate anything, but she was not made of tin nor straw, and could not live unless she was fed.

Chapter VI

· The Cowardly Lion ·

All this time Dorothy and her companions had been walking through the thick woods. The road was still paved with yellow brick, but these were much covered by dried branches and dead leaves from the trees, and the walking was not at all good.

There were few birds in this part of the forest, for birds love the open country where there is plenty of sunshine; but now and then there came a deep growl from some wild animal hidden among the trees. These sounds made the little girl's heart beat fast, for she did not know what made them; but Toto knew, and he walked close to Dorothy's side, and did not even bark in return.

"How long will it be," the child asked of the Tin Woodman, "before we are out of the forest?"

"I cannot tell," was the answer, "for I have never been to the Emerald City. But my father went there once, when I was a boy, and he said it was a long journey through a dangerous country, although nearer to the city where Oz dwells the country is beautiful. But I am not afraid so long as I have my oil-can, and nothing can hurt the Scarecrow, while you bear upon your forehead the mark of the good Witch's kiss, and that will protect you from harm."

"But Toto!" said the girl, anxiously; "what will protect him?"

"We must protect him ourselves, if he is in danger," replied the Tin Woodman.

Just as he spoke there came from the forest a terrible roar, and the next moment a great Lion bounded into the road. With one blow of his paw he sent the Scarecrow spinning over and over to the edge of the road, and then he struck at the Tin Woodman with his sharp claws. But, to the Lion's surprise, he could make no impression on the tin, although the Woodman fell over in the road and lay still.

Little Toto, now that he had an enemy to face, ran barking toward the Lion, and the great beast had opened his mouth to bite the dog, when Dorothy, fearing Toto would be killed, and heedless of danger, rushed forward and slapped the Lion upon his nose as hard as she could, while she cried out:

"Don't you dare to bite Toto! You ought to be ashamed of yourself, a big beast like you, to bite a poor little dog!"

"I didn't bite him," said the Lion, as he rubbed his nose with his paw where Dorothy had hit it.

"No, but you tried to," she retorted. "You are nothing but a big coward."

"I know it," said the Lion, hanging his head in shame; "I've always known it. But how can I help it?"

"I don't know, I'm sure. To think of your striking a stuffed man, like the poor Scarecrow!"

"Is he stuffed?" asked the Lion, in surprise, as he watched her

pick up the Scarecrow and set him upon his feet, while she patted him into shape again.

"Of course he's stuffed," replied Dorothy, who was still angry.

"That's why he went over so easily," remarked the Lion. "It astonished me to see him whirl around so. Is the other one stuffed, also?"

"No," said Dorothy, "he's made of tin." And she helped the Woodman up again.

"That's why he nearly blunted my claws," said the Lion. "When they scratched against the tin it made a cold shiver run down my back. What is that little animal you are so tender of?"

"He is my dog, Toto," answered Dorothy.

"Is he made of tin, or stuffed?" asked the Lion.

"Neither. He's a—a—a meat dog," said the girl.

"Oh. He's a curious animal, and seems remarkably small, now that I look at him. No one would think of biting such a little thing except a coward like me," continued the Lion, sadly.

"What makes you a coward?" asked Dorothy, looking at the great beast in wonder, for he was as big as a small horse.

"It's a mystery," replied the Lion. "I suppose I was born that way. All the other animals in the forest naturally expect me to be brave, for the Lion is everywhere thought to be the King of Beasts. I learned that if I roared very loudly every living thing was frightened and got out of my way. Whenever I've met a man I've been awfully scared; but I just roared at him, and he has always run away as fast as he could go. If the elephants and the tigers and the bears had ever tried to fight me, I should have run myself—I'm such a coward; but just as soon as they hear me roar they all try to get away from me, and of course I let them go."

"But that isn't right. The King of Beasts shouldn't be a coward," said the Scarecrow.

"I know it," returned the Lion, wiping a tear from his eye with the tip of his tail; "it is my great sorrow, and makes my life very unhappy. But whenever there is danger my heart begins to beat fast."

"Perhaps you have heart disease," said the Tin Woodman.

"It may be," said the Lion.

"If you have," continued the Tin Woodman, "you ought to be

glad, for it proves you have a heart. For my part, I have no heart; so I cannot have heart disease."

"Perhaps," said the Lion, thoughtfully, "if I had no heart I should not be a coward."

"Have you brains?" asked the Scarecrow.

"I suppose so. I've never looked to see," replied the Lion.

"I am going to the great Oz to ask him to give me some," remarked the Scarecrow, "for my head is stuffed with straw."

"And I am going to ask him to give me a heart," said the Woodman.

"And I am going to ask him to send Toto and me back to Kansas," added Dorothy.

"Do you think Oz could give me courage?" asked the cowardly Lion.

"Just as easily as he could give me brains," said the Scarecrow.

"Or give me a heart," said the Tin Woodman.

"Or send me back to Kansas," said Dorothy.

"Then, if you don't mind, I'll go with you," said the Lion, "for my life is simply unbearable without a bit of courage."

"You will be very welcome," answered Dorothy, "for you will help to keep away the other wild beasts. It seems to me they must be more cowardly than you are if they allow you to scare them so easily."

"They really are," said the Lion; "but that doesn't make me any braver, and as long as I know myself to be a coward I shall be unhappy."

So once more the little company set off upon the journey, the Lion walking with stately strides at Dorothy's side. Toto did not approve this new comrade at first, for he could not forget how nearly he had been crushed between the Lion's great jaws; but after a time he became more at ease, and presently Toto and the Cowardly Lion had grown to be good friends.

During the rest of that day there was no other adventure to mar the peace of their journey. Once, indeed, the Tin Woodman stepped upon a beetle that was crawling along the road, and killed the poor little thing. This made the Tin Woodman very unhappy, for he was always careful not to hurt any living creature; and as he walked along he wept several tears of sorrow and regret. These tears ran slowly down his face and over the hinges of his jaw, and there they rusted. When Dorothy presently asked him a question the Tin Woodman could not open his mouth, for his jaws were tightly rusted together. He became greatly frightened at this and made many motions to Dorothy to relieve him, but she could not understand. The Lion was also puzzled to know what was wrong. But the Scarecrow seized the oil-can from Dorothy's basket and oiled the Woodman's jaws, so that after a few moments he could talk as well as before.

"This will serve me a lesson," said he, "to look where I step. For if I should kill another bug or beetle I should surely cry again, and crying rusts my jaw so that I cannot speak."

Thereafter he walked very carefully, with his eyes on the road, and when he saw a tiny ant toiling by he would step over it, so as not to harm it. The Tin Woodman knew very well he had no heart, and therefore he took great care never to be cruel or unkind to anything.

"You people with hearts," he said, "have something to guide you, and need never do wrong; but I have no heart, and so I must be very careful, When Oz gives me a heart of course I needn't mind so much."

Chapter VII

· The Journey to the Great Oz ·

They were obliged to camp out that night under a large tree in the forest, for there were no houses near. The tree made a good, thick covering to protect them from the dew, and the Tin Woodman chopped a great pile of wood with his axe and Dorothy built a splendid fire that warmed her and made her feel less lonely. She and Toto ate the last of their bread, and now she did not know what they would do for breakfast.

"If you wish," said the Lion, "I will go into the forest and kill a deer for you. You can roast it by the fire, since your tastes are so peculiar that you prefer cooked food, and then you will have a very good breakfast."

"Don't! please don't," begged the Tin Woodman. "I should

certainly weep if you killed a poor deer, and then my jaws would rust again."

But the Lion went away into the forest and found his own supper, and no one ever knew what it was, for he didn't mention it. And the Scarecrow found a tree full of nuts and filled Dorothy's basket with them, so that she would not be hungry for a long time. She thought this was very kind and thoughtful of the Scarecrow, but she laughed heartily at the awkward way in which the poor creature picked up the nuts. His padded hands were so clumsy and the nuts were so small that he dropped almost as many as he put in the basket. But the Scarecrow did not mind how long it took him to fill the basket, for it enabled him to keep away from the fire, as he feared a spark might get into his straw and burn him up. So he kept a good distance away from the flames, and only came near to cover Dorothy with dry leaves when she lay down to sleep. These kept her very snug and warm and she slept soundly until morning.

When it was daylight the girl bathed her face in a little rippling brook and soon after they all started toward the Emerald City.

This was to be an eventful day for the travellers. They had hardly been walking an hour when they saw before them a great ditch that crossed the road and divided the forest as far as they could see on either side. It was a very wide ditch, and when they crept up to the edge and looked into it they could see it was also very deep, and there were many jagged rocks at the bottom. The sides were so steep that none of them could climb down, and for a moment it seemed that their journey must end.

"What shall we do?" asked Dorothy, despairingly.

"I haven't the faintest idea," said the Tin Woodman; and the Lion shook his shaggy mane and looked thoughtful. But the Scarecrow said:

"We cannot fly, that is certain; neither can we climb down into this great ditch. Therefore, if we cannot jump over it, we must stop where we are."

"I think I could jump over it," said the Cowardly Lion, after measuring the distance carefully in his mind.

"Then we are all right," answered the Scarecrow, "for you can carry us all over on your back, one at a time."

"Well, I'll try it," said the Lion. "Who will go first?"

"I will," declared the Scarecrow; "for, if you found that you could not jump over the gulf, Dorothy would be killed, or the Tin Woodman badly dented on the rocks below. But if I am on your back it will not matter so much, for the fall would not hurt me at all."

"I am terribly afraid of falling, myself," said the Cowardly Lion, "but I suppose there is nothing to do but try it. So get on my back and we will make the attempt."

The Scarecrow sat upon the Lion's back, and the big beast walked to the edge of the gulf and crouched down.

"Why don't you run and jump?" asked the Scarecrow.

"Because that isn't the way we Lions do these things," he replied. Then giving a great spring, he shot through the air and landed safely on the other side. They were all greatly pleased to see how easily he did it, and after the Scarecrow had got down from his back the Lion sprang across the ditch again.

Dorothy thought she would go next; so she took Toto in her arms and climbed on the Lion's back, holding tightly to his mane with one hand. The next moment it seemed as if she was flying through the air; and then, before she had time to think about it, she was safe on the other side. The Lion went back a third time and got the Tin Woodman, and then they all sat down for a few moments to give the beast a chance to rest, for his great leaps had made his breath short, and he panted like a big dog that has been running too long.

They found the forest very thick on this side, and it looked dark and gloomy. After the Lion had rested they started along the road of yellow brick, silently wondering, each in his own mind, if ever they would come to the end of the woods and reach the bright sunshine again. To add to their discomfort, they soon heard strange noises in the depths of the forest, and the Lion whispered to them that it was in this part of the country that the Kalidahs lived.

"What are the Kalidahs?" asked the girl.

"They are monstrous beasts with bodies like bears and heads like tigers," replied the Lion; "and with claws so long and sharp that they could tear me in two as easily as I could kill Toto. I'm terribly afraid of the Kalidahs."

"I'm not surprised that you are," returned Dorothy. "They must be dreadful beasts."

The Lion was about to reply when suddenly they came to another gulf across the road; but this one was so broad and deep that the Lion knew at once he could not leap across it.

So they sat down to consider what they should do, and after serious thought the Scarecrow said,

"Here is a great tree, standing close to the ditch. If the Tin Woodman can chop it down, so that it will fall to the other side, we can walk across it easily."

"That is a first rate idea," said the Lion. "One would almost suspect you had brains in your head, instead of straw."

The Woodman set to work at once, and so sharp was his axe that the tree was soon chopped nearly through. Then the Lion put his strong front legs against the tree and pushed with all his might, and slowly the big tree tipped and fell with a crash across the ditch, with its top branches on the other side.

They had just started to cross this queer bridge when a sharp growl made them all look up, and to their horror they saw running toward them two great beasts with bodies like bears and heads like tigers.

"They are the Kalidahs!" said the Cowardly Lion, beginning to tremble.

"Quick!" cried the Scarecrow, "let us cross over."

So Dorothy went first, holding Toto in her arms; the Tin Woodman followed, and the Scarecrow came next. The Lion, although he was certainly afraid, turned to face the Kalidahs, and then he gave so loud and terrible a roar that Dorothy screamed and the Scarecrow fell over backwards, while even the fierce beasts stopped short and looked at him in surprise.

But, seeing they were bigger than the Lion, and remembering that there were two of them and only one of him, the Kalidahs again rushed forward, and the Lion crossed over the tree and turned to see what they would do next. Without stopping an instant the fierce beasts also began to cross the tree, and the Lion said to Dorothy,

"We are lost, for they will surely tear us to pieces with their sharp claws. But stand close behind me, and I will fight them as long as I am alive."

"Wait a minute!" called the Scarecrow. He had been thinking what was best to be done, and now he asked the Woodman to chop away the end of the tree that rested on their side of the ditch. The Tin Woodman began to use his axe at once, and, just as the two Kalidahs were nearly across, the tree fell with a crash into the gulf, carrying the ugly, snarling brutes with it, and both were dashed to pieces on the sharp rocks at the bottom.

"Well," said the Cowardly Lion, drawing a long breath of relief, "I see we are going to live a little while longer, and I am glad of it, for it must be a very uncomfortable thing not to be alive. Those creatures frightened me so badly that my heart is beating yet."

"Ah," said the Tin Woodman, sadly, "I wish I had a heart to beat."

This adventure made the travellers more anxious than ever to get out of the forest, and they walked so fast that Dorothy became tired, and had to ride on the Lion's back. To their great joy the trees became thinner the further they advanced, and in the afternoon they suddenly came upon a broad river, flowing swiftly just before them. On the other side of the water they could see the road of yellow brick running through a beautiful country, with green meadows dotted with bright flowers and all the road bordered with trees hanging full of delicious fruits. They were greatly pleased to see this delightful country before them.

"How shall we cross the river?" asked Dorothy.

"That is easily done," replied the Scarecrow. "The Tin Woodman must build us a raft, so we can float to the other side."

So the Woodman took his axe and began to chop down small trees to make a raft, and while he was busy at this the Scarecrow found on the river bank a tree full of fine fruit. This pleased Dorothy, who had eaten nothing but nuts all day, and she made a hearty meal of the ripe fruit.

But it takes time to make a raft, even when one is as industrious and untiring as the Tin Woodman, and when night came the work was not done. So they found a cozy place under the trees where they slept well until the morning; and Dorothy dreamed of the Emerald City, and of the good Wizard Oz, who would soon send her back to her own home again.

Chapter VIII

· The Deadly Poppy Field ·

Our little party of travellers awakened next morning refreshed and full of hope, and Dorothy breakfasted like a princess off peaches and plums from the trees beside the river. Behind them was the dark forest they had passed safely through, although they had suffered many discouragements; but before them was a lovely, sunny country that seemed to beckon them on to the Emerald City.

To be sure, the broad river now cut them off from this beautiful land; but the raft was nearly done, and after the Tin Woodman had cut a few more logs and fastened them together with wooden pins, they were ready to start. Dorothy sat down in the middle of the raft and held Toto in her arms. When the Cowardly Lion stepped upon the raft it tipped badly, for he was big and heavy; but the Scarecrow and the Tin Woodman stood upon the other end to steady it, and they had long poles in their hands to push the raft through the water.

They got along quite well at first, but when they reached the middle of the river the swift current swept the raft down stream, farther and farther away from the road of yellow brick; and the water grew so deep that the long poles would not touch the bottom.

"This is bad," said the Tin Woodman, "for if we cannot get to the land we shall be carried into the country of the wicked Witch of the West, and she will enchant us and make us her slaves."

"And then I should get no brains," said the Scarecrow.

"And I should get no courage," said the Cowardly Lion.

"And I should get no heart," said the Tin Woodman.

"And I should never get back to Kansas," said Dorothy.

"We must certainly get to the Emerald City if we can," the Scarecrow continued, and he pushed so hard on his long pole that it stuck fast in the mud at the bottom of the river, and before he could pull it out again, or let go, the raft was swept away and the poor Scarecrow left clinging to the pole in the middle of the river.

"Good-bye!" he called after them, and they were very sorry to leave him; indeed, the Tin Woodman began to cry, but fortunately remembered that he might rust, and so dried his tears on Dorothy's apron.

Of course this was a bad thing for the Scarecrow.

"I am now worse off than when I first met Dorothy," he thought. "Then, I was stuck on a pole in a cornfield, where I could make believe scare the crows, at any rate; but surely there is no use for a Scarecrow stuck on a pole in the middle of a river. I am afraid I shall never have any brains, after all!"

Down the stream the raft floated, and the poor Scarecrow was left far behind. Then the Lion said:

"Something must be done to save us. I think I can swim to the shore and pull the raft after me, if you will only hold fast to the tip of my tail."

So he sprang into the water and the Tin Woodman caught fast hold of his tail, when the Lion began to swim with all his might toward the shore. It was hard work, although he was so big; but by and by they were drawn out of the current, and then Dorothy took the Tin Woodman's long pole and helped push the raft to the land.

They were all tired out when they reached the shore at last and stepped off upon the pretty green grass, and they also knew that the stream had carried them a long way past the road of yellow brick that led to the Emerald City.

"What shall we do now?" asked the Tin Woodman, as the Lion lay down on the grass to let the sun dry him.

"We must get back to the road, in some way," said Dorothy.

"The best plan will be to walk along the river bank until we come to the road again," remarked the Lion.

So, when they were rested, Dorothy picked up her basket and they started along the grassy bank, back to the road from which the river had carried them. It was a lovely country, with plenty of flowers and fruit trees and sunshine to cheer them, and had they not felt so sorry for the poor Scarecrow they could have been very happy.

They walked along as fast as they could, Dorothy only stopping once to pick a beautiful flower; and after a time the Tin Woodman cried out,

"Look!"

Then they all looked at the river and saw the Scarecrow perched upon his pole in the middle of the water, looking very lonely and sad.

"What can we do to save him?" asked Dorothy.

The Lion and the Woodman both shook their heads, for they did not know. So they sat down upon the bank and gazed wistfully at the Scarecrow until a Stork flew by, which, seeing them, stopped to rest at the water's edge.

"Who are you, and where are you going?" asked the Stork.

"I am Dorothy," answered the girl; "and these are my friends, the Tin Woodman and the Cowardly Lion; and we are going to the Emerald City."

"This isn't the road," said the Stork, as she twisted her long neck and looked sharply at the queer party.

"I know it," returned Dorothy, "but we have lost the Scarecrow, and are wondering how we shall get him again."

"Where is he?" asked the Stork.

"Over there in the river," answered the girl.

"If he wasn't so big and heavy I would get him for you," remarked the Stork.

"He isn't heavy a bit," said Dorothy, eagerly, "for he is stuffed with straw; and if you will bring him back to us we shall thank you ever and ever so much."

"Well, I'll try," said the Stork; "but if I find he is too heavy to carry I shall have to drop him in the river again."

So the big bird flew into the air and over the water till she came to where the Scarecrow was perched upon his pole. Then the Stork with her great claws grabbed the Scarecrow by the arm and carried him up into the air and back to the bank, where Dorothy and the Lion and the Tin Woodman and Toto were sitting.

When the Scarecrow found himself among his friends again he was so happy that he hugged them all, even the Lion and Toto; and as they walked along he sang "Tol-de-ri-de-oh!" at every step, he felt so gay.

"I was afraid I should have to stay in the river forever," he

said, "but the kind Stork saved me, and if I ever get any brains I shall find the Stork again and do it some kindness in return."

"That's all right," said the Stork, who was flying along beside them. "I always like to help anyone in trouble. But I must go now, for my babies are waiting in the nest for me. I hope you will find the Emerald City and that Oz will help you."

"Thank you," replied Dorothy, and then the kind Stork flew into the air and was soon out of sight.

They walked along listening to the singing of the bright-colored birds and looking at the lovely flowers which now became so thick that the ground was carpeted with them. There were big yellow and white and blue and purple blossoms, besides great clusters of scarlet poppies, which were so brilliant in color they almost dazzled Dorothy's eyes.

"Aren't they beautiful?" the girl asked, as she breathed in the spicy scent of the flowers.

"I suppose so," answered the Scarecrow. "When I have brains I shall probably like them better."

"If I only had a heart I should love them," added the Tin Woodman.

"I always did like flowers," said the Lion; "they seem so helpless and frail. But there are none in the forest so bright as these."

They now came upon more and more of the big scarlet poppies, and fewer and fewer of the other flowers; and soon they found themselves in the midst of a great meadow of poppies. Now it is well known that when there are many of these flowers together their odor is so powerful that anyone who breathes it falls asleep, and if the sleeper is not carried away from the scent of the flowers he sleeps on and on forever. But Dorothy did not know this, nor could she get away from the bright red flowers that were everywhere about; so presently her eyes grew heavy and she felt she must sit down to rest and to sleep.

But the Tin Woodman would not let her do this.

"We must hurry and get back to the road of yellow brick before dark," he said; and the Scarecrow agreed with him. So they kept walking until Dorothy could stand no longer. Her eyes closed in spite of herself and she forgot where she was and fell among the poppies, fast asleep.

"What shall we do?" asked the Tin Woodman.

"If we leave her here she will die," said the Lion. "The smell of the flowers is killing us all. I myself can scarcely keep my eyes open and the dog is asleep already."

It was true; Toto had fallen down beside his little mistress. But the Scarecrow and the Tin Woodman, not being made of flesh, were not troubled by the scent of the flowers.

"Run fast," said the Scarecrow to the Lion, "and get out of this deadly flower-bed as soon as you can. We will bring the little girl with us, but if you should fall asleep you are too big to be carried."

So the Lion aroused himself and bounded forward as fast as he could go. In a moment he was out of sight.

"Let us make a chair with our hands, and carry her," said the Scarecrow. So they picked up Toto and put the dog in Dorothy's lap, and then they made a chair with their hands for the seat and their arms for the arms and carried the sleeping girl between them through the flowers.

On and on they walked, and it seemed that the great carpet of deadly flowers that surrounded them would never end. They followed the bend of the river, and at last came upon their friend the Lion, lying fast asleep among the poppies. The flowers had been too strong for the huge beast and he had given up, at last, and fallen only a short distance from the end of the poppy-bed, where the sweet grass spread in beautiful green fields before them.

"We can do nothing for him," said the Tin Woodman, sadly; "for he is much too heavy to lift. We must leave him here to sleep on forever, and perhaps he will dream that he has found courage at last."

"I'm sorry," said the Scarecrow; "the Lion was a very good comrade for one so cowardly. But let us go on."

They carried the sleeping girl to a pretty spot beside the river, far enough from the poppy field to prevent her breathing any more of the poison of the flowers, and here they laid her gently on the soft grass and waited for the fresh breeze to waken her.

Chapter IX

· The Queen of the Field Mice ·

"We cannot be far from the road of yellow brick, now," remarked the Scarecrow, as he stood beside the girl, "for we have come nearly as far as the river carried us away."

The Tin Woodman was about to reply when he heard a low growl, and turning his head (which worked beautifully on hinges) he saw a strange beast come bounding over the grass towards them. It was, indeed, a great, yellow wildcat, and the Woodman thought it must be chasing something, for its ears were lying close to its head and its mouth was wide open, showing two rows of ugly teeth, while its red eyes glowed like balls of fire. As it came nearer the Tin Woodman saw that running before the beast was a little gray field-mouse, and although he had no heart he knew it was wrong for the wildcat to try to kill such a pretty, harmless creature.

So the Woodman raised his axe, and as the wildcat ran by he gave it a quick blow that cut the beast's head clean off from its body, and it rolled over at his feet in two pieces.

The field-mouse, now that it was freed from its enemy, stopped short; and coming slowly up to the Woodman it said, in a squeaky little voice,

"Oh, thank you! Thank you ever so much for saving my life."

"Don't speak of it, I beg of you," replied the Woodman. "I have no heart, you know, so I am careful to help all those who may need a friend, even if it happens to be only a mouse."

"Only a mouse!" cried the little animal, indignantly; "why, I am a Queen—the Queen of all the field-mice!"

"Oh, indeed," said the Woodman, making a bow.

"Therefore you have done a great deed, as well as a brave one, in saving my life," added the Queen.

At that moment several mice were seen running up as fast as their little legs could carry them, and when they saw their Queen they exclaimed,

"Oh, your Majesty, we thought you would be killed! How did you manage to escape the great Wildcat?" and they all bowed so low to the little Queen that they almost stood upon their heads.

"This funny tin man," she answered, "killed the Wildcat and saved my life. So hereafter you must all serve him, and obey his slightest wish."

"We will!" cried all the mice, in a shrill chorus. And then they scampered in all directions, for Toto had awakened from his sleep, and seeing all these mice around him he gave one bark of delight and jumped right into the middle of the group. Toto had always loved to chase mice when he lived in Kansas, and he saw no harm in it.

But the Tin Woodman caught the dog in his arms and held him tight, while he called to the mice: "Come back! come back! Toto shall not hurt you."

At this the Queen of the Mice stuck her head out from a clump of grass and asked, in a timid voice,

"Are you sure he will not bite us?"

"I will not let him," said the Woodman; "so do not be afraid."

One by one the mice came creeping back, and Toto did not bark again, although he tried to get out of the Woodman's arms, and would have bitten him had he not known very well he was made of tin. Finally one of the biggest mice spoke.

"Is there anything we can do," it asked, "to repay you for saving the life of our Queen?"

"Nothing that I know of," answered the Woodman; but the Scarecrow, who had been trying to think, but could not because his head was stuffed with straw, said, quickly,

"Oh, yes; you can save our friend, the Cowardly Lion, who is asleep in the poppy bed."

"A Lion!" cried the little Queen; "why, he would eat us all up."

"Oh, no;" declared the Scarecrow; "this Lion is a coward."

"Really?" asked the Mouse.

"He says so himself," answered the Scarecrow, "and he would never hurt anyone who is our friend. If you will help us to save him I promise that he shall treat you all with kindness."

"Very well," said the Queen, "we will trust you. But what shall we do?"

"Are there many of these mice which call you Queen and are willing to obey you?"

"Oh, yes; there are thousands," she replied.

"Then send for them all to come here as soon as possible, and let each one bring a long piece of string."

The Queen turned to the mice that attended her and told them to go at once and get all her people. As soon as they heard her orders they ran away in every direction as fast as possible.

"Now," said the Scarecrow to the Tin Woodman, "you must go to those trees by the river-side and make a truck that will carry the Lion."

So the Woodman went at once to the trees and began to work; and he soon made a truck out of the limbs of trees, from which he chopped away all the leaves and branches. He fastened it together with wooden pegs and made the four wheels out of short pieces of a big tree-trunk. So fast and so well did he work that by the time the mice began to arrive the truck was all ready for them.

They came from all directions, and there were thousands of them: big mice and little mice and middle-sized mice; and each one brought a piece of string in his mouth. It was about this time that Dorothy woke from her long sleep and opened her eyes. She was greatly astonished to find herself lying upon the grass, with thousands of mice standing around and looking at her timidly. But the Scarecrow told her about everything, and turning to the dignified little Mouse, he said,

"Permit me to introduce to you her Majesty, the Queen."

Dorothy nodded gravely and the Queen made a courtesy, after which she became quite friendly with the little girl.

The Scarecrow and the Woodman now began to fasten the mice to the truck, using the strings they had brought. One end of a string was tied around the neck of each mouse and the other end to the truck. Of course the truck was a thousand times bigger than any of the mice who were to draw it; but when all the mice had been harnessed they were able to pull it quite easily. Even the Scarecrow and the Tin Woodman could sit on it, and were drawn swiftly by their queer little horses to the place where the Lion lay asleep.

After a great deal of hard work, for the Lion was heavy, they managed to get him up on the truck. Then the Queen hurriedly gave her people the order to start, for she feared if the mice stayed among the poppies too long they also would fall asleep.

At first the little creatures, many though they were, could hardly stir the heavily loaded truck; but the Woodman and the Scarecrow both pushed from behind, and they got along better. Soon they rolled the Lion out of the poppy bed to the green fields, where he could breathe the sweet, fresh air again, instead of the poisonous scent of the flowers.

Dorothy came to meet them and thanked the little mice warmly for saving her companion from death. She had grown so fond of the big Lion she was glad he had been rescued.

Then the mice were unharnessed from the truck and scampered away through the grass to their homes. The Queen of the Mice was the last to leave.

"If ever you need us again," she said, "come out into the field and call, and we shall hear you and come to your assistance. Good-bye!"

"Good-bye!" they all answered, and away the Queen ran, while Dorothy held Toto tightly lest he should run after her and frighten her.

After this they sat down beside the Lion until he should awaken; and the Scarecrow brought Dorothy some fruit from a tree near by, which she ate for her dinner.

Chapter X

· The Guardian of the Gates ·

It was some time before the Cowardly Lion awakened, for he had lain among the poppies a long while, breathing in their deadly fragrance; but when he did open his eyes and roll off the truck he was very glad to find himself still alive.

"I ran as fast as I could," he said, sitting down and yawning; "but the flowers were too strong for me. How did you get me out?"

Then they told him of the field-mice, and how they had generously saved him from death; and the Cowardly Lion laughed, and said,

"I have always thought myself very big and terrible; yet such small things as flowers came near to killing me, and such small animals as mice have saved my life. How strange it all is! But, comrades, what shall we do now?"

"We must journey on until we find the road of yellow brick again," said Dorothy; "and then we can keep on to the Emerald City."

So, the Lion being fully refreshed, and feeling quite himself again, they all started upon the journey, greatly enjoying the walk through the soft, fresh grass; and it was not long before they reached the road of yellow brick and turned again toward the Emerald City where the great Oz dwelt.

The road was smooth and well paved, now, and the country about was beautiful; so that the travelers rejoiced in leaving the forest far behind, and with it the many dangers they had met in its gloomy shades. Once more they could see fences built beside the road; but these were painted green, and when they came to a small house, in which a farmer evidently lived, that also was painted green. They passed by several of these houses during the afternoon, and sometimes people came to the doors and looked at them as if they would like to ask questions; but no one came near them nor spoke to them because of the great Lion, of which they were much afraid. The people were all dressed in clothing of a lovely emerald green color and wore peaked hats like those of the Munchkins.

"This must be the Land of Oz," said Dorothy, "and we are surely getting near the Emerald City."

"Yes," answered the Scarecrow; "everything is green here, while in the country of the Munchkins blue was the favorite color. But the people do not seem to be as friendly as the Munchkins and I'm afraid we shall be unable to find a place to pass the night."

"I should like something to eat besides fruit," said the girl, "and I'm sure Toto is nearly starved. Let us stop at the next house and talk to the people."

So, when they came to a good sized farm house, Dorothy walked boldly up to the door and knocked. A woman opened it just far enough to look out, and said,

"What do you want, child, and why is that great Lion with you?"

"We wish to pass the night with you, if you will allow us," answered Dorothy; "and the Lion is my friend and comrade, and would not hurt you for the world."

"Is he tame?" asked the woman, opening the door a little wider.

"Oh, yes;" said the girl, "and he is a great coward, too; so that he will be more afraid of you than you are of him."

"Well," said the woman, after thinking it over and taking another peep at the Lion, "if that is the case you may come in, and I will give you some supper and a place to sleep."

So they all entered the house, where there were, besides the woman, two children and a man. The man had hurt his leg, and was lying on the couch in a corner. They seemed greatly surprised to see so strange a company, and while the woman was busy laying the table the man asked,

"Where are you all going?"

"To the Emerald City," said Dorothy, "to see the Great Oz."

"Oh, indeed!" exclaimed the man. "Are you sure that Oz will see you?"

"Why not?" she replied.

"Why, it is said that he never lets any one come into his presence. I have been to the Emerald City many times, and it is a beautiful and wonderful place; but I have never been permitted to see the Great Oz, nor do I know of any living person who has seen him."

"Does he never go out?" asked the Scarecrow.

"Never. He sits day after day in the great throne room of his palace, and even those who wait upon him do not see him face to face."

"What is he like?" asked the girl.

"That is hard to tell," said the man, thoughtfully. "You see, Oz is a great Wizard, and can take on any form he wishes. So that some say he looks like a bird; and some say he looks like an elephant; and some say he looks like a cat. To others he appears as a beautiful fairy, or a brownie, or in any other form that pleases him. But who the real Oz is, when he is in his own form, no living person can tell."

"That is very strange," said Dorothy; "but we must try, in

some way, to see him, or we shall have made our journey for nothing."

"Why do you wish to see the terrible Oz?" asked the man.

"I want him to give me some brains," said the Scarecrow, eagerly.

"Oh, Oz could do that easily enough," declared the man. "He has more brains than he needs."

"And I want him to give me a heart," said the Tin Woodman.

"That will not trouble him," continued the man, "for Oz has a large collection of hearts, of all sizes and shapes."

"And I want him to give me courage," said the Cowardly Lion.

"Oz keeps a great pot of courage in his throne room," said the man, "which he has covered with a golden plate, to keep it from running over. He will be glad to give you some."

"And I want him to send me back to Kansas," said Dorothy.

"Where is Kansas?" asked the man, in surprise.

"I don't know," replied Dorothy, sorrowfully; "but it is my home, and I'm sure it's somewhere."

"Very likely. Well, Oz can do anything; so I suppose he will find Kansas for you. But first you must get to see him, and that will be a hard task; for the great Wizard does not like to see anyone, and he usually has his own way. But what do you want?" he continued, speaking to Toto. Toto only wagged his tail; for, strange to say, he could not speak.

The woman now called to them that supper was ready, so they gathered around the table and Dorothy ate some delicious porridge and a dish of scrambled eggs and a plate of nice white bread, and enjoyed her meal. The Lion ate some of the porridge, but did not care for it, saying it was made from oats and oats were food for horses, not for lions. The Scarecrow and the Tin Woodman ate nothing at all. Toto ate a little of everything, and was glad to get a good supper again.

The woman now gave Dorothy a bed to sleep in, and Toto lay down beside her, while the Lion guarded the door of her room so she might not be disturbed. The Scarecrow and the Tin Woodman stood up in a corner and kept quiet all night, although of course they could not sleep.

The next morning, as soon as the sun was up, they started on

their way, and soon saw a beautiful green glow in the sky just before them.

"That must be the Emerald City," said Dorothy.

As they walked on, the green glow became brighter and brighter, and it seemed that at last they were nearing the end of their travels. Yet it was afternoon before they came to the great wall that surrounded the City. It was high, and thick, and of a bright green color.

In front of them, and at the end of the road of yellow brick, was a big gate, all studded with emeralds that glittered so in the sun that even the painted eyes of the Scarecrow were dazzled by their brilliancy.

There was a bell beside the gate, and Dorothy pushed the button and heard a silvery tinkle sound within. Then the big gate swung slowly open, and they all passed through and found themselves in a high arched room, the walls of which glistened with countless emeralds.

Before them stood a little man about the same size as the Munchkins. He was clothed all in green, from his head to his feet, and even his skin was of a greenish tint. At his side was a large green box.

When he saw Dorothy and her companions the man asked, "What do you wish in the Emerald City?"

"We came here to see the Great Oz," said Dorothy.

The man was so surprised at this answer that he sat down to think it over.

"It has been many years since anyone asked me to see Oz," he said, shaking his head in perplexity. "He is powerful and terrible, and if you come on an idle or foolish errand to bother the wise reflections of the Great Wizard, he might be angry and destroy you all in an instant."

"But it is not a foolish errand, nor an idle one," replied the Scarecrow; "it is important. And we have been told that Oz is a good Wizard."

"So he is," said the green man; "and he rules the Emerald City wisely and well. But to those who are not honest, or who approach him from curiosity, he is most terrible, and few have ever dared ask to see his face. I am the Guardian of the Gates, and since you demand to see the Great Oz I must take you to his palace. But first you must put on the spectacles."

"Why?" asked Dorothy.

"Because if you did not wear spectacles the brightness and glory of the Emerald City would blind you. Even those who live in the City must wear spectacles night and day. They are all locked on, for Oz so ordered it when the City was first built, and I have the only key that will unlock them."

He opened the big box, and Dorothy saw that it was filled with spectacles of every size and shape. All of them had green glasses in them. The Guardian of the gates found a pair that would just fit Dorothy and put them over her eyes. There were two golden bands fastened to them that passed around the back of her head, where they were locked together by a little key that was at the end of a chain the Guardian of the Gates wore around his neck. When they were on, Dorothy could not take them off had she wished, but of course she did not want to be blinded by the glare of the Emerald City, so she said nothing.

Then the green man fitted spectacles for the Scarecrow and the Tin Woodman and the Lion, and even on little Toto; and all were locked fast with the key.

Then the Guardian of the Gates put on his own glasses and told them he was ready to show them to the palace. Taking a big golden key from a peg on the wall he opened another gate, and they all followed him through the portal into the streets of the Emerald City.

Chapter XI

· The Wonderful Emerald City of Oz ·

Even with eyes protected by the green spectacles Dorothy and her friends were at first dazzled by the brilliancy of the wonderful City. The streets were lined with beautiful houses all built of green marble and studded everywhere with sparkling emeralds. They walked over a pavement of the same green marble, and where the blocks were joined together were rows of emeralds, set closely, and glittering in the brightness of the sun. The window panes were of green glass; even the sky above the City had a green tint, and the rays of the sun were green.

There were many people, man, women and children, walking about, and these were all dressed in green clothes and had greenish skins. They looked at Dorothy and her strangely assorted company with wondering eyes, and the children all ran away and hid behind their mothers when they saw the Lion; but no one spoke to them. Many shops stood in the street, and Dorothy saw that everything in them was green. Green candy and green pop-corn were offered for sale, as well as green shoes, green hats and green clothes of all sorts. At one place a man was selling green lemonade, and when the children bought it Dorothy could see that they paid for it with green pennies.

There seemed to be no horses nor animals of any kind; the men carried things around in little green carts, which they pushed before them. Everyone seemed happy and contented and prosperous.

The Guardian of the Gates led them through the streets until they came to a big building, exactly in the middle of the City, which was the Palace of Oz, the Great Wizard. There was a soldier before the door, dressed in a green uniform and wearing a long green beard.

"Here are strangers," said the Guardian of the Gates to him, "and they demand to see the Great Oz."

"Step inside," answered the soldier, "and I will carry your message to him."

So they passed through the Palace gates and were led into a big room with a green carpet and lovely green furniture set with emeralds. The soldier made them all wipe their feet upon a green mat before entering this room, and when they were seated he said, politely,

"Please make yourselves comfortable while I go to the door of the Throne Room and tell Oz you are here."

They had to wait a long time before the soldier returned. When, at last, he came back, Dorothy asked,

"Have you seen Oz?"

"Oh, no;" returned the soldier; "I have never seen him. But I spoke to him as he sat behind his screen, and gave him your message. He says he will grant you an audience, if you so desire; but each one of you much enter his presence alone, and he will admit but one each day. Therefore, as you must remain in the Palace for several days, I will have you shown to rooms where you may rest in comfort after your journey."

"Thank you," replied the girl; "that is very kind of Oz."

The soldier now blew upon a green whistle, and at once a young girl, dressed in a pretty green silk gown, entered the room. She had lovely green hair and green eyes, and she bowed low before Dorothy as she said,

"Follow me and I will show you your room."

So Dorothy said good-bye to all her friends except Toto, and taking the dog in her arms followed the green girl through seven passages and up three flights of stairs until they came to a room at the front of the Palace. It was the sweetest little room in the world, with a soft, comfortable bed that had sheets of green silk and a green velvet counterpane. There was a tiny fountain in the middle of the room, that shot a spray of green perfume into the air, to fall back into a beautifully carved green marble basin. Beautiful green flowers stood in the windows, and there was a shelf with a row of little green books. When Dorothy had time to open these books she found them full of queer green pictures that made her laugh, they were so funny.

In a wardrobe were many green dresses, made of silk and satin and velvet; and all of them fitted Dorothy exactly.

"Make yourself perfectly at home," said the green girl, "and if you wish for anything ring the bell. Oz will send for you to-morrow morning."

She left Dorothy alone and went back to the others. These she also led to rooms, and each one of them found himself lodged in a very pleasant part of the Palace. Of course this politeness was wasted on the Scarecrow; for when he found himself alone in his room he stood stupidly in one spot, just within the doorway, to wait till morning. It would not rest him to lie down, and he could not close his eyes; so he remained all night staring at a little spider which was weaving its web in a corner of the room, just as if it were not one of the most wonderful rooms in the world. The Tin Woodman lay down on his bed from force of habit, for he remembered when he was made of flesh; but not

being able to sleep he passed the night moving his joints up and
down to make sure they kept in good working order. The Lion
would have preferred a bed of dried leaves in the forest, and did
not like being shut up in a room; but he had too much sense to
let this worry him, so he sprang upon the bed and rolled himself
up like a cat and purred himself asleep in a minute.

The next morning, after breakfast, the green maiden came to
fetch Dorothy, and she dressed her in one of the prettiest
gowns—made of green brocaded satin. Dorothy put on a green
silk apron and tied a green ribbon around Toto's neck, and they
started for the Throne Room of the Great Oz.

First they came to a great hall in which were many ladies and
gentlemen of the court, all dressed in rich costumes. These
people had nothing to do but talk to each other, but they always
came to wait outside the Throne Room every morning, although
they were never permitted to see Oz. As Dorothy entered they
looked at her curiously, and one of them whispered,

"Are you really going to look upon the face of Oz the Terrible?"

"Of course," answered the girl, "if he will see me."

"Oh, he will see you," said the soldier who had taken her
message to the Wizard, "although he does not like to have
people ask to see him. Indeed, at first he was angry, and said I
should send you back where you came from. Then he asked me
what you looked like, and when I mentioned your silver shoes
he was very much interested. At last I told him about the mark
upon your forehead, and he decided he would admit you to his
presence."

Just then a bell rang, and the green girl said to Dorothy,

"That is the signal. You must go into the Throne Room
alone."

She opened a little door and Dorothy walked boldly through
and found herself in a wonderful place. It was a big, round room
with a high arched roof, and the walls and ceiling and floor were
covered with large emeralds set closely together. In the center of
the roof was a great light, as bright as the sun, which made the
emeralds sparkle in a wonderful manner.

But what interested Dorothy most was the big throne of green
marble that stood in the middle of the room. It was shaped like a
chair and sparkled with gems, as did everything else. In the

center of the chair was an enormous Head, without body to support it or any arms or legs whatever. There was no hair upon this head, but it had eyes and nose and mouth, and was bigger than the head of the biggest giant.

As Dorothy gazed upon this in wonder and fear the eyes turned slowly and looked at her sharply and steadily. Then the mouth moved, and Dorothy heard a voice say:

"I am Oz, the Great and Terrible. Who are you, and why do you seek me?"

It was not such an awful voice as she had expected to come from the big Head; so she took courage and answered,

"I am Dorothy, the Small and Meek. I have come to you for help."

The eyes looked at her thoughtfully for a full minute. Then said the voice:

"Where did you get the silver shoes?"

"I got them from the wicked Witch of the East, when my house fell on her and killed her," she replied.

"Where did you get the mark upon your forehead?" continued the voice.

"That is where the good Witch of the North kissed me when she bade me good-bye and sent me to you," said the girl.

Again the eyes looked at her sharply, and they saw she was telling the truth. Then Oz asked,

"What do you wish me to do?"

"Send me back to Kansas, where my Aunt Em and Uncle Henry are," she answered, earnestly. "I don't like your country, although it is so beautiful. And I am sure Aunt Em will be dreadfully worried over my being away so long."

The eyes winked three times, and then they turned up to the ceiling and down to the floor and rolled around so queerly that they seemed to see every part of the room. And at last they looked at Dorothy again.

"Why should I do this for you?" asked Oz.

"Because you are strong and I am weak; because you are a Great Wizard and I am only a helpless little girl," she answered.

"But you were strong enough to kill the wicked Witch of the East," said Oz.

"That just happened," returned Dorothy, simply; "I could not help it."

"Well," said the Head, "I will give you my answer. You have no right to expect me to send you back to Kansas unless you do something for me in return. In this country everyone must pay for everything he gets. If you wish me to use my magic power to send you home again you must do something for me first. Help me and I will help you."

"What must I do?" asked the girl.

"Kill the wicked Witch of the West," answered Oz.

"But I cannot!" exclaimed Dorothy, greatly surprised.

"You killed the Witch of the East and you wear the silver shoes, which bear a powerful charm. There is now but one Wicked Witch left in all this land, and when you can tell me she is dead I will sent you back to Kansas—but not before."

The little girl began to weep, she was so much disappointed; and the eyes winked again and looked upon her anxiously, as if the Great Oz felt that she could help him if she would.

"I never killed anything, willingly," she sobbed; "and even if I want to, how could I kill the Wicked Witch? If you, who are Great and Terrible, cannot kill her yourself, how do you expect me to do it?"

"I do not know," said the Head; "but that is my answer, and until the Wicked Witch dies you will not see your Uncle and Aunt again. Remember that the Witch is Wicked—tremendously Wicked—and ought to be killed. Now go, and do not ask to see me again until you have done your task."

Sorrowfully Dorothy left the Throne Room and went back where the Lion and the Scarecrow and the Tin Woodman were waiting to hear what Oz had said to her.

"There is no hope for me," she said, sadly, "for Oz will not send me home until I have killed the Wicked Witch of the West; and that I can never do."

Her friends were sorry, but could do nothing to help her; so she went to her own room and lay down on the bed and cried herself to sleep.

The next morning the soldier with the green whiskers came to the Scarecrow and said,

"Come with me, for Oz has sent for you."

So the Scarecrow followed him and was admitted into the great Throne Room, where he saw, sitting in the emerald throne, a most lovely lady. She was dressed in green silk gauze and wore upon her flowing green locks a crown of jewels. Growing from her shoulders were wings, gorgeous in color and so light that they fluttered if the slightest breath of air reached them.

When the Scarecrow had bowed, as prettily as his straw stuffing would let him, before this beautiful creature, she looked upon him sweetly, and said,

"I am Oz, the Great and Terrible. Who are you, and why do you seek me?"

Now the Scarecrow, who had expected to see the great Head Dorothy had told him of, was much astonished; but he answered her bravely.

"I am only a Scarecrow, stuffed with straw. Therefore I have no brains, and I come to you praying that you will put brains in my head instead of straw, so that I may become as much a man as any other in your dominions."

"Why should I do this for you?" asked the lady.

"Because you are wise and powerful, and no one else can help me," answered the Scarecrow.

"I never grant favors without some return," said Oz; "but this much I will promise. If you will kill for me the Wicked Witch of the West I will bestow upon you a great many brains, and such good brains that you will be the wisest man in all the Land of Oz."

"I thought you asked Dorothy to kill the Witch," said the Scarecrow, in surprise.

"So I did. I don't care who kills her. But until she is dead I will not grant your wish. Now go, and do not seek me again until you have earned the brains you so greatly desire."

The Scarecrow went sorrowfully back to his friends and told them what Oz had said; and Dorothy was surprised to find that the great Wizard was not a Head, as she had seen him, but a lovely lady.

"All the same," said the Scarecrow, "she needs a heart as much as the Tin Woodman."

On the next morning the soldier with the green whiskers came to the Tin Woodman and said,

"Oz has sent for you. Follow me."

So the Tin Woodman followed him and came to the great Throne Room. He did not know whether he would find Oz a lovely lady or a Head, but he hoped it would be the lovely lady. "For," he said to himself, "if it is the Head, I am sure I shall not be given a heart, since a head has no heart of its own and therefore cannot feel for me. But if it is the lovely lady I shall beg hard for a heart, for all ladies are themselves said to be kindly hearted."

But when the Woodman entered the great Throne Room he saw neither the Head nor the Lady, for Oz had taken the shape of a most terrible Beast. It was nearly as big as an elephant, and the green throne seemed hardly strong enough to hold its weight. The Beast had a head like that of a rhinoceros, only there were five eyes in its face. There were five long arms growing out of its body and it also had five long, slim legs. Thick, woolly hair covered every part of it, and a more dreadful looking monster could not be imagined. It was fortunate the Tin Woodman had no heart at that moment, for it would have beat loud and fast from terror. But being only tin, the Woodman was not at all afraid, although he was much disappointed.

"I am Oz, the Great and Terrible," spake the Beast, in a voice that was one great roar. "Who are you, and why do you seek me?"

"I am a Woodman, and made of tin. Therefore I have no heart, and cannot love. I pray you to give me a heart that I may be as other men are."

"Why should I do this?" demanded the Beast.

"Because I ask it, and you alone can grant my request," answered the Woodman.

Oz gave a low growl at this, but said, gruffly,

"If you indeed desire a heart, you must earn it."

"How?" asked the Woodman.

"Help Dorothy to kill the Wicked Witch of the West," replied the Beast. "When the Witch is dead, come to me, and I will then give you the biggest and kindest and most loving heart in all the Land of Oz."

So the Tin Woodman was forced to return sorrowfully to his friends and tell them of the terrible Beast he had seen. They all wondered greatly at the many forms the great Wizard could take upon himself, and the Lion said,

"If he is a beast when I go to see him, I shall roar my loudest, and so frighten him that he will grant all I ask. And if he is the lovely lady, I shall pretend to spring upon her, and so compel her to do my bidding. And if he is the great Head, he will be at my mercy; for I will roll this head all about the room until he promises to give us what we desire. So be of good cheer my friends, for all will yet be well."

The next morning the soldier with the green whiskers led the Lion to the great Throne Room and bade him enter the presence of Oz.

The Lion at once passed through the door, and glancing around saw, to his surprise, that before the throne was a Ball of Fire, so fierce and glowing he could scarcely bear to gaze upon it. His first thought was that Oz had by accident caught on fire and was burning up; but, when he tried to go nearer, the heat was so intense that it singed his whiskers, and he crept back tremblingly to a spot nearer the door.

Then a low, quiet voice came from the Ball of Fire, and these were the words it spoke:

"I am Oz, the Great and Terrible. Who are you, and why do you seek me?" And the Lion answered,

"I am a Cowardly Lion, afraid of everything. I come to you to beg that you give me courage, so that in reality I may become the King of Beasts, as men call me."

"Why should I give you courage?" demanded Oz.

"Because of all Wizards you are the greatest, and alone have power to grant my request," answered the Lion.

The Ball of Fire burned fiercely for a time, and the voice said,

"Bring me proof that the Wicked Witch is dead, and that moment I will give you courage. But so long as the Witch lives you must remain a coward."

The Lion was angry at this speech, but could say nothing in reply, and while he stood silently gazing at the Ball of Fire it became so furiously hot that he turned tail and rushed from the room. He was glad to find his friends waiting for him, and told them of his terrible interview with the Wizard.

"What shall we do now?" asked Dorothy, sadly.

"There is only one thing we can do," returned the Lion, "and that is to go to the land of the Winkies, seek out the Wicked Witch, and destroy her."

"But suppose we cannot?" said the girl.

"Then I shall never have courage," declared the Lion.

"And I shall never have brains," added the Scarecrow.

"And I shall never have a heart," spoke the Tin Woodman.

"And I shall never see Aunt Em and Uncle Henry," said Dorothy, beginning to cry.

"Be careful!" cried the green girl, "the tears will fall on your green silk gown, and spot it."

So Dorothy dried her eyes and said,

"I suppose we must try it; but I am sure I do not want to kill anybody, even to see Aunt Em again."

"I will go with you; but I'm too much of a coward to kill the Witch," said the Lion.

"I will go too," declared the Scarecrow; "but I shall not be of much help to you, I am such a fool."

"I haven't the heart to harm even a Witch," remarked the Tin Woodman; "but if you go I certainly shall go with you."

Therefore it was decided to start upon their journey the next morning, and the Woodman sharpened his axe on a green grindstone and had all his joints properly oiled. The Scarecrow stuffed himself with fresh straw and Dorothy put new paint on his eyes that he might see better. The green girl, who was very kind to them, filled Dorothy's basket with good things to eat, and fastened a little bell around Toto's neck with a green ribbon.

They went to bed quite early and slept soundly until daylight, when they were awakened by the crowing of a green cock that lived in the back yard of the palace, and the cackling of a hen that had laid a green egg.

Chapter XII

· The Search for the Wicked Witch ·

The soldier with the green whiskers led them through the streets of the Emerald City until they reached the room where

the Guardian of the Gates lived. This officer unlocked their spectacles to put them back in his great box, and then he politely opened the gate for our friends.

"Which road leads to the Wicked Witch of the West?" asked Dorothy.

"There is no road," answered the Guardian of the Gates; "no one ever wishes to go that way."

"How, then, are we to find her?" enquired the girl.

"That will be easy," replied the man; "for when she knows you are in the Country of the Winkies she will find you, and make you all her slaves."

"Perhaps not," said the Scarecrow, "for we mean to destroy her."

"Oh, that is different," said the Guardian of the Gates. "No one has ever destroyed her before, so I naturally thought she would make slaves of you, as she has of all the rest. But take care; for she is wicked and fierce, and may not allow you to destroy her. Keep to the West, where the sun sets, and you cannot fail to find her."

They thanked him and bade him good-bye, and turned toward the West, walking over fields of soft grass dotted here and there with daisies and buttercups. Dorothy still wore the pretty silk dress she had put on in the palace, but now, to her surprise, she found it was no longer green, but pure white. The ribbon around Toto's neck had also lost its green color and was as white as Dorothy's dress.

The Emerald City was soon left far behind. As they advanced the ground became rougher and hillier, for there were no farms nor houses in this country of the West, and the ground was untilled.

In the afternoon the sun shone hot in their faces, for there were no trees to offer them shade; so that before night Dorothy and Toto and the Lion were tired, and lay down upon the grass and fell asleep, with the Woodman and the Scarecrow keeping watch.

Now the Wicked Witch of the West had but one eye, yet that was as powerful as a telescope, and could see everywhere. So, as she sat in the door of her castle, she happened to look around and saw Dorothy lying asleep, with her friends all about her. They were a long distance off, but the Wicked Witch was angry to find them in her country; so she blew upon a silver whistle that hung around her neck.

At once there came running to her from all directions a pack of great wolves. They had long legs and fierce eyes and sharp teeth.

"Go to those people," said the Witch, "and tear them to pieces."

"Are you not going to make them your slaves?" asked the leader of the wolves.

"No," she answered, "one is of tin, and one of straw; one is a girl and another a Lion. None of them is fit to work, so you may tear them into small pieces."

"Very well," said the wolf, and he dashed away at full speed, followed by the others.

It was lucky the Scarecrow and the Woodman were wide awake and heard the wolves coming.

"This is my fight," said the Woodman; "so get behind me and I will meet them as they come."

He seized his axe, which he had made very sharp, and as the leader of the wolves came on the Tin Woodman swung his arm and chopped the wolf's head from its body, so that it immediately died. As soon as he could raise his axe another wolf came up, and he also fell under the sharp edge of the Tin Woodman's weapon. There were forty wolves, and forty times a wolf was killed; so that at last they all lay dead in a heap before the Woodman.

Then he put down his axe and sat beside the Scarecrow, who said,

"It was a good fight, friend."

They waited until Dorothy awoke the next morning. The little girl was quite frightened when she saw the great pile of shaggy wolves, but the Tin Woodman told her all. She thanked him for saving them and sat down to breakfast, after which they started again upon their journey.

Now this same morning the Wicked Witch came to the door of her castle and looked out with her one eye that could see afar off. She saw all her wolves lying dead, and the strangers still travelling through her country. This made her angrier than before, and she blew her silver whistle twice.

Straightway a great flock of wild crows came flying toward her, enough to darken the sky. And the Wicked Witch said to the King Crow,

"Fly at once to the strangers; peck out their eyes and tear them to pieces."

The wild crows flew in one great flock toward Dorothy and her companions. When the little girl saw them coming she was afraid. But the Scarecrow said,

"This is my battle; so lie down beside me and you will not be harmed."

So they all lay upon the ground except the Scarecrow, and he stood up and stretched out his arms. And when the crows saw him they were frightened, as these birds always are by scarecrows, and did not dare to come any nearer. But the King Crow said,

"It is only a stuffed man. I will peck his eyes out."

The King Crow flew at the Scarecrow, who caught it by the head and twisted its neck until it died. And then another crow flew at him, and the Scarecrow twisted its neck also. There were forty crows, and forty times the Scarecrow twisted a neck, until at last all were lying dead beside him. Then he called to his companions to rise, and again they went upon their journey.

When the Wicked Witch looked out again and saw all her crows lying in a heap, she got into a terrible rage, and blew three times upon her silver whistle.

Forthwith there was heard a great buzzing in the air, and a swarm of black bees came flying towards her.

"Go to the strangers and sting them to death!" commanded the Witch, and the bees turned and flew rapidly until they came to where Dorothy and her friends were walking. But the Woodman had seen them coming and the Scarecrow had decided what to do.

"Take out my straw and scatter it over the little girl and the dog and the lion," he said to the Woodman, "and the bees cannot sting them." This the Woodman did, and as Dorothy lay close beside the Lion and held Toto in her arms, the straw covered them entirely.

The bees came and found no one but the Woodman to sting, so they flew at him and broke off all ther stings against the tin, without hurting the Woodman at all. And as bees cannot live when their stings are broken that was the end of the black bees, and they lay scattered thick about the Woodman, like little heaps of fine coal.

Then Dorothy and the Lion got up, and the girl helped the Tin Woodman put the straw back into the Scarecrow again, until he was as good as ever. So they started upon their journey once more.

The Wicked Witch was so angry when she saw her black bees in little heaps like fine coal that she stamped her foot and tore her hair and gnashed her teeth. And then she called a dozen of her slaves, who were the Winkies, and gave them sharp spears, telling them to go to the strangers and destroy them.

The Winkies were not a brave people, but they had to do as they were told; so they marched away until they came near to Dorothy. Then the Lion gave a great roar and sprang toward them, and the poor Winkies were so frightened that they ran back as fast as they could.

When they returned to the castle the Wicked Witch beat them well with a strap, and sent them back to their work, after which she sat down to think what she should do next. She could not understand how all her plans to destroy these strangers had failed; but she was a powerful Witch, as well as a wicked one, and she soon made up her mind how to act.

There was, in her cupboard, a Golden Cap, with a circle of diamonds and rubies running round it. This Golden Cap had a charm. Whoever owned it could call three times upon the Winged Monkeys, who would obey any order they were given. But no person could command these strange creatures more than three times. Twice already the Wicked Witch had used the charm of the Cap. Once was when she had made the Winkies her slaves, and set herself to rule over their country. The Winged Monkeys had helped her do this. The second time was when she had fought against the Great Oz himself, and driven him out of the land of the West. The Winged Monkeys had also helped her in doing this. Only once more could she use this Golden Cap, for which reason she did not like to do so until all her other powers were exhausted. But now that her fierce wolves and her wild crows and her stinging bees were gone, and her slaves had been scared away by the Cowardly Lion, she saw there was only one way left to destroy Dorothy and her friends.

So the Wicked Witch took the Golden Cap from her cupboard and placed it upon her head. Then she stood upon her left foot and said, slowly,

"Ep-pe, pep-pe, kak-ke!"

Next she stood upon her right foot and said,

"Hil-lo, hol-lo, hel-lo!"

After this she stood upon both feet and cried in a loud voice,

"Ziz-zy, zuz-zy, zik!"

Now the charm began to work. The sky was darkened, and a low rumbling sound was heard in the air. There was a rushing of many wings; a great chattering and laughing; and the sun came out of the dark sky to show the Wicked Witch surrounded by a crowd of monkeys, each with a pair of immense and powerful wings on his shoulders.

One, much bigger than the others, seemed to be their leader. He flew close to the Witch and said,

"You have called us for the third and last time. What do you command?"

"Go to the strangers who are within my land and destroy them all except the Lion," said the Wicked Witch. "Bring that beast to me, for I have a mind to harness him like a horse, and make him work."

"Your commands shall be obeyed," said the leader; and then, with a great deal of chattering and noise, the Winged Monkeys flew away to the place where Dorothy and her friends were walking.

Some of the Monkeys seized the Tin Woodman and carried him through the air until they were over a country thickly covered with sharp rocks. Here they dropped the poor Woodman, who fell a great distance to the rocks, where he lay so battered and dented that he could neither move nor groan.

Others of the Monkeys caught the Scarecrow, and with their long fingers pulled all of the straw out of his clothes and head. They made his hat and boots and clothes into a small bundle and threw it into the top branches of a tall tree.

The remaining Monkeys threw pieces of stout rope around the Lion and wound many coils about his body and head and legs, until he was unable to bite or scratch or struggle in any way. Then they lifted him up and flew away with him to the Witch's castle, where he was placed in a small yard with a high iron fence around it, so that he could not escape.

But Dorothy they did not harm at all. She stood, with Toto in her arms, watching the sad fate of her comrades and thinking it would soon be her turn. The leader of the Winged Monkeys flew up to her, his long, hairy arms stretched out and his ugly face grinning terribly; but he saw the mark of the Good Witch's kiss upon her forehead and stopped short, motioning the others not to touch her.

"We dare not harm this little girl," he said to them, "for she is protected by the Power of Good, and that is greater than the Power of Evil. All we can do is to carry her to the castle of the Wicked Witch and leave her there."

So, carefully and gently, they lifted Dorothy in their arms and carried her swiftly through the air until they came to the castle, where they set her down upon the front door step. Then the leader said to the Witch,

"We have obeyed you as far as we were able. The Tin Woodman and the Scarecrow are destroyed, and the Lion is tied up in your yard. The little girl we dare not harm, nor the dog she carries in her arms. Your power over our band is now ended, and you will never see us again."

Then all the Winged Monkeys, with much laughing and chattering and noise, flew into the air and were soon out of sight.

The Wicked Witch was both surprised and worried when she saw the mark on Dorothy's forehead, for she knew well that neither the Winged Monkeys nor she, herself, dare hurt the girl in any way. She looked down at Dorothy's feet, and seeing the Silver Shoes, began to tremble with fear, for she knew what a powerful charm belonged to them. At first the Witch was tempted to run away from Dorothy; but she happened to look into the child's eyes and saw how simple the soul behind them was, and that the little girl did not know of the wonderful power the Silver Shoes gave her. So the Wicked Witch laughed to herself, and thought, "I can still make her my slave, for she does

not know how to use her power." Then she said to Dorothy, harshly and severely,

"Come with me; and see that you mind everything I tell you, for if you do not I will make an end of you, as I did of the Tin Woodman and the Scarecrow."

Dorothy followed her through many of the beautiful rooms in her castle until they came to the kitchen, where the Witch bade her clean the pots and kettles and sweep the floor and keep the fire fed with wood.

Dorothy went to work meekly, with her mind made up to work as hard as she could; for she was glad the Wicked Witch had decided not to kill her.

With Dorothy hard at work the Witch thought she would go into the court-yard and harness the Cowardly Lion like a horse; it would amuse her, she was sure, to make him draw her chariot whenever she wished to go to drive. But as she opened the gate the Lion gave a loud roar and bounded at her so fiercely that the Witch was afraid, and ran out and shut the gate again.

"If I cannot harness you," said the Witch to the Lion, speaking through the bars of the gate, "I can starve you. You shall have nothing to eat until you do as I wish."

So after that she took no food to the imprisoned Lion; but every day she came to the gate at noon and asked,

"Are you ready to be harnessed like a horse?"

And the Lion would answer,

"No. If you come in this yard I will bite you."

The reason the Lion did not have to do as the Witch wished was that every night, while the woman was asleep Dorothy carried him food from the cupboard. After he had eaten he would lie down on his bed of straw, and Dorothy would lie beside him and put her head on his soft, shaggy mane, while they talked of their troubles and tried to plan some way to escape. But they could find no way to get out of the castle, for it was constantly guarded by the yellow Winkies, who were the slaves of the Wicked Witch and too afraid of her not to do as she told them.

The girl had to work hard during the day, and often the Witch threatened to beat her with the same old umbrella she always carried in her hand. But, in truth, she did not dare to strike Dorothy, because of the mark upon her forehead. The child did not know this, and was full of fear for herself and Toto. Once the Witch struck Toto a blow with her umbrella and the brave little dog flew at her and bit her leg, in return. The Witch did not bleed where she was bitten, for she was so wicked that the blood in her had dried up many years before.

Dorothy's life became very sad as she grew to understand that it would be harder than ever to get back to Kansas and Aunt Em again. Sometimes she would cry bitterly for hours, with Toto sitting at her feet and looking into her face, whining dismally to show how sorry he was for his little mistress. Toto did not really care whether he was in Kansas or the Land of Oz so long as Dorothy was with him; but he knew the little girl was unhappy, and that made him unhappy too.

Now the Wicked Witch had a great longing to have for her own the Silver Shoes which the girl always wore. Her Bees and her Crows and her Wolves were lying in heaps and drying up, and she had used up all the power of the Golden Cap; but if she could only get hold of the Silver Shoes they would give her more power than all the other things she had lost. She watched Dorothy carefully, to see if she ever took off her shoes, thinking she might steal them. But the child was so proud of her pretty shoes that she never took them off except at night and when she took her bath. The Witch was too much afraid of the dark to dare go in Dorothy's room at night to take the shoes, and her dread of water was greater than her fear of the dark, so she never came near when Dorothy was bathing. Indeed, the old Witch never touched water, nor ever let water touch her in any way.

But the wicked creature was very cunning, and she finally thought of a trick that would give her what she wanted. She placed a bar of iron in the middle of the kitchen floor, and then by her magic arts made the iron invisible to human eyes. So that when Dorothy walked across the floor she stumbled over the bar, not being able to see it, and fell at full length. She was not much hurt, but in her fall one of the Silver Shoes came off, and before she could reach it the Witch had snatched it away and put it on her own skinny foot.

The wicked woman was greatly pleased with the success of her trick, for as long as she had one of the shoes she owned half the power of their charm, and Dorothy could not use it against her, even had she known how to do so.

The little girl, seeing she had lost one of her pretty shoes, grew angry, and said to the Witch,

"Give me back my shoe!"

"I will not," retorted the Witch, "for it is now my shoe, and not yours."

"You are a wicked creature!" cried Dorothy. "You have no right to take my shoe from me."

"I shall keep it, just the same," said the Witch, laughing at her, "and some day I shall get the other one from you, too."

This made Dorothy so very angry that she picked up the bucket of water that stood near and dashed it over the Witch, wetting her from head to foot.

Instantly the wicked woman gave a loud cry of fear; and then, as Dorothy looked at her in wonder, the Witch began to shrink and fall away.

"See what you have done!" she screamed. "In a minute I shall melt away."

"I'm very sorry, indeed," said Dorothy, who was truly frightened to see the Witch actually melting away like brown sugar before her very eyes.

"Didn't you know water would be the end of me?" asked the Witch, in a wailing, despairing voice.

"Of course not," answered Dorothy; "how should I?"

"Well, in a few minutes I shall be all melted, and you will have the castle to yourself. I have been wicked in my day, but I never thought a little girl like you would ever be able to melt me and end my wicked deeds. Look out—here I go!"

With these words the Witch fell down in a brown, melted, shapeless mass and began to spread over the clean boards of the kitchen floor. Seeing that she had really melted away to nothing, Dorothy drew another bucket of water and threw it over the mess. She then swept it all out the door. After picking out the silver shoe, which was all that was left of the old woman, she cleaned and dried it with a cloth, and put it on her foot again. Then, being at last free to do as she chose, she ran out to the court-yard to tell the Lion that the Wicked Witch of the West had come to an end, and that they were no longer prisoners in a strange land.

Chapter XIII

· The Rescue ·

The Cowardly Lion was much pleased to hear that the Wicked Witch had been melted by a bucket of water, and Dorothy at once unlocked the gate of his prison and set him free. They went in together to the castle, where Dorothy's first act was to call all the Winkies together and tell them that they were no longer slaves.

There was great rejoicing among the yellow Winkies, for they had been made to work hard during many years for the Wicked Witch, who had always treated them with great cruelty. They kept this day as a holiday, then and ever after, and spent the time in feasting and dancing.

"If our friends, the Scarecrow and the Tin Woodman, were only with us," said the Lion, "I should be quite happy."

"Don't you suppose we could rescue them?" asked the girl, anxiously.

"We can try," answered the Lion.

So they called the yellow Winkies and asked them if they would help to rescue their friends, and the Winkies said that they would be delighted to do all in their power for Dorothy, who had set them free from bondage. So she chose a number of Winkies who looked as if they knew the most, and they all started away. They travelled that day and part of the next until they came to the rocky plain where the Tin Woodman lay, all battered and bent. His axe was near him, but the blade was rusted and the handle broken off short.

The Winkies lifted him tenderly in their arms, and carried him back to the yellow castle again, Dorothy shedding a few tears by the way at the sad plight of her old friend, and the Lion looking sober and sorry. When they reached the castle Dorothy said to the Winkies,

"Are any of your people tinsmiths?"

"Oh, yes; some of us are very good tinsmiths," they told her.

"Then bring them to me," she said. And when the tinsmiths came, bringing with them all their tools in baskets, she enquired,

"Can you straighten out those dents in the Tin Woodman, and bend him back into shape again, and solder him together where he is broken?"

The tinsmiths looked the Woodman over carefully and then answered that they thought they could mend him so he would be as good as ever. So they set to work in one of the big yellow rooms of the castle and worked for three days and four nights, hammering and twisting and bending and soldering and polishing and pounding at the legs and body and head of the Tin Woodman, until at last he was straightened out into his old form, and his joints worked as well as ever. To be sure, there were several patches on him, but the tinsmiths did a good job, and as the Woodman was not a vain man he did not mind the patches at all.

When, at last, he walked into Dorothy's room and thanked her for rescuing him, he was so pleased that he wept tears of joy, and Dorothy had to wipe every tear carefully from his face with her apron, so his joints would not be rusted. At the same time her own tears fell thick and fast at the joy of meeting her old friend again, and these tears did not need to be wiped away. As for the Lion, he wiped his eyes so often with the tip of his tail that it became quite wet, and he was obliged to go out into the courtyard and hold it in the sun till it dried.

"If we only had the Scarecrow with us again," said the Tin Woodman, when Dorothy had finished telling him everything that had happened, "I should be quite happy."

"We must try to find him," said the girl.

So she called the Winkies to help her, and they walked all that day and part of the next until they came to the tall tree in the branches of which the Winged Monkeys had tossed the Scarecrow's clothes.

It was a very tall tree, and the trunk was so smooth that no one could climb it; but the Woodman said at once,

"I'll chop it down, and then we can get the Scarecrow's clothes."

Now while the tinsmiths had been at work mending the Woodman himself, another of the Winkies, who was a goldsmith, had made an axe-handle of solid gold and fitted it to the Woodman's axe, instead of the old broken handle. Others polished the blade until all the rust was removed and it glistened like burnished silver.

As soon as he had spoken, the Tin Woodman began to chop, and in a short time the tree fell over with a crash, when the Scarecrow's clothes fell out of the branches and rolled off on the ground.

Dorothy picked them up and had the Winkies carry them back to the castle, where they were stuffed with nice, clean straw; and, behold! here was the Scarecrow, as good as ever, thanking them over and over again for saving him.

Now they were reunited, Dorothy and her friends spent a few happy days at the Yellow Castle, where they found everything they needed to make them comfortable. But one day the girl thought of Aunt Em, and said,

"We must go back to Oz, and claim his promise."

"Yes," said the Woodman, "at last I shall get my heart."

"And I shall get my brains," added the Scarecrow, joyfully.

"And I shall get my courage," said the Lion, thoughtfully.

"And I shall get back to Kansas," cried Dorothy, clapping her hands. "Oh, let us start for the Emerald City to-morrow!"

This they decided to do. The next day they called the Winkies together and bade them good-bye. The Winkies were sorry to have them go, and they had grown so fond of the Tin Woodman that they begged him to stay and rule over them, and the Yellow Land of the West. Finding they were determined to go, the Winkies gave Toto and the Lion each a golden collar; and to Dorothy they presented a beautiful bracelet, studded with diamonds; and to the Scarecrow they gave a gold-headed walking stick, to keep him from stumbling; and to the Tin Woodman they offered a silver oil-can, inlaid with gold and set with precious jewels.

Every one of the travellers made the Winkies a pretty speech in return, and all shook hands with them until their arms ached.

Dorothy went to the Witch's cupboard to fill her basket with food for the journey, and there she saw the Golden Cap. She tried it on her own head and found that it fitted her exactly. She did not know anything about the charm of the Golden Cap, but she saw that it was pretty, so she made up her mind to wear it and carry her sunbonnet in the basket.

Then, being prepared for the journey, they all started for the Emerald City; and the Winkies gave them three cheers and many good wishes to carry with them.

Chapter XIV

· The Winged Monkeys ·

You will remember there was no road—not even a pathway—between the castle of the Wicked Witch and the Emerald City. When the four travellers went in search of the Witch she had seen them coming, and so sent the Winged Monkeys to bring them to her. It was much harder to find their way back through the big fields of buttercups and yellow daisies than it was being carried. They knew, of course, they must go straight east, toward the rising sun; and they started off in the right way. But at noon, when the sun was over their heads, they did not know which was east and which was west, and that was the reason they were lost in the great fields. They kept on walking, however, and at night the moon came out and shone brightly. So they lay down among the sweet smelling yellow flowers and slept soundly until morning—all but the Scarecrow and the Tin Woodman.

The next morning the sun was behind a cloud, but they started on, as if they were quite sure which way they were going.

"If we walk far enough," said Dorothy, "we shall sometime come to some place, I am sure."

But day by day passed away, and they still saw nothing before them but the yellow fields. The Scarecrow began to grumble a bit.

"We have surely lost our way," he said, "and unless we find it again in time to reach the Emerald City I shall never get my brains."

"Nor I my heart," declared the Tin Woodman. "It seems to me I can scarcely wait till I get to Oz, and you must admit this is a very long journey."

"You see," said the Cowardly Lion, with a whimper, "I haven't the courage to keep tramping forever, without getting anywhere at all."

Then Dorothy lost heart. She sat down on the grass and looked at her companions, and they sat down and looked at her, and Toto found that for the first time in his life he was too tired to chase a butterfly that flew past his head; so he put out his tongue and panted and looked at Dorothy as if to ask what they should do next.

"Suppose we call the Field Mice," she suggested. "They could probably tell us the way to the Emerald City."

"To be sure they could," cried the Scarecrow; "why didn't we think of that before?"

Dorothy blew the little whistle she had always carried about her neck since the Queen of the Mice had given it to her. In a few minutes they heard the pattering of tiny feet, and many of the small grey mice came running up to her. Among them was the Queen herself, who asked, in her squeaky little voice,

"What can I do for my friends?"

"We have lost our way," said Dorothy. "Can you tell us where the Emerald City is?"

"Certainly," answered the Queen; "but it is a great way off, for you have had it at your backs all this time." Then she noticed Dorothy's Golden Cap, and said, "Why don't you use the charm of the Cap, and call the Winged Monkeys to you? They will carry you to the City of Oz in less than an hour."

"I didn't know there was a charm," answered Dorothy, in surprise. "What is it?"

"It is written inside the Golden Cap," replied the Queen of the Mice; "but if you are going to call the Winged Monkeys we must run away, for they are full of mischief and think it great fun to plague us."

"Won't they hurt me?" asked the girl, anxiously.

"Oh, no; they must obey the wearer of the Cap. Good-bye!"

And she scampered out of sight, with all the mice hurrying after her.

Dorothy looked inside the Golden Cap and saw some words written upon the lining. These, she thought, must be the charm, so she read the directions carefully and put the Cap upon her head.

"Ep-pe, pep-pe, kak-ke!" she said, standing on her left foot.

"What did you say?" asked the Scarecrow, who did not know what she was doing.

"Hil-lo, hol-lo, hel-lo!" Dorothy went on, standing this time on her right foot.

"Hello!" replied the Tin Woodman, calmly.

"Ziz-zy, zuz-zy, zik!" said Dorothy, who was now standing on both feet. This ended the saying of the charm, and they heard a great chattering and flapping of wings, as the band of Winged Monkeys flew up to them. The King bowed low before Dorothy, and asked,

"What is your command?"

"We wish to go to the Emerald City," said the child, "and we have lost our way."

"We will carry you," replied the King, and no sooner had he spoken than two of the Monkeys caught Dorothy in their arms and flew away with her. Others took the Scarecrow and the Woodman and the Lion, and one little Monkey seized Toto and flew after them, although the dog tried hard to bite him.

The Scarecrow and the Tin Woodman were rather frightened at first, for they remembered how badly the Winged Monkeys had treated them before; but they saw that no harm was intended, so they rode through the air quite cheerfully, and had a find time looking at the pretty gardens and woods far below them.

Dorothy found herself riding easily between two of the biggest Monkeys, one of them the King himself. They had made a chair of their hands and were careful not to hurt her.

"Why do you have to obey the charm of the Golden Cap?" she asked.

"That is a long story," answered the King, with a laugh; "but as we have a long journey before us I will pass the time by telling you about it, if you wish."

"I shall be glad to hear it," she replied.

"Once," began the leader, "we were a free people, living happily in the great forest, flying from tree to tree, eating nuts and fruit, and doing just as we pleased without calling anybody master. Perhaps some of us were rather too full of mischief at times, flying down to pull the tails of the animals that had no wings, chasing birds, and throwing nuts at the people who walked in the forest. But we were careless and happy and full of fun, and enjoyed every minute of the day. This was many years ago, long before Oz came out of the clouds to rule over this land.

"There lived here then, away at the North, a beautiful princess, who was also a powerful sorceress. All her magic was used to help the people, and she was never known to hurt anyone who was good. Her name was Gayelette, and she lived in a handsome palace built from great blocks of ruby. Everyone loved her, but her greatest sorrow was that she could find no one to love in return, since all the men were much too stupid and ugly to mate with one so beautiful and wise. At last, however, she found a boy who was handsome and manly and wise beyond his years. Gayelette made up her mind that when he grew to be a man she would make him her husband, so she took him to her ruby palace and used all her magic powers to make him as strong and good and lovely as any woman could wish. When he grew to manhood, Quelala, as he was called, was said to be the best and wisest man in all the land, while his manly beauty was so great that Gayelette loved him dearly, and hastened to make everything ready for the wedding.

"My grandfather was at that time the King of the Winged Monkeys which lived in the forest near Gayelette's palace, and the old fellow loved a joke better than a good dinner. One day, just before the wedding, my grandfather was flying out with his band when he saw Quelala walking beside the river. He was dressed in a rich costume of pink silk and purple velvet, and my grandfather thought he would see what he could do. At his word the band flew down and seized Quelala, carried him in their arms until they were over the middle of the river, and then dropped him into the water.

" 'Swim out, my fine fellow,' cried my grandfather, 'and see if the water has spotted your clothes.' Quelala was much too wise not to swim, and he was not in the least spoiled by all his good fortune. He laughed, when he came to the top of the water, and swam in to shore. But when Gayelette came running out to him she found his silks and velvet all ruined by the river.

"The princess was very angry, and she knew, of course, who did it. She had all the Winged Monkeys brought before her, and she said at first that their wings should be tied and they should be treated as they had treated Quelala, and dropped in the river. But my grandfather pleaded hard, for he knew the Monkeys would drown in the river with their wings tied, and Quelala said a kind word for them also; so that Gayelette finally spared them, on condition that the Winged Monkeys should ever after do three times the bidding of the owner of the Golden Cap. This Cap had been made for a wedding present to Quelala, and it is said to have cost the princess half her kingdom. Of course my grandfather and all the other Monkeys at once agreed to the condition, and that is how it happens that we are three times the slaves of the owner of the Golden Cap, whomsoever he may be."

"And what became of them?" asked Dorothy, who had been greatly interested in the story.

"Quelala being the first owner of the Golden Cap," replied the Monkey, "he was the first to lay his wishes upon us. As his bride could not bear the sight of us, he called us all to him in the forest after he had married her and ordered us to always keep where she could never again set eyes on a Winged Monkey, which we were glad to do, for we were all afraid of her.

"This was all we ever had to do until the Golden Cap fell into the hands of the Wicked Witch of the West, who made us enslave the Winkies, and afterward drive Oz himself out of the Land of the West. Now the Golden Cap is yours, and three times you have the right to lay your wishes upon us."

As the Monkey King finished his story Dorothy looked down and saw the green, shining walls of the Emerald City before them. She wondered at the rapid flight of the Monkeys, but was glad the journey was over. The strange creatures set the travellers down carefully before the gate of the City, the King bowed low to Dorothy, and then flew swiftly away, followed by all his band.

"That was a good ride," said the little girl.

"Yes, and a quick way out of our troubles," replied the Lion. "How lucky it was you brought away that wonderful Cap!"

Chapter XV

· The Discovery of Oz, the Terrible ·

The four travellers walked up to the great gate of the Emerald City and rang the bell. After ringing several times it was opened by the same Guardian of the Gates they had met before.

"What! are you back again?" he asked, in surprise.

"Do you not see us?" answered the Scarecrow.

"But I thought you had gone to visit the Wicked Witch of the West."

"We did visit her," said the Scarecrow.

"And she let you go again?" asked the man, in wonder.

"She could not help it, for she is melted," explained the Scarecrow.

"Melted! Well, that is good news, indeed," said the man. "Who melted her?"

"It was Dorothy," said the Lion, gravely.

"Good gracious!" exclaimed the man, and he bowed very low indeed before her.

Then he led them into his little room and locked the spectacles from the great box on all their eyes, just as he had done before. Afterward they passed on through the gate into the Emerald City, and when the people heard from the Guardian of the Gates that they had melted the Wicked Witch of the West they all gathered around the travellers and followed them in a great crowd to the Palace of Oz.

The soldier with the green whiskers was still on guard before the door, but he let them in at once and they were again met by the beautiful green girl, who showed each of them to their old rooms at once, so they might rest until the Great Oz was ready to receive them.

The soldier had the news carried straight to Oz that Dorothy and the other travellers had come back again, after destroying the Wicked Witch; but Oz made no reply. They thought the Great Wizard would send for them at once, but he did not. They had no word from him the next day, nor the next, nor the next. The waiting was tiresome and wearing, and at last they grew vexed that Oz should treat them in so poor a fashion, after sending them to undergo hardships and slavery. So the Scarecrow at last asked the green girl to take another message to Oz, saying if he did not let them in to see him at once they would call the Winged Monkeys to help them, and find out whether he kept his promises or not. When the Wizard was given this message he was so frightened that he sent word for them to come to the Throne Room at four minutes after nine o'clock the next morning. He had once met the Winged Monkeys in the Land of the West, and he did not wish to meet them again.

The four travellers passed a sleepless night, each thinking of the gift Oz had promised to bestow upon him. Dorothy fell asleep only once, and then she dreamed she was in Kansas, where Aunt Em was telling her how glad she was to have her little girl at home again.

Promptly at nine o'clock the next morning the green whiskered soldier came to them, and four minutes later they all went into the Throne Room of the Great Oz.

Of course each one of them expected to see the Wizard in the shape he had taken before, and all were greatly surprised when they looked about and saw no one at all in the room. They kept close to the door and closer to one another, for the stillness of the empty room was more dreadful than any of the forms they had seen Oz take.

Presently they heard a Voice, seeming to come from somewhere near the top of the great dome, and it said, solemnly,

"I am Oz, the Great and Terrible. Why do you seek me?"

They looked again in every part of the room, and then, seeing no one, Dorothy asked,

"Where are you?"

"I am everywhere," answered the Voice, "but to the eyes of common mortals I am invisible. I will now seat myself upon my throne, that you may converse with me." Indeed, the Voice seemed just then to come straight from the throne itself; so they walked toward it and stood in a row while Dorothy said:

"We have come to claim our promise, O Oz."

"What promise?" asked Oz.

"You promised to send me back to Kansas when the Wicked Witch was destroyed," said the girl.

"And you promised to give me brains," said the Scarecrow.

"And you promised to give me a heart," said the Tin Woodman.

"And you promised to give me courage," said the Cowardly Lion.

"Is the Wicked Witch really destroyed?" asked the Voice, and Dorothy thought it trembled a little.

"Yes," she answered, "I melted her with a bucket of water."

"Dear me," said the Voice; "how sudden! Well, come to me to-morrow, for I must have time to think it over."

"You've had plenty of time already," said the Tin Woodman, angrily.

"We shan't wait a day longer," said the Scarecrow.

"You must keep your promises to us!" exclaimed Dorothy.

The Lion thought it might be as well to frighten the Wizard, so he gave a large, loud roar, which was so fierce and dreadful that Toto jumped away from him in alarm and tipped over the screen that stood in a corner. As it fell with a crash they looked that way, and the next moment all of them were filled with wonder. For they saw, standing in just the spot the screen had hidden, a little, old man, with a bald head and a wrinkled face, who seemed to be as much surprised as they were. The Tin Woodman, raising his axe, rushed toward the little man and cried out,

"Who are you?"

"'I am Oz, the Great and Terrible," said the little man, in a trembling voice, "but don't strike me—please don't!—and I'll do anything you want me to."

Our friends looked at him in surprise and dismay.

"I thought Oz was a great Head," said Dorothy.

"And I thought Oz was a lovely Lady," said the Scarecrow,

"And I thought Oz was a terrible Beast," said the Tin Woodman.

"And I thought Oz was a Ball of Fire," exclaimed the Lion.

"No; you are all wrong," said the little man, meekly. "I have been making believe."

"Making believe!" cried Dorothy. "Are you not a great Wizard?"

"Hush, my dear," he said; "don't speak so loud, or you will be overheard—and I should be ruined. I'm supposed to be a Great Wizard."

"And aren't you?" she asked.

"Not a bit of it, my dear; I'm just a common man."

"You're more than that," said the Scarecrow, in a grieved tone; "you're a humbug."

"Exactly so!" declared the little man, rubbing his hands together as if it pleased him; "I am a humbug."

"But this is terrible," said the Tin Woodman; "how shall I ever get my heart?"

"Or I my courage?" asked the Lion.

"Or I my brains?" wailed the Scarecrow, wiping the tears from his eyes with his coat-sleeve.

"My dear friends," said Oz, "I pray you not to speak of these little things. Think of me, and the terrible trouble I'm in at being found out."

"Doesn't anyone else know you're a humbug?" asked Dorothy.

"No one knows it but you four—and myself," replied Oz. "I have fooled everyone so long that I thought I should never be found out. It was a great mistake my ever letting you into the Throne Room. Usually I will not see even my subjects, and so they believe I am something terrible."

"But, I don't understand," said Dorothy, in bewilderment. "How was it that you appeared to me as a great Head?"

"That was one of my tricks," answered Oz. "Step this way, please, and I will tell you all about it."

He led the way to a small chamber in the rear of the Throne Room, and they all followed him. He pointed to one corner, in which lay the Great Head, made out of many thicknesses of paper, and with a carefully painted face.

"This I hung from the ceiling by a wire," said Oz; "I stood behind the screen and pulled a thread, to make the eyes move and the mouth open."

"But how about the voice?" she enquired.

"Oh, I am a ventriloquist," said the little man, "and I can throw the sound of my voice wherever I wish; so that you

thought it was coming out of the Head. Here are the other things I used to deceive you." He showed the Scarecrow the dress and the mask he had worn when he seemed to be the lovely Lady; and the Tin Woodman saw that his Terrible Beast was nothing but a lot of skins, sewn together, with slats to keep their sides out. As for the Ball of Fire, the false Wizard had hung that also from the ceiling. It was really a ball of cotton, but when oil was poured upon it the ball burned fiercely.

"Really," said the Scarecrow, "you ought to be ashamed of yourself for being such a humbug."

"I am—I certainly am," answered the little man, sorrowfully; "but it was the only thing I could do. Sit down, please, there are plenty of chairs; and I will tell you my story."

So they sat down and listened while he told the following tale:

"I was born in Omaha—"

"Why, that isn't very far from Kansas!" cried Dorothy.

"No; but it's farther from here," he said, shaking his head at her, sadly. "When I grew up I became a ventriloquist, and at that I was very well trained by a great master. I can imitate any kind of a bird or beast." Here he mewed so like a kitten that Toto pricked up his ears and looked everywhere to see where she was. "After a time," continued Oz, "I tired of that, and became a balloonist."

"What is that?" asked Dorothy.

"A man who goes up in a balloon on circus day, so as to draw a crowd of people together and get them to pay to see the circus," he explained.

"Oh," she said; "I know."

"Well, one day I went up in a balloon and the ropes got twisted, so that I couldn't come down again. It went way up above the clouds, so far that a current of air struck it and carried it many, many miles away. For a day and a night I travelled through the air, and on the morning of the second day I awoke and found the balloon floating over a strange and beautiful country.

"It came down gradually, and I was not hurt a bit. But I found myself in the midst of a strange people, who, seeing me come from the clouds, thought I was a great Wizard. Of course I let them think so, because they were afraid of me, and promised to do anything I wished them to.

"Just to amuse myself, and keep the good people busy, I ordered them to build this City, and my palace; and they did it all willingly and well. Then I thought, as the country was so green and beautiful, I would call it the Emerald City, and to make the name fit better I put green spectacles on all the people, so that everything they saw was green."

"But isn't everything here green?" asked Dorothy.

"No more than in any other city," replied Oz; "but when you wear green spectacles, why of course everthing you see looks green to you. The Emerald City was built a great many years ago, for I was a young man when the balloon brought me here, and I am a very old man now. But my people have worn green glasses on their eyes so long that most of them think it really is an Emerald City, and it certainly is a beautiful place, abounding in jewels and precious metals, and every good thing that is needed to make one happy. I have been good to the people, and they like me; but ever since this Palace was built I have shut myself up and would not see any of them.

"One of my greatest fears was the Witches, for while I had no magical powers at all I soon found out that the Witches were really able to do wonderful things. There were four of them in this country, and they ruled the people who live in the North and South and East and West. Fortunately, the Witches of the North and South were good, and I knew they would do me no harm; but the Witches of the East and West were terribly wicked, and had they not thought I was more powerful than they themselves, they would surely have destroyed me. As it was, I lived in deadly fear of them, for many years; so you can imagine how pleased I was when I heard your house had fallen on the Wicked Witch of the East. When you came to me I was willing to promise anything if you would only do away with the other Witch; but, now that you have melted her, I am ashamed to say that I cannot keep my promises."

"I think you are a very bad man," said Dorothy.

"Oh, no, my dear; I'm really a very good man; but I'm a very bad Wizard, I must admit."

"Can't you give me brains?" asked the Scarecrow.

"You don't need them. You are learning something every day.

A baby has brains, but it doesn't know much. Experience is the only thing that brings knowledge, and the longer you are on earth the more experience you are sure to get."

"That may all be true," said the Scarecrow, "but I shall be very unhappy unless you give me brains."

The false wizard looked at him carefully.

"Well," he said, with a sigh, "I'm not much of a magician, as I said; but if you will come to me to-morrow morning, I will stuff your head with brains. I cannot tell you how to use them, however; you must find that out for yourself."

"Oh, thank you—thank you!" cried the Scarecrow. "I'll find a way to use them, never fear!"

"But how about my courage?" asked the Lion, anxiously.

"You have plenty of courage, I am sure," answered Oz. "All you need is confidence in yourself. There is no living thing that is not afraid when it faces danger. True courage is in facing danger when you are afraid, and that kind of courage you have in plenty."

"Perhaps I have, but I'm scared just the same," said the Lion. "I shall really be very unhappy unless you give me the sort of courage that makes one forget he is afraid."

"Very well; I will give you that sort of courage to-morrow," replied Oz.

"How about my heart?" asked the Tin Woodman.

"Why, as for that," answered Oz, "I think you are wrong to want a heart. It makes most people unhappy. If you only knew it, you are in luck not to have a heart."

"That must be a matter of opinion," said the Tin Woodman. "For my part, I will bear all the unhappiness without a murmur, if you will give me the heart."

"Very well," answered Oz, meekly. "Come to me to-morrow and you shall have a heart. I have played Wizard for so many years that I may as well continue the part a little longer."

"And now," said Dorothy, "how am I to get back to Kansas?"

"We shall have to think about that," replied the little man. "Give me two or three days to consider the matter and I'll try to find a way to carry you over the desert. In the meantime you shall all be treated as my guests, and while you live in the Palace my people will wait upon you and obey your slightest wish. There is only one thing I ask in return for my help—such as it is. You must keep my secret and tell no one I am a humbug."

They agreed to say nothing of what they had learned, and went back to their rooms in high spirits. Even Dorothy had hope that "The Great and Terrible Humbug," as she called him, would find a way to send her back to Kansas, and if he did that she was willing to forgive him everything.

Chapter XVI

· The Magic Art of the Great Humbug ·

Next morning the Scarecrow said to his friends:

"Congratulate me. I am going to Oz to get my brains at last. When I return I shall be as other men are."

"I have always liked you as you were," said Dorothy, simply.

"It is kind of you to like a Scarecrow," he replied. "But surely you will think more of me when you hear the splendid thoughts my new brain is going to turn out." Then he said good-bye to them all in a cheerful voice and went to the Throne Room, where he rapped upon the door.

"Come in," said Oz.

The Scarecrow went in and found the little man sitting down by the window, engaged in deep thought.

"I have come for my brains," remarked the Scarecrow, a little uneasily.

"Oh, yes; sit down in that chair, please," replied Oz. "You must excuse me for taking your head off, but I shall have to do it in order to put your brains in their proper place."

"That's all right," said the Scarecrow. "You are quite welcome to take my head off, as long as it will be a better one when you put it on again."

So the Wizard unfastened his head and emptied out the straw. Then he entered the back room and took up a measure of bran, which he mixed with a great many pins and needles. Having shaken them together thoroughly, he filled the top of the Scarecrow's head with the mixture and stuffed the rest of the space with straw, to hold it in place. When he had fastened the Scarecrow's head on his body again he said to him,

"Hereafter you will be a great man, for I have given you a lot of bran-new brains."

The Scarecrow was both pleased and proud at the fulfillment of his greatest wish, and having thanked Oz warmly he went back to his friends.

Dorothy looked at him curiously. His head was quite bulging out at the top with brains.

"How do you feel?" she asked.

"I feel wise, indeed," he answered, earnestly. "When I get used to my brains I shall know everything."

"Why are those needles and pins sticking out of your head?" asked the Tin Woodman.

"That is proof that he is sharp," remarked the Lion.

"Well, I must go to Oz and get my heart," said the Woodman. So he walked to the Throne Room and knocked at the door.

"Come in," called Oz, and the Woodman entered and said, "I have come for my heart."

"Very well," answered the little man. "But I shall have to cut a hole in your breast, so I can put your heart in the right place. I hope it won't hurt you."

"Oh, no;" answered the Woodman. "I shall not feel it at all."

So Oz brought a pair of tinners' shears and cut a small, square hole in the left side of the Tin Woodman's breast. Then, going to a chest of drawers, he took out a pretty heart, made entirely of silk and stuffed with sawdust.

"Isn't it a beauty?" he asked.

"It is, indeed!" replied the Woodman, who was greatly pleased. "But is it a kind heart?"

"Oh, very!" answered Oz. He put the heart in the Woodman's breast and then replaced the square of tin, soldering it neatly together where it had been cut.

"There," said he; "now you have a heart that any man might be proud of. I'm sorry I had to put a patch on your breast, but it really couldn't be helped."

"Never mind the patch," exclaimed the happy Woodman. "I am very grateful to you, and shall never forget your kindness."

"Don't speak of it," replied Oz.

Then the Tin Woodman went back to his friends, who wished him every joy on account of his good fortune.

The Lion now walked to the Throne Room and knocked at the door.

"Come in," said Oz.

"I have come for my courage," announced the Lion, entering the room.

"Very well," answered the little man; "I will get it for you."

He went to a cupboard and reaching up to a high shelf took down a square green bottle, the contents of which he poured into a green-gold dish, beautifully carved. Placing this before the Cowardly Lion, who sniffed at it as if he did not like it, the Wizard said,

"Drink."

"What is it?" asked the Lion.

"Well," answered Oz, "if it were inside of you, it would be courage. You know, of course, that courage is always inside one; so that this really cannot be called courage until you have swallowed it. Therefore I advise you to drink it as soon as possible."

The Lion hesitated no longer, but drank till the dish was empty.

"How do you feel now?" asked Oz.

"Full of courage," replied the Lion, who went joyfully back to his friends to tell them of his good fortune.

Oz, left to himself, smiled to think of his success in giving the Scarecrow and the Tin Woodman and the Lion exactly what they thought they wanted. "How can I help being a humbug," he said, "when all these people make me do things that everybody knows can't be done? It was easy to make the Scarecrow and the Lion and the Woodman happy, because they imagined I could do anything. But it will take more than imagination to carry Dorothy back to Kansas, and I'm sure I don't know how it can be done."

Chapter XVII

· How the Balloon was Launched ·

For three days Dorothy heard nothing from Oz. These were sad days for the little girl, although her friends were all quite happy and contented. The Scarecrow told them there were wonderful thoughts in his head; but he would not say what they were because he knew no one could understand them but himself. When the Tin Woodman walked about he felt his heart rattling around in his breast; and he told Dorothy he had discovered it to be a kinder and more tender heart than the one he had owned when he was made of flesh. The Lion declared he was afraid of nothing on earth, and would gladly face an army of men or a dozen of the fierce Kalidahs.

Thus each of the little party was satisfied except Dorothy, who longed more than ever to get back to Kansas.

On the fourth day, to her great joy, Oz sent for her, and when she entered the Throne Room he said, pleasantly:

"Sit down, my dear; I think I have found the way to get you out of this country."

"And back to Kansas?" she asked, eagerly.

"Well, I'm not sure about Kansas," said Oz; "for I haven't the faintest notion which way it lies. But the first thing to do is to cross the desert, and then it should be easy to find your way home."

"How can I cross the desert?" she enquired.

"Well, I'll tell you what I think," said the little man. "You see, when I came to this country it was in a balloon. You also came through the air, being carried by a cyclone. So I believe the best way to get across the desert will be through the air. Now, it is quite byond my powers to make a cyclone; but I've been thinking the matter over, and I believe I can make a balloon."

"How?" asked Dorothy.

"A balloon," said Oz, "is made of silk, which is coated with glue to keep the gas in it. I have plenty of silk in the Palace, so it will be no trouble for us to make the balloon. But in all this country there is no gas to fill the balloon with, to make it float."

"If it won't float," remarked Dorothy, "it will be of no use to us."

"True, answered Oz. "But there is another way to make it float, which is to fill it with hot air. Hot air isn't as good as gas, for if the air should get cold the balloon would come down in the desert, and we should be lost."

"We!" exclaimed the girl; "are you going with me?"

"Yes, of course," replied Oz. "I am tired of being such a humbug. If I should go out of this Palace my people would soon discover I am not a Wizard, and then they would be vexed with me for having deceived them. So I have to stay shut up in these rooms all day, and it gets tiresome. I'd much rather go back to Kansas with you and be in a circus again."

"I shall be glad to have your company," said Dorothy.

"Thank you," he answered. "Now, if you will help me sew the silk together, we will begin to work on our balloon."

So Dorothy took a needle and thread, and as fast as Oz cut the strips of silk into proper shape the girl sewed them neatly together. First there was a strip of light green silk, then a strip of dark green and then a strip of emerald green; for Oz had a fancy to make the balloon in different shades of the color about them. It took three days to sew all the strips together, but when it was finished they had a big bag of green silk more than twenty feet long.

Then Oz painted it on the inside with a coat of thin glue, to make it air-tight, after which he announced that the balloon was ready.

"But we must have a basket to ride in," he said. So he sent the soldier with the green whiskers for a big clothes basket, which he fastened with many ropes to the bottom of the balloon.

When it was all ready, Oz sent word to his people that he was going to make a visit to a great brother Wizard who lived in the clouds. The news spread rapidly throughout the city and everyone came to see the wonderful sight.

Oz ordered the balloon carried out in front of the Palace, and the people gazed upon it with much curiosity. The Tin Woodman had chopped a big pile of wood, and now he made a fire of it, and Oz held the bottom of the balloon over the fire so that the hot air that arose from it would be caught in the silken bag. Gradually the balloon swelled and rose into the air, until finally the basket just touched the ground.

Then Oz got into the basket and said to all the people in a loud voice:

"I am now going away to make a visit. While I am gone the Scarecrow will rule over you. I command you to obey him as you would me."

The balloon was by this time tugging hard at the rope that held it to the ground, for the air within it was hot, and this made it so much lighter in weight than the air without that it pulled hard to rise into the sky.

"Come, Dorothy!" cried the Wizard; "hurry up, or the balloon will fly away."

"I can't find Toto anywhere," replied Dorothy, who did not wish to leave her little dog behind. Toto had run into the crowd to bark at a kitten, and Dorothy at last found him. She picked him up and ran toward the balloon.

She was within a few steps of it, and Oz was holding out his hands to help her into the basket, when, crack! went the ropes, and the balloon rose into the air without her.

"Come back!" she screamed; "I want to go, too!"

"I can't come back, my dear," called Oz from the basket. "Good-bye!"

"Good-bye!" shouted everyone, and all eyes were turned upward to where the Wizard was riding in the basket, rising every moment farther and father into the sky.

And that was the last any of them ever saw of Oz, the Wonderful Wizard, though he may have reached Omaha safely, and be there now, for all we know. But the people remembered him lovingly, and said to one another,

"Oz was always our friend. When he was here he built for us this beautiful Emerald City, and now he is gone he has left the Wise Scarecrow to rule over us,"

Still, for many days they grieved over the loss of the Wonderful Wizard, and would not be comforted.

Chapter XVIII

· Away to the South ·

D orothy wept bitterly at the passing of her hope to get home to Kansas again; but when she thought it all over she was glad she had not gone up in a balloon. And she also felt sorry at losing Oz, and so did her companions.

The Tin Woodman came to her and said,

"Truly I should be ungrateful if I failed to mourn for the man who gave me my lovely heart. I should like to cry a little because Oz is gone, if you will kindly wipe away my tears, so that I shall not rust."

"With pleasure," she answered, and brought a towel at once. Then the Tin Woodman wept for several minutes, and she watched the tears carefully and wiped them away with the towel. When he had finished he thanked her kindly and oiled himself thoroughly with his jewelled oil-can, to guard against mishap.

The Scarecrow was now the ruler of the Emerald City, and although he was not a Wizard the people were proud of him. "For," they said, "there is not another city in all the world that is ruled by a stuffed man." And, so far as they knew, they were quite right.

The morning after the balloon had gone up with Oz the four travellers met in the Throne Room and talked matters over. The Scarecrow sat in the big throne and the others stood respectfully before him.

"We are not so unlucky," said the new ruler; "for this Palace and the Emerald City belong to us, and we can do just as we please. When I remember that a short time ago I was up on a pole in a farmer's cornfield, and that I am now the ruler of this beautiful City, I am quite satisfied with my lot."

"I also," said the Tin Woodman, "am well pleased with my new heart; and, really, that was the only thing I wished in all the world."

"For my part, I am content in knowing I am as brave as any beast that ever lived, if not braver," said the Lion, modestly.

"If Dorothy would only be contented to live in the Emerald City," continued the Scarecrow, "we might all be happy together."

"But I don't want to live here," cried Dorothy. "I want to go to Kansas, and live with Aunt Em and Uncle Henry."

"Well, then, what can be done?" enquired the Woodman.

The Scarecrow decided to think, and he thought so hard that the pins and needles began to stick out of his brains. Finally he said:

"Why not call the Winged Monkeys, and ask them to carry you over the desert?"

"I never thought of that!" said Dorothy, joyfully. "It's just the thing. I'll go at once for the Golden Cap."

When she brought it into the Throne Room she spoke the magic words, and soon the band of Winged Monkeys flew in through an open window and stood beside her.

"This is the second time you have called us," said the Monkey King, bowing before the little girl. "What do you wish?"

"I want you to fly with me to Kansas," said Dorothy.

But the Monkey King shook his head.

"That cannot be done," he said. "We belong to this country alone, and cannot leave it. There has never been a Winged Monkey in Kansas yet, and I suppose there never will be, for they don't belong there. We shall be glad to serve you in any way in our power, but we cannot cross the desert. Good-bye."

And with another bow the Monkey King spread his wings and flew away through the window, followed by all his band.

Dorothy was almost ready to cry with disappointment.

"I have wasted the charm of the Golden Cap to no purpose," she said, "for the Winged Monkeys cannot help me."

"It is certainly too bad!" said the tender hearted Woodman.

The Scarecrow was thinking again, and his head bulged out so horribly that Dorothy feared it would burst.

"Let us call in the soldier with the green whiskers," he said, "and ask his advice."

So the soldier was summoned and entered the Throne Room timidly, for while Oz was alive he never was allowed to come further than the door.

"This little girl," said the Scarecrow to the soldier, "wishes to cross the desert. How can she do so?"

"I cannot tell," answered the soldier; "for nobody has ever crossed the desert, unless it is Oz himself."

"Is there no one who can help me?" asked Dorothy, earnestly.

"Glinda might," he suggested.

"Who is Glinda?" enquired the Scarecrow.

"The Witch of the South. She is the most powerful of all the Witches, and rules over the Quadlings. Besides, her castle stands on the edge of the desert, so she may know a way to cross it."

"Glinda is a good Witch, isn't she?" asked the child.

"The Quadlings think she is good," said the soldier, "and she is kind to everyone. I have heard that Glinda is a beautiful woman, who knows how to keep young in spite of the many years she has lived."

"How can I get to her castle?" asked Dorothy.

"The road is straight to the South," he answered, "but it is said to be full of dangers to travellers. There are wild beasts in the woods, and a race of queer men who do not like strangers to cross their country. For this reason none of the Quadlings ever come to the Emerald City."

The soldier then left them and the Scarecrow said,

"It seems, in spite of dangers, that the best thing Dorothy can do is to travel to the Land of the South and ask Glinda to help her. For, of course, if Dorothy stays here she will never get back to Kansas."

"You must have been thinking again," remarked the Tin Woodman.

"I have," said the Scarecrow.

"I shall go with Dorothy," declared the Lion, "for I am tired of your city and long for the woods and the country again. I am really a wild beast, you know. Besides, Dorothy will need some-one to protect her."

"That is true," agreed the Woodman. "My axe may be of ser-vice to her; so I, also, will go with her to the Land of the South."

"When shall we start?" asked the Scarecrow.

"Are you going?" they asked, in surprise.

"Certainly. If it wasn't for Dorothy I should never have had brains. She lifted me from the pole in the cornfield and brought me to the Emerald City. So my good luck is all due to her, and I shall never leave her until she starts back to Kansas for good and all."

"Thank you," said Dorothy, gratefully. "You are all very kind to me. But I should like to start as soon as possible."

"We shall go to-morrow morning," returned the Scarecrow. So now let us all get ready, for it will be a long journey."

Chapter XIX

· Attacked by the Fighting Trees ·

The next morning Dorothy kissed the pretty green girl good-bye, and they all shook hands with the soldier with the green whiskers, who had walked with them as far as the gate. When the Guardian of the Gates saw them again he wondered greatly that they could leave the beautiful City to get into new trouble. But he at once unlocked their spectacles, which he put back into the green box, and gave them many good wishes to carry with them.

"You are now our ruler," he said to the Scarecrow; "so you must come back to us as soon as possible."

"I certainly shall if I am able," the Scarecrow replied; "but I must help Dorothy to get home, first."

As Dorothy bade the good-natured Guardian a last farewell she said,

"I have been very kindly treated in your lovely City, and everyone has been good to me. I cannot tell you how grateful I am."

"Don't try, my dear," he answered. "We should like to keep you with us, but if it is your wish to return to Kansas I hope you will find a way." He then opened the gate of the outer wall and they walked forth and started upon their journey.

The sun shone brightly as our friends turned their faces toward the Land of the South. They were all in the best of spirits, and laughed and chatted together. Dorothy was once more filled with the hope of getting home, and the Scarecrow and the Tin

Woodman were glad to be of use to her. As for the Lion, he sniffed the fresh air with delight and whisked his tail from side to side in pure joy at being in the country again, while Toto ran around them and chased the moths and butterflies, barking merrily all the time.

"City life does not agree with me at all," remarked the Lion, as they walked along at a brisk pace. "I have lost much flesh since I lived there, and now I am anxious for a chance to show the other beasts how courageous I have grown."

They now turned and took a last look at the Emerald City. All they could see was a mass of towers and steeples behind the green walls, and high up above everything the spires and dome of the Palace of Oz.

"Oz was not such a bad Wizard, after all," said the Tin Woodman, as he felt his heart rattling around in his breast.

"He knew how to give me brains, and very good brains, too," said the Scarecrow.

"If Oz had taken a dose of the same courage he gave me," added the Lion, "he would have been a brave man."

Dorothy said nothing. Oz had not kept the promise he made her, but he had done his best, so she forgave him. As he said, he was a good man, even if he was a bad Wizard.

The first day's journey was through the green fields and bright flowers that stretched about the Emerald City on every side. They slept that night on the grass, with nothing but the stars over them; and they rested very well indeed.

In the morning they travelled on until they came to a thick wood. There was no way of going around it, for it seemed to extend to the right and left as far as they could see; and, besides, they did not dare change the direction of their journey for fear of getting lost. So they looked for the place where it would be easaiest to get into the forest.

The Scarecrow, who was in the lead, finally discovered a big tree with such wide spreading branches that there was room for the party to pass underneath. So he walked forward to the tree, but just as he came under the first branches they bent down and twined around him, and the next minute he was raised from the ground and flung headlong among his fellow travellers.

This did not hurt the Scarecrow, but it surprised him, and he looked rather dizzy when Dorothy picked him up.

"Here is another space between the trees," called the Lion.

"Let me try it first," said the Scarecrow, "for it doesn't hurt me to get thrown about." He walked up to another tree, as he spoke, but its branches immediately seized him and tossed him back again.

"This is strange," exclaimed Dorothy; "what shall we do?"

"The trees seem to have made up their minds to fight us, and stop our journey," remarked the Lion.

"I believe I will try it myself," said the Woodman, and shouldering his axe he marched up to the first tree that had handled the Scarecrow so roughly. When a big branch bent down to seize him the Woodman chopped at it so fiercely that he cut it in two. At once the tree began shaking all its branches as if in pain, and the Tin Woodman passed safely under it.

"Come on!" he shouted to the others; "be quick!"

They all ran forward and passed under the tree without injury, except Toto, who was caught by a small branch and shaken until he howled. But the Woodman promptly chopped off the branch and set the little dog free.

The other trees of the forest did nothing to keep them back, so they made up their minds that only the first row of trees could bend down their branches, and that probably these were the policemen of the forest, and given this wonderful power in order to keep strangers out of it.

The four travellers walked with ease through the trees until they came to the further edge of the wood. Then, to their surprise, they found before them a high wall, which seemed to be made of white china. It was smooth, like the surface of a dish, and higher than their heads.

"What shall we do now?" asked Dorothy.

"I will make a ladder," said the Tin Woodman, "for we certainly must climb over the wall."

Chapter XX

· The Dainty China Country ·

While the Woodman was making a ladder from wood which he found in the forest Dorothy lay down and slept, for she was tired by the long walk. The Lion also curled himself up to sleep and Toto lay beside him.

The Scarecrow watched the Woodman while he worked, and said to him:

"I cannot think why this wall is here, nor what it is made of."

"Rest your brains and do not worry about the wall," replied the Woodman; "when we have climbed over it we shall know what is on the other side."

After a time the ladder was finished. It looked clumsy, but the Tin Woodman was sure it was strong and would answer their purpose. The Scarecrow waked Dorothy and the Lion and Toto, and told them that the ladder was ready. The Scarecrow climbed up the ladder first, but he was so awkward that Dorothy had to follow close behind and keep him from falling off. When he got his head over the top of the wall the Scarecrow said,

"Oh, my!"

"Go on," exclaimed Dorothy.

So the Scarecrow climbed further up and sat down on the top of the wall, and Dorothy put her head over and cried,

"Oh, my!" just as the Scarecrow had done.

Then Toto came up, and immediately began to bark, but Dorothy made him be still.

The Lion climbed the ladder next, and the Tin Woodman came last; but both of them cried, "Oh, my!" as soon as they looked over the wall. When they were all sitting in a row on the top of the wall they looked down and saw a strange sight.

Before them was a great stretch of country having a floor as smooth and shining and white as the bottom of a big platter. Scattered around were many houses made entirely of china and painted in the brightest colours. These houses were quite small, the biggest of them reaching only as high as Dorothy's waist. There were also pretty little barns, with china fences around them, and many cows and sheep and horses and pigs and chickens, all made of china, were standing about in groups.

But the strangest of all were the people who lived in this queer country. There were milk-maids and shepherdesses, with bright-colored bodices and golden spots all over their gowns; and princesses with most gorgeous frocks of silver and gold and purple; and shepherds dressed in knee-breeches with pink and yellow and blue stripes down them, and golden buckles on their shoes; and princes with jewelled crowns upon their heads, wearing ermine robes and satin doublets; and funny clowns in ruffled gowns, with round red spots upon their cheeks and tall, pointed caps. And, strangest of all, these people were all made of china, even to their clothes, and were so small that the tallest of them was no higher than Dorothy's knee.

No one did so much as look at the travellers at first, except one little purple china dog with an extra-large head, which came to the wall and barked at them in a tiny voice, afterwards running away again.

"How shall we get down?" asked Dorothy.

They found the ladder so heavy they could not pull it up, so the Scarecrow fell off the wall and the others jumped down upon him so that the hard floor would not hurt their feet. Of course they took pains not to light on his head and get the pins in their feet. When all were safely down they picked up the Scarecrow, whose body was quite flattened out, and patted his straw into shape again.

"We must cross this strange place in order to get to the other side," said Dorothy; "for it would be unwise for us to go any other way except due South."

They began walking through the country of the china people, and the first thing they came to was a china milk-maid milking a china cow. As they drew near the cow suddenly gave a kick and kicked over the stool, the pail, and even the milk-maid herself, all falling on the china ground with a great clatter.

Dorothy was shocked to see that the cow had broken her leg short off, and that the pail was lying in several small pieces, while the poor milk-maid had a nick in her left elbow.

"There!" cried the milk-maid, angrily; "see what you have done! My cow has broken her leg, and I must take her to the

mender's shop and have it glued on again. What do you mean by coming here and frightening my cow?"

"I'm very sorry," returned Dorothy; "please forgive us."

But the pretty milk-maid was much too vexed to make any answer. She picked up the leg sulkily and led her cow away, the poor animal limping on three legs. As she left them the milk-maid cast many reproachful glances over her shoulder at the clumsy strangers, holding her nicked elbow close to her side.

Dorothy was quite grieved at this mishap.

"We must be very careful here," said the kind-hearted Woodman, "or we may hurt these pretty little people so they will never get over it."

A little farther on Dorothy met a most beautiful dressed young princess, who stopped short as she saw the strangers and started to run away.

Dorothy wanted to see more of the Princess, so she ran after her; but the china girl cried out,

"Don't chase me! don't chase me!"

She had such a frightened little voice that Dorothy stopped and said,

"Why not?"

"Because," answered the princess, also stopping, a safe distance away, "if I run I may fall down and break myself."

"But couldn't you be mended?" asked the girl.

"Oh, yes; but one is never so pretty after being mended, you know," replied the princess.

"I suppose not," said Dorothy.

"Now there is Mr. Joker, one of our clowns," continued the china lady, "who is always trying to stand upon his head. He has broken himself so often that he is mended in a hundred places, and doesn't look at all pretty. Here he comes now, so you can see for yourself."

Indeed, a jolly little Clown now came walking toward them, and Dorothy could see that in spite of his pretty clothes of red and yellow and green he was completely covered with cracks, running every which way and showing plainly that he had been mended in many places.

The Clown put his hands in his pockets, and after puffing out his cheeks and nodding his head at them saucily he said,

"My lady fair,
Why do you stare
At poor old Mr. Joker?
You're quite as stiff
And prim as if
You'd eaten up a poker!"

"Be quiet, sir!" said the princess; "can't you see these are strangers, and should be treated with respect?"

"Well, that's respect, I expect," declared the Clown, and immediately stood upon his head.

"Don't mind Mr. Joker," said the princess to Dorothy; "he is considerably cracked in his head, and that makes him foolish."

"Oh, I don't mind him a bit," said Dorothy. "But you are so beautiful," she continued, "that I am sure I could love you dearly. Won't you let me carry you back to Kansas and stand you on Aunt Em's mantel-shelf? I could carry you in my basket."

"That would make me very unhappy," answered the china princess. "You see, here in our own country we live contentedly, and can talk and move around as we please. But whenever any of us are taken away our joints at once stiffen, and we can only stand straight and look pretty. Of course that is all that is expected of us when we are on mantel-shelves and cabinets and drawing-room tables, but our lives are much pleasanter here in our own country."

"I would not make you unhappy for all the world!" exclaimed Dorothy; "so I'll just say good-bye."

"Good-bye," replied the princess.

They walked carefully through the china country. The little animals and all the people scampered out of their way, fearing the strangers would break them, and after an hour or so the travellers reached the other side of the country and came to another china wall.

It was not as high as the first, however, and by standing upon the Lion's back they all managed to scramble to the top. Then the Lion gathered his legs under him and jumped on the wall; but just as he jumped he upset a china church with his tail and smashed it all to pieces.

"That was too bad," said Dorothy, "but really I think we were lucky in not doing these little people more harm than breaking a cow's leg and a church. They are all so brittle!"

"They are, indeed," said the Scarecrow, "and I am thankful I am made of straw and cannot be easily damaged. There are worse things in the world than being a Scarecrow."

Chapter XXI
· The Lion Becomes the King of Beasts ·

After climbing down from the china wall the travellers found themselves in a disagreeable country, full of bogs and marshes and covered with tall, rank grass. It was difficult to walk far without falling into muddy holes, for the grass was so thick that it hid them from sight. However, by carefully picking their way, they got safely along until they reached solid ground. But here the country seemed wilder than ever, and after a long and tiresome walk through the underbrush they entered another forest, where the trees were bigger and older than any they had ever seen.

"This forest is perfectly delightful," declared the Lion, looking around him with joy; "never have I seen a more beautiful place."

"It seems gloomy," said the Scarecrow.

"Not a bit of it," answered the Lion; "I should like to live here all my life. See how soft the dried leaves are under your feet and how rich and green the moss is that clings to these old trees. Surely no wild beast could wish a pleasanter home."

"Perhaps there are wild beasts in the forest now," said Dorothy.

"I suppose there are," returned the Lion; "but I do not see any of them about."

They walked through the forest until it became too dark to go any farther. Dorothy and Toto and the Lion lay down to sleep, while the Woodman and the Scarecrow kept watch over them as usual.

When morning came they started again. Before they had gone far they heard a low rumble, as of the growling of many wild animals. Toto whimpered a little but none of the others was frightened and they kept along the well-trodden path until they came to an opening in the wood, in which were gathered hundreds of beasts of every variety. There were tigers and elephants and bears and wolves and foxes and all the others in the natural history, and for a moment Dorothy was afraid. But the Lion explained that the animals were holding a meeting, and he judged by their snarling and growling that they were in great trouble.

As he spoke several of the beasts caught sight of him, and at once the great assemblage hushed as if by magic. The biggest of the tigers came up to the Lion and bowed, saying,

"Welcome, O King of Beasts! You have come in good time to fight our enemy and bring peace to all the animals of the forest once more."

"What is your trouble?" asked the Lion, quietly.

"We are all threatened," answered the tiger, "by a fierce enemy which has lately come into this forest. It is a most tremendous monster, like a great spider, with a body as big as an elephant and legs as long as a tree trunk. It has eight of these long legs, and as the monster crawls through the forest he seizes an animal with a leg and drags it to his mouth, where he eats it as a spider does a fly. Not one of us is safe while this fierce creature is alive, and we had called a meeting to decide how to take care of ourselves when you came among us."

The Lion thought for a moment.

"Are there any other lions in this forest?" he asked.

"No; there were some, but the monster has eaten them all. And, besides, they were none of them nearly so large and brave as you."

"If I put an end to your enemy will you bow down to me and obey me as King of the Forest?" enquired the Lion.

"We will do that gladly," returned the tiger; and all the other beasts roared with a mighty roar: "We will!"

"Where is this great spider of yours now?" asked the Lion.

"Yonder, among the oak trees," said the tiger, pointing with his fore-foot."

"Take good care of these friends of mine," said the Lion, "and I will go at once to fight the monster."

He bade his comrades good-bye and marched proudly away to do battle with the enemy.

The great spider was lying asleep when the Lion found him, and it looked so ugly that its foe turned up his nose in disgust. Its legs were quite as long as the tiger had said, and its body covered with coarse black hair. It had a great mouth, with a row of sharp teeth a foot long; but its head was joined to the pudgy body by a neck as slender as a wasp's waist. This gave the Lion a hint of the best way to attack the creature, and as he knew it was easier to fight it asleep than awake, he gave a great spring and landed directly upon the monster's back. Then, with one blow of his heavy paw, all armed with sharp claws, he knocked the spider's head from its body. Jumping down, he watched it until the long legs stopped wiggling, when he knew it was quite dead.

The Lion went back to the opening where the beasts of the forest were waiting for him and said, proudly,

"You need fear your enemy no longer."

Then the beasts bowed down to the Lion as their King, and he promised to come back and rule over them as soon as Dorothy was safely on her way to Kansas.

Chapter XXII

· The Country of the Quadlings ·

The four travellers passed through the rest of the forest in safety, and when they came out from its gloom saw before them a steep hill, covered from top to bottom with great pieces of rock.

"That will be a hard climb," said the Scarecrow, "but we must get over the hill, nevertheless."

So he led the way and the others followed. They had nearly reached the first rock when they heard a rough voice cry out,

"Keep back!"

"Who are you?" asked the Scarecrow. Then a head showed itself over the rock and the same voice said,

"This hill belongs to us, and we don't allow anyone to cross it."

"But we must cross it," said the Scarecrow. "We're going to the country of the Quadlings."

"But you shall not!" replied the voice, and there stepped from behind the rock the strangest man the travellers had ever seen.

He was quite short and stout and had a big head, which was flat at the top and supported by a thick neck full of wrinkles. But he had no arms at all, and, seeing this, the Scarecrow did not fear that so helpless a creature could prevent them from climbing the hill. So he said,

"I'm sorry not to do as you wish, but we must pass over your hill whether you like it or not," and he walked boldly forward.

As quick as lightning the man's head shot forward and his neck stretched out until the top of the head, where it was flat, struck the Scarecrow in the middle and sent him tumbling, over and over, down the hill. Almost as quickly as it came the head went back to the body, and the man laughed harshly as he said,

"It isn't as easy as you think!"

A chorus of boisterous laughter came from the other rocks, and Dorothy saw hundreds of the armless Hammer-Heads upon the hillside, one behind every rock.

The Lion became quite angry at the laughter caused by the Scarecrow's mishap, and giving a loud roar that echoed like thunder he dashed up the hill.

Again a head shot swiftly out, and the great Lion went rolling down the hill as if he had been struck by a cannon ball.

Dorothy ran down and helped the Scarecrow to his feet, and the Lion came up to her, feeling rather bruised and sore, and said,

"It is useless to fight people with shooting heads; no one can withstand them."

"What can we do, then?" she asked.

"Call the Winged Monkeys," suggested the Tin Woodman; "you have still the right to command them once more."

"Very well," she answered, and putting on the Golden Cap she

uttered the magic words. The Monkeys were as prompt as ever, and in a few moments the entire band stood before her.

"What are your commands?" enquired the King of the Monkeys, bowing low.

"Carry us over the hill to the country of the Quadlings," answered the girl.

"It shall be done," said the King, and at once the Winged Monkeys caught the four travellers and Toto up in their arms and flew away with them. As they passed over the hill the Hammer-Heads yelled with vexation, and shot their heads high in the air; but they could not reach the Winged Monkeys, which carried Dorothy and her comrades safely over the hill and set them down in the beautiful country of the Quadlings.

"This is the last time you can summon us," said the leader to Dorothy; "so good-bye and good luck to you."

"Good-bye, and thank you very much," returned the girl; and the Monkeys rose into the air and were out of sight in a twinkling.

The country of the Quadlings seemed rich and happy. There was field upon field of ripening grain, with well-paved roads running between, and pretty rippling brooks with strong bridges across them. The fences and houses and bridges were all painted bright red, just as they had been painted yellow in the country of the Winkies and blue in the country of the Munchkins. The Quadlings themselves, who were short and fat and looked chubby and good natured, were dressed all in red, which showed bright against the green grass and the yellowing grain.

The Monkeys had set them down near a farm house, and the four travellers walked up to it and knocked at the door. It was opened by the farmer's wife, and when Dorothy asked for something to eat the woman gave them all a good dinner, with three kinds of cake and four kinds of cookies, and a bowl of milk for Toto.

"How far is it to the Castle of Glinda?" asked the child.

"It is not a great way," answered the farmer's wife. "Take the road to the South and you will soon reach it."

Thanking the good woman, they started afresh and walked by the fields and across the pretty bridges until they saw before them a very beautiful Castle. Before the gates were three young girls, dressed in handsome red uniforms trimmed with gold braid; and as Dorothy approached one of them said to her,

"Why have you come to the South Country?"

"To see the Good Witch who rules here," she answered. "Will you take me to her?"

"Let me have your name and I will ask Glinda if she will receive you." They told who they were, and the girl soldier went into the Castle. After a few moments she came back to say that Dorothy and the others were to be admitted at once.

Chapter XXIII

· The Good Witch Grants Dorothy's Wish ·

Before they went to see Glinda, however, they were taken to a room of the Castle, where Dorothy washed her face and combed her hair, and the Lion shook the dust out of his mane, and the Scarecrow patted himself into his best shape, and the Woodman polished his tin and oiled his joints.

When they were all quite presentable they followed the soldier girl into a big room where the Witch Glinda sat upon a throne of rubies.

She was both beautiful and young to their eyes. Her hair was a rich red in color and fell in flowing ringlets over her shoulders. Her dress was pure white; but her eyes were blue, and they looked kindly upon the little girl.

"What can I do for you, my child?" she asked.

Dorothy told the Witch all her story; how the cyclone had brought her to the Land of Oz, how she had found her companions, and of the wonderful adventures they had met with.

"My greatest wish now," she added, "is to get back to Kansas, for Aunt Em will surely think something dreadful has happened to me, and that will make her put on mourning; and unless the crops are better this year than they were last I am sure Uncle Henry cannot afford it."

Glinda leaned forward and kissed the sweet, upturned face of the loving little girl.

"Bless your dear heart," she said, "I am sure I can tell you of a way to get back to Kansas." Then she added:

"But, if I do, you must give me the Golden Cap."

"Willingly!" exclaimed Dorothy; "indeed, it is of no use to me now, and when you have it you can command the Winged Monkeys three times."

"And I think I shall need their service just those three times," answered Glinda, smiling.

Dorothy then gave her the Golden Cap, and the Witch said to the Scarecrow,

"What will you do when Dorothy has left us?"

"I will return to the Emerald City," he replied, "for Oz has made me its ruler and the people like me. The only thing that worries me is how to cross the hill of the Hammer-Heads."

"By means of the Golden Cap I shall command the Winged Monkeys to carry you to the gates of the Emerald City," said Glinda, "for it would be a shame to deprive the people of so wonderful a ruler."

"Am I really wonderful?" asked the Scarecrow.

"You are unusual," replied Glinda.

Turning to the Tin Woodman, she asked:

"What will become of you when Dorothy leaves this country?"

He leaned on his axe and thought a moment. Then he said,

"The Winkies were very kind to me, and wanted me to rule over them after the Wicked Witch died. I am fond of the Winkies, and if I could get back again to the country of the West I should like nothing better than to rule over them forever."

"My second command to the Winged Monkeys," said Glinda, "will be that they carry you safely to the land of the Winkies. Your brains may not be so large to look at as those of the Scarecrow, but you are really brighter than he is—when you are well polished—and I am sure you will rule the Winkies wisely and well."

Then the Witch looked at the big, shaggy Lion and asked,

"When Dorothy has returned to her own home, what will become of you?"

"Over the hill of the Hammer-Heads," he answered, "lies a grand old forest, and all the beasts that live there have made me their King. If I could only get back to this forest I would pass my life very happily there."

"My third command to the Winged Monkeys," said Glinda, "shall be to carry you to your forest. Then, having used up the powers of the Golden Cap, I shall give it to the King of the Monkeys, that he and his band may thereafter be free for evermore."

The Scarecrow and the Tin Woodman and the Lion now thanked the Good Witch earnestly for her kindness, and Dorothy exclaimed,

"You are certainly as good as you are beautiful! But you have not yet told me how to get back to Kansas."

"Your Silver Shoes will carry you over the desert," replied Glinda. "If you had known their power you could have gone back to your Aunt Em the very first day you came to this country."

"But then I should not have had my wonderful brains!" cried the Scarecrow. "I might have passed my whole life in the farmer's cornfield."

"And I should not have had my lovely heart," said the Tin Woodman. "I might have stood and rusted in the forest till the end of the world."

"And I should have lived a coward forever," declared the Lion, "and no beast in all the forest would have had a good word to say to me."

"This is all true," said Dorothy, "and I am glad I was of use to these good friends. But now that each of them has had what he most desired, and each is happy in having a kingdom to rule beside, I think I should like to go back to Kansas."

"The Silver Shoes," said the Good Witch, "have wonderful powers. And one of the most curious things about them is that they can carry you to any place in the world in three steps, and each step will be made in the wink of an eye. All you have to do is to knock the heels together three times and command the shoes to carry you wherever you wish to go."

"If that is so," said the child, joyfully, "I will ask them to carry me back to Kansas at once."

She threw her arms around the Lion's neck and kissed him, patting his big head tenderly. Then she kissed the Tin Woodman, who was weeping in a way most dangerous to his joints. But she hugged the soft, stuffed body of the Scarecrow in her arms instead of kissing his painted face, and found she was crying herself at this sorrowful parting from her loving comrades.

Glinda the Good stepped down from her ruby throne to give the little girl a good-bye kiss, and Dorothy thanked her for all the kindness she had shown to her friends and herself.

Dorothy now took Toto up solemnly in her arms, and having said one last good-bye she clapped the heels of her shoes together three times, saying,

"Take me home to Aunt Em!"

Instantly she was whirling through the air, so swiftly that all she could see or feel was the wind whistling past her ears.

The Silver Shoes took but three steps, and then she stopped so suddenly that she rolled over upon the grass several times before she knew where she was.

At length, however, she sat up and looked about her.

"Good gracious!" she cried.

For she was sitting on the broad Kansas prairie, and just before her was the new farm-house Uncle Henry built after the cyclone had carried away the old one. Uncle Henry was milking the cows in the barnyard, and Toto had jumped out of her arms and was running toward the barn, barking joyously.

Dorothy stood up and found she was in her stocking-feet. For the Silver Shoes had fallen off in her flight through the air, and were lost forever in the desert.

Chapter XXIV

· Home Again ·

Aunt Em had just come out of the house to water the cabbages when she looked up and saw Dorothy running toward her.

"My darling child!" she cried, folding the little girl in her arms and covering her face with kisses; "where in the world did you come from?"

"From the Land of Oz," said Dorothy, gravely. "And here is Toto, too. And oh, Aunt Em! I'm so glad to be at home again!"

Early Opinions

A New Book for Children

It is impossible to conceive of a greater contrast than exists between the children's books of antiquity that were new publications during the sixteenth century and modern children's books of which *The Wonderful Wizard of Oz* is typical. The crudeness that was characteristic of the oldtime publications that were intended for the delectation and amusement of ancestral children would now be enough to cause the modern child to yell with rage and vigor and to instantly reject the offending volume, if not to throw it out the window. The time when anything was considered good enough for children has long since passed, and the volumes devoted to our youth are based upon the fact that they are the future citizens: that they are the country's hope, and are thus worthy of the best, not the worst, that art can give. Kate Greenaway has forever

Reprinted from *The New York Times*, September 8, 1900, p. 605.

driven out the lottery book and the horn book. In *The Wonderful Wizard of Oz* the fact is clearly recognized that the young as well as their elders love novelty. They are pleased with dashes of color and something new in the place of the old, familiar, and winged fairies of Grimm and Andersen.

Neither the tales of Aesop and other fabulists, nor the stories such as "The Three Bears" will ever pass utterly away, but a welcome place remains and will easily be found for such stories as *Father Goose, His Book, The Songs of Father Goose,* and now *The Wonderful Wizard of Oz,* that have all come from the hands of Baum and Denslow.

This last story of *The Wizard* is ingenuously woven out of commonplace material. It is of course an extravaganza, but will safely be found to appeal strongly to child readers as well as to the younger children, to whom it will be read by mothers or those having charge of the entertaining of children. There seems to be an inborn love of stories in child minds, and one of the most familiar and pleading requests of children is to be told another story.

The drawing as well as the introduced color work vies with the texts drawn, and the result has been a book that rises far above the average children's book of today, high as is the present standard. Dorothy, the little girl, and her strangely assorted companions, whose adventures are many and whose dangers are often very great, have experiences that seem in some respects like a leaf out of one of the old English fairy tales that Andrew Lang or Joseph Jacobs has rescued for us. A difference there is, however, and Baum has done with mere words what Denslow has done with his delightful draughtsmanship. The story has humor and here and there stray bits of philosophy that will be a moving power on the child mind and will furnish fields of study and investigation for the future students and professors of psychology. Several new features and ideals of fairy life have been introduced into the "Wonderful Wizard," who turns out in the end to be only a wonderful humbug after all. A scarecrow stuffed with straw, a tin woodman, and a cowardly lion do not at first blush promise well as moving heroes in a tale when merely mentioned, but in actual practice they take on something of the living and breathing quality that is so gloriously exemplified in "The Story of the Three Bears," that has become a classic.

The book has a bright and joyous atmosphere, and does not dwell upon killing and deeds of violence. Enough stirring adventure enters into it, however, to flavor it with zest, and it will indeed be strange if there be a normal child who will not enjoy the story.

Modern Fairy Tales

· by L. Frank Baum ·

The earliest literature of which we have knowledge is that of fairy lore, and the fairy tale has survived through all the changing ages to this day, and is still as popular with childish minds as in the beginning. Yet it has necessarily undergone considerable evolution, and the modern fairy tale differs materially from the folk tales of the ancients.

It is only experience in life and contact with the world that changes the childish viewpoint to the adult viewpoint. When the world was young, and life's experiences were few, men and women had simple minds and craved the same class of wonder tales that childhood has always loved. They were then told by professional story-tellers, and sung by wandering minstrels, and the folk tales—the legends and romances handed down from age to age by word of mouth—teemed with relations of fairy elves who assisted mankind in time of need; for it is to be remarked that even the oldest known fairy legends carried their morals, and never has a fairy tale lived, if one has been told or written, wherein the good did not conquer the evil and virtue finally reign supreme. Indeed, the editors of the first printed books of fairy tales took especial pains to place a moral at the end of each story, so that if by chance the reader carelessly missed it in the narration it would stare him in the face before he could finally escape. So that the fairies were originally intended, and are today, to be the benefactors of mankind, and the acquaintance of our children with them can lead to no harm at all.

I once asked a little fellow, a friend of mine, to tell me what a "fairy" is. He replied, quite promptly: "A fairy has wings, and is much like an angel, only smaller." Now that, I believe, is the general conception of fairies; and it is a pretty conception, is it not? Yet we know the family of immortals generally termed "fairies" has many branches and includes fays, sprites, elves, nymphs, ryls, knooks, gnomes, brownies and many other subdivisions.

There is no blue book or history of the imaginative little creatures to guide us in classifying them, but they all have their uses and peculiar characteristics; as, for example, the little ryls, who carry around paint-pots, with which they color, most brilliantly and artistically, the blossoms of the flowers.

No one knows who invented fairies. The earliest record of intelligent man shows him conversant with fairy lore. Perhaps a dim realization

Reprinted from *The Advance*, August 19, 1909, pp. 236–237.

that a beneficent guiding power directs our mortal footsteps first led to the conception of fairies. Anyway, they were one of the first fruits of human imagination, and the idea of the quaint, merry helpful, and sometimes mischievous, little immortals proved so fascinating that it has never for a day been forgotten since the world has had a history.

Nor is the authorship of the oldest and most popular fairy tales known. They belong to legendary folk lore of nations, and no man can claim them for his own. It was once declared that Charles Perrault, a Frenchman who lived in the seventeenth century, wrote the first authentic fairy tales; but this has since been disproved. "The Sleeping Beauty," "Cinderella," and "Little Red Riding-Hood" are found to be folk tales of various nations, differing but slightly in form in each instance; so that Perrault must be classed with the Brothers Grimm, and later with Andrew Lang, as a collector and editor of the fairy literature prevalent in his time. Doubtless Perrault, the Grimms, and Lang deserve undying fame for having thus rescued so many beautiful stories from threatened oblivion, for it has been impossible for modern authors to equal the charming imagery of those ancient tales.

The first known creator of fairy tales, and perhaps the best known of all who have since followed him, is Hans Christian Andersen, the immortal friend of the childhood days of our grandparents. This great Dane had not only a marvelous imagination but he was a poet as well, and surrounded his tales with some of the most beautiful descriptive passages known to our literature. As children you skipped those passages—I can guess that, because as a child I skipped them myself—but as women you ought to read Andersen again, that you may revel in the beauties of his splendid descriptions, and enjoy the fascination of his poesy. Andersen wrote but one book of short fairy tales, yet that book will live forever, and all else that he wrote—and he wrote many books—is long since forgotten.

Singularly enough, we have no recognized author of fairy literature between Andersen's day and that of Lewis Carroll, the quaint and clever old clergyman who recorded *Alice's Adventures in Wonderland.* Carroll's method of handling fairies was as whimsical as Andersen's was reverential, yet it is but fair to state that the children loved Alice better than any prince or princess that Andersen ever created. The secret of Alice's success lay in the fact that she was a real child, and any normal child could sympathize with her all through her adventures. The story may often bewilder the little one—for it is bound to bewilder us, having neither plot nor motive in its relation—but Alice is doing something every moment, and doing something strange and marvelous, too; so the child follows her with rapturous delight. It is said that Dr. Dodgson, the author, was so ashamed of having written a child's book that he would only allow it to be published under the pen name of Lewis Carroll; but it made him famous, even then, and *Alice in Wonderland,* rambling and incoherent as it is, is one of the best and perhaps the most famous of all modern fairy tales.

Frank Stockton once wrote a most bewitching story of the good class called "The Floating Prince," and Howard Pyle's dragon stories are unsurpassed in drollery and imaginative power. Another famous book is by Tudor Jenks, and is called *Imaginations.* Then there are Albert Stearns' entertaining story books, and the clever stories of the English author, E. Nesbit. Just recently Mrs. Frances Hodgson Burnett has written some little books of fairy tales that are all about children and the things children love. I do not wholly approve Miss Mulock's famous story of *The Little Lame Prince,* for although it is charmingly written it is too pitiful in sentiment. Doubtless many crippled children have derived a degree of comfort from the adventures of the little lame prince and his magic cloak; but a normal child should not be harassed with pitiful subjects, and even the maimed ones prefer to idolize the well and strong.

Yes; there are many books to be had of the right sort; books that will entertain and delight your little ones without putting a single bad or repulsive idea into their heads. So I entreat parents, and those who present books to children, to be particular in selecting modern, up-to-date fairy tales, for in this way you will feed the imaginative instinct of the little ones and develop the best side of child nature. Glance into the book yourself, and see that the story is not marred by murders or cruelties, by terrifying characters, or by mawkish sentimentality, love and marriage. Because some fairy tales have these faults it would be folly to withhold all fairy tales from children. You do not ostracize all novels because you know some of them are vicious. Life at any period is robbed of half its pleasure if good books do not enter into it.

The child skips descriptive passages because it cannot understand or appreciate them, and such writers as Andersen, with all their kindly sympathy for the little ones, forget that their own keen appreciation of the beauties of nature is not yet shared by their youthful and inexperienced readers. Some years ago good old Dr. Skinner, pastor of the Mercer Street Church, in New York, made a ponderous attempt to do his duty by the lambs of his flock by preaching a special sermon to children every month. "My children," said he, on one of those painful occasions, "I propose to give you this morning an epitome of the life of St. Paul. Perhaps some of you, my children, do not know what the word 'epitome' means. Now 'epitome,' my children, is in its signification synonymous with synopsis."

It is folly to place before the little ones a class of literature they cannot comprehend and which is sure to bore them and to destroy their pleasure in reading. What they want is action—"something doing every minute"—exciting adventures, unexpected difficulties to be overcome, and marvelous escapes.

To my mind a good book of this sort is just as necessary to the proper promotion of a child's welfare as baths, exercise, or wholesome food. There is no danger of deceiving the little one, or giving it a false impression of life. The children know very well that fairies and fairylands are apart from human life, even if they believe for a time that such things really exist. The myth concerning Santa Claus deceives few modern children, but delights them all; and so it is with the fairies. Childhood loves the vivid interest of fairy tales and the glamor of fairyland just as we adults love the play and the glamor of the stage, and there is no particle of harm in the entertainment thus afforded them if proper care is taken in the selection of their books.

Fairy Tales

L. Frank Baum is dead, and the children, if they knew it, would mourn. That endless procession of "Oz" books, coming out just before Christmas, is to cease. *The Wizard of Oz, Queen Zixi of Ix, Dorothy and the Wizard [in Oz], John Dough and the Cherub,* there will never be any more of them, and the children have suffered a loss they do not know. Years from now, though the children cannot clamor for the newest Oz book, the crowding generations will plead for the old ones.

Baum brought the fairy tale up to date. He had competitors. The thing has always been well done, because children like stories and are not discriminating. There was Samuel McCord Crothers' infant acquaintance, who, asked what stories she liked best, replied without hesitation, " 'Cinderella,' 'The Probable Son,' and—" well, we have forgotten the last of the trilogy. Nevertheless, the modern fairy tale, even Baum's, is not a real fairy tale. Walt McDougall wrote *The Rambillicus Book,* a perfectly good book of fairy stories for children on the principle above outlined, but no sort of fairy story for people who know what the real thing is. For a fairy story has to be written by one who believes in fairies, and they who write them nowadays, whether a Baum or a

McDougall, do not believe in fairies. There is something pathetic in Peter Pan's appeal to the audience as Tinker Bell flutters away into death: "Do you believe in fairies? Oh, say you do!" The audience rises en masse and says it does; but it is Maude Adams who makes them do it, not any real belief in fairies.

But the men who wrote the real fairy tales did believe in them. Baum did not believe in his Tin Woodman and his Scarecrow; behind the scenes you could see the smile of the showman. No more did Barrie, whatever he may say, believe in Peter Pan. But how about the serious-minded peasants who composed the fairy legends of Ireland, long before they were put on paper? We could not go so far as to say that Charles Perrault really believed in "Little Red Riding Hood," "Cinderella," "Puss in Boots," "Hop o' My Thumb," "The Sleeping Beauty," and "Bluebeard," for he lived in far too artificial an age; but those stories, or most of them, were not originated by him; he put them on paper from old legends and gave them his inimitable literary twist. Even at that, it took a man with a child's heart to give that vivid touch.

So with the Brothers Grimm, Wilhelm and Jacob, who came so long after Perrault. They had the child heart, just as Baum had it, and they were able to conceal any skepticism about the truth of what they wrote, which he was not and which no fairy-tale writer since has been able to do, not even Emile Zola with his *Stories to Ninon*. One can see that Zola did not believe in fairies; one can see the tender, half-mocking smile with which he told his *Stories to Ninon*, just as one can see Baum's cheerful grin behind *The Wizard of Oz*. But the Brothers Grimm were serious about it; they went intently to work, as scientists (which they were), to reproduce the very atmosphere of the old folk stories. That was a shade beyond Perrault, who did preserve the atmosphere, but only because he wanted first of all to tell a good story.

And how close their work is to his. Aschenbroedel is the same as Cinderella; in fact, the very name is the same, only German instead of French. Nearly all of the stories date back to Norse mythology or even further. The Grimms were not concerned with origins or with morals, though the morals they found they planted in their stories as in duty bound. It was not until Hans Christian Andersen's day that any prominent writer thought of making his own fairy stories; and Andersen was a moralist and a theorist. There is a truth peeping out from all the greater stories, such as the story (we forget the name) of the coquettish ball or the faithful tin soldier, or the fakirs who made a new robe for the King. That was a thing not seen since the tenth century when the various versions of "Reynard the Fox" were popular.

Reynard was a political character, and the stories about him were all satirical; but then, ten centuries later, the satire has all been forgotten and Reynard is merely the hero of a fairy story, as much as Puss in Boots. What a strange fate has overtaken so many of these old stories! Take Swift's *Gulliver's Travels*, of which Bulwer wrote:

> *Swift wrote this book to wreak a ribald scorn*
> *On all that Man should love or Priest should mourn—*
> *And lo! the book, from all its ends beguiled,*
> *A harmless wonder to some happy child!*

"The age of chivalry is dead." Is the age of fairy-tale writing? Not so long as men like Baum can counterfeit it. But the real note of sincerity can never come back in this age. We cannot write about fairies with honesty any more than we can write about Greek gods. The nearest we can get to that old reality is when W. Butler Yeats, or somebody like him, can collect the old fairy tales that were told in ages of belief, and retell them with an accent of sincerity, which he can get only by subduing his own personality and sitting like a child at the feet of wiser men than he, the few faint relics of an older time who believe in what they tell him. And this, if we knew it, is why Geoffrey Keating's *General History of Ireland*, wild and fanciful as it is, is dearer to many hearts than Gibbon and Carlyle and Macaulay and Froude put together. For poor Keating wrote as a believer.

Utopia Americana

· by Edward Wagenknecht ·

I

The theory has sometimes been advanced that human misery is the source of all artistic expression. If we could live completely satisfactory lives in this actual world that we inhabit, if we could perfectly adjust ourselves to our environment, why—it is asked—should we seek to create and escape into another world and one which at best is only imaginary? Primitive man, the argument goes, has few wants and fewer aspirations. He is able very readily to harmonize with his environment—or if disharmony exists, he is not sensitive enough, not

Reprinted from *Utopia Americana*. Seattle: University of Washington Book Store, 1929. Copyright © 1929 and 1957 by Edward Wagenknecht. Reprinted by permission of Edward Wagenknecht.

sufficiently the philosopher to be aware of the fact: consequently he has no art. But once man begins to think, to aspire, he becomes painfully aware of the difference between his aspirations and his achievements: thus dissatisfaction is born and with it comes the birth of art. Denied satisfaction in his personal living, man now turns away from the world of the senses to enter that of the imagination. Here he may create things to suit himself.

The theory is at least suggestive. There are cases, like that of Robert Louis Stevenson, that it seems at first glance quite adequately to explain. Temperamentally, as Stuart Sherman conveniently pointed out not so very long ago, Stevenson was one of the healthiest, most red-blooded spirits that ever lived. Even with tuberculosis holding him back, he "consorted with thieves and harlots in the slums of Edinburgh and London, ran through the professions of engineering and law before he was twenty-five, explored the Scotch coast in a sailboat, canoed the Sambre and Oise, slept in a lonely bivouac *à la belle étoile* in the Cévennes, fled to San Francisco by emigrant train, ran away with a wife and family, camped on Mount St. Helena, chartered his own schooner, sailed the South Seas for three years, feasted with cannibal chiefs, refused to sleep with their wives, conspired with Kanaka kings, was threatened with deportation, planted a wilderness, governed a small tribe of savages and died in his boots."* But even so this was not enough to satisfy him: even so, he did not have anything like the adventurous career he desired and which he might have had if his health had been good. Consequently he turned to literature, pouring out here the superabundant energy that his life could not contain, dreaming the adventures he was never destined to experience.

But of course all artists are not Stevensons, nor are they all embittered or disappointed idealists. Personally I believe the sacred mystery of man's creative impulse—his self-expression in art—is much too complicated ever to be fully explained within the bounds of a single theory. Yet there can be no doubt that for many this factor looms large. It will be remembered that in Bernard Shaw's utopia in *Back to Methuselah*, the Ancients—who represent the goal of Creative Evolution—have outgrown their need of art. They have a direct sense of life, receive impressions without intermediary: consequently they have no need of painting or of literature.

It is in connection with the romantic movement that the escape-theory finds its best apparent justification. So far as the realists are concerned, many of them, just at present, are engaged in the business of

---

* *Critical Wood-Cuts* (New York: Charles Scribner's Sons, 1925), p. 165.

making worlds so very much *less* attractive than the one in which we live that it is surely not unfair to say that if they are seeking escape through art, it must be because our world is too good for them, rather than because it is not good enough. With the romancer it is quite otherwise. The famous quatrain from *The Rubáiyát of Omar Khayyám* is inscribed on his banners:

> *Ah Love! could you and I with Him conspire*
> *To grasp this sorry Scheme of Things entire,*
> *Would not we shatter it to bits—and then*
> *Remould it nearer to the Heart's Desire!*

The romancer will have none of our world: he constructs a world of his own—a world which operates by virtue of laws peculiar to itself but not applicable here.

The ordinary romancer, to be sure, is not overburdened with spiritual ambitions. Discontented with the somewhat vulgar ritual of the God of Things as They Are, he simply runs away with his followers into the magic land of Never-Never-Was, where fountains play in the sunshine and all the problems of life are left behind. His purpose is frankly that of the entertainer—all that he offers is a momentary, possibly recreative respite from the serious business of life.

But there is another and a higher type of romance, in which material which transcends human experience altogether, sometimes even material apparently fantastic and wholly unreal, is used for the purpose of interpreting life and of helping us to understand it better. This is the sort of romance that we get in *Gulliver's Travels,* in *The Pilgrim's Progress,* in *The Tempest,* and even in *The Divine Comedy.*

The advantages of choosing the romantic rather than the realistic method of presenting definite teaching or interpretation are, I suppose, fairly obvious. It is no accident that George Bernard Shaw, by all odds the most earnest, the most consciously ethical of all contemporary writers, has so often chosen to work through fantasy and extravaganza. For the realist is bound to represent conditions as they are. He may change some things but he must not change too much, or those who know the scene of which he is writing will refuse to accept his picture. The romancer, on the other hand, is bound only by such laws as the nature of his own specific creation imposes upon him. Not content with elaborating specific instances or with gazing upon detached sections of life, he demands, with an ambition worthy of a greater being than man, the privilege of seeing life steadily and seeing it whole. Consequently the very constitution of his world expresses the viewpoint of its artist-creator. Here, says the romancer, my readers may be expected to lay aside the prejudices of daily living and to see life as I want them to see it. The same persons who thrill to the fine idealism of King Cophetua's love for a beggar-maid would only sneer if I gave them the story of a romance between a Chicago bank president and his manicurist. Here, on a ridiculously reduced scale, are the reasons why Dante carried the action of *The Divine Comedy* over into the world beyond the grave. He did not want the practical conditions of this world—with which all his readers were familiar—to be continually getting in the way of what he wanted to teach about life.

A few years ago, in a very interesting review of Walter de la Mare's *Broomsticks,* Mr. Robert Cortes Holiday half-seriously contended that the fairy tale is the highest type of literature:

"Fairy stories," of course, the miraculous accounts full of far-fetched wisdom are older than Father Time. This "realism" kind of thing only came about, by the clock, the other day. Anybody, almost, can write passably well, because it only takes a little workaday brains. But the wonder tale, that is another matter. It is not hatched in the school-educated head of this smart chap or that, but lurks in the blood of the race, like a sense of religion. Now and then, Seers come on the earth and give it voice; and the battlements of our mundane being are riven like a veil, and for an instant we know that we are not merely people in store clothes, but as good as goblins in our own right.

I think that is absolutely sound. The fairy tale is the highest type of literature. The Elizabethans knew it: hence the honor they paid to Edmund Spenser and *The Faerie Queene.* It was not only because they were aristocrats that the sordid, unimportant happenings of daily life did not appeal to them as susceptible of artistic recreation: it was because, with all their sins, they had not lost the habit of idealism. To lose your love for fairy tales is almost as terrible as to lose your sense of religion. Indeed at bottom it is very much the same thing, for religion and fairy lore alike spring from a sense of reverence and a sense of wonder in the face of the unexplored and unexplained mystery of life. One of the most terrifying things about modern society is that there are so few fairy tales for adults. One of the most hopeful signs of the present hour is the fact that there is among very recent writers a turn away from drab realism and in the direction of the romance and the wonder tale. What is Robert Nathan doing except fairy tales, and what that is now being produced in America is likely to live longer than his books? It will be a very sad day for civilization when we relegate the dreams of life to the nursery and confine adult attention to lands and mortgages, stocks and bonds. Myself, I always watch out for the man who finds *Peter Pan* or *The Blue Bird* or *A Good Little Devil* silly. He thinks he has outgrown them: in nine cases out of ten, the point is that he has not yet grown up to them. He is a walking illustration of the idea advanced by William Wordsworth in his "Ode on the Intimations of Immortality": the conflict of life has rubbed off all the beauty and poetry and tenderness he once knew; the gates to the land of mystery from whence he came have been closed to him forever.

Some foolish people seek to discredit the fairy tale on the ground that fairy tales are "made up." What nonsense! Fairy tales are no more "made up" (in the sense of being fabricated) than Theodore Dreiser's novels are "made up." The fairies have had their share in the history of humanity quite as certainly as the thieves and the harlots have had theirs, for—thank God!—our dreams belong to our spiritual experience and not merely our sins. All art—realistic as well as romantic—consists in the rearrangement of life experiences. Only, in the case of the wonder tale the rearrangement is more thoroughgoing: it is carried through at an intenser degree of pressure and it reaches farther than can ever be the case in a realistic work.

There is much sound sense in John Galsworthy's contention that only through fostering a sense of beauty in mankind can we hope to abolish war. Anatôle France has said: "Without the Utopians of other times, men would still live in caves, miserable and naked. It was Utopians who traced the lines of the first city. . . . Out of generous dreams come beneficial realities. Utopia is the principle of all progress, and the essay into a better future."

The distinction between utopia and fairyland is of course very thin. The word may have originated in the sixteenth century with Sir Thomas More. But many utopias—many ideal commonwealths—existed before the days of Sir Thomas More: indeed they run clear back to the days of Plato's *Republic* and Isaiah's vision of the ideal Jerusalem. And there have been many of them since, and wide are the differences between them. But all of them connect very definitely with the program for social reform. As Lewis Mumford pointed out in his interesting book, *The Story of Utopias*, utopias generally come to be written in transitional ages—when the need for a new social order is seriously felt. On paper, the idealist creates an imaginary commonwealth—in form a fairy tale, in practice a model for a better society. Even when they seem to be having little effect, such utopias provide an ideal toward which men can aspire.

II

America is not rich in distinctive fairy lore. We have indeed, among older books, those of the great American illustrator, Howard Pyle. Considered simply as fairy tales, such books as *The Wonder Clock* and *Pepper and Salt* leave little or nothing to be desired. I am amazed every time I look at them at the work that went into them—the wealth of story, the great profusion of exquisitely drawn pictures. Such books could hardly be made nowadays—certainly not as popular books: the conditions of manufacture have become too expensive. Fortunately the old plates have lasted, so that the children of today may meet the children of yesterday at the gentle feet of Howard Pyle.

Only, it can hardly be claimed that Pyle's fairy tales are in any definite or distinctive sense American. They happened to be written in America—that is all: the materials of which they are compounded is the fairy lore of the Old World. There is little in them that a European romancer could not have included.

This is surely not the case with the writings of L. Frank Baum. Indeed it is in *The Wizard of Oz* that we meet the first distinctive attempt to construct a fairyland out of American materials. Baum's long series of Oz books represents thus an important pioneering work: they may even be considered an American utopia.

Lyman Frank Baum was an American journalist, born in Chittenango, New York, in 1856. He was educated at Syracuse and later came on to Chicago, where he was the editor of a periodical called *The Show Window* from 1897 to 1901. He was a voluminous writer, the author of some fifty odd volumes, nearly all of them for children. *The Wizard of Oz*, the book which made his fame, appeared in 1900. In addition he was a playwright, his best known plays being *The Maid of Arran*, 1882, and *The Queen of Killarney*, 1885. *The Wizard of Oz* itself became a musical extravaganza for Montgomery and Stone, an enormously successful show which undoubtedly contributed in large measure to the continued success of the book. In addition, it determined the Fred Stone type of musical play and widely influenced other extravaganzas. Later on Mr. Baum went west, settling finally at Hollywood, California. Here he became known also for his success in raising fine varieties of chrysanthemums, and here he died in May of 1919.

It is interesting to see how accidentally as it were Baum discovered the Land of Oz, and how little he realized at first just what a mine he had struck. He had written in 1897 a book called *Mother Goose in Prose*. This is a volume of charming stories inspired by the historic jingles, the general idea being to tell that part of the story which Mother Goose did not tell. The book is excellent in its way and should be read along with Sarah Addington's recent volumes about the Mother Goose characters, *The Boy That Lived in Pudding Lane* and the others. For our purpose, however, the point to be noted is that *Mother Goose in*

Prose is English not American in its inspiration. That is to say, Mr. Baum's fancy plays about and transforms not things that he has seen but things he has read about. Nor is there anything distinctively American about Maxfield Parrish's pictures for the volume. And the same assertion might be made about some of the later Baum books—for example, *The Life and Adventures of Santa Claus* and *Queen Zixi of Ix*, the latter certainly one of the best fairy tales in the world.

When he finished *The Wizard of Oz*, Baum at first regarded it as one of his books, no more and no less than the others. It caught on immediately and went through enormous sales the very year of its publication. This of course gratified him immensely, and the next year he came forth with *Dot and Tot of Merryland*, the story of a candy country ruled over by a doll, to me at least one of the least interesting of his books. Indeed the idea for a series of Oz books did not originate with Mr. Baum: it came from the children who after the publication of *The Wizard* deluged him with letters begging that the story might be continued. In 1904 he yielded to this clamor and produced *The Land of Oz*, A Sequel to The Wizard of Oz. Youthful appetites still proving insatiable, he wrote in 1907 the third of the series, *Ozma of Oz*. By this time he was more or less resigned to his fate and the three succeeding years saw the publication of *Dorothy and the Wizard in Oz*, *The Road to Oz*, and *The Emerald City of Oz*. Then, in 1910, he once more rebelled. He knew a great many other stories he wanted to write down: he was probably afraid also that if he continued indefinitely in one field the stream of his fancy would run thin. Accordingly in *The Emerald City of Oz*, he invented an elaborate fiction about how that fairyland had been permanently cut off from communication with the rest of the world and himself, as historian of Oz, therefore made incapable of securing further information concerning it.

But a little thing like that could not stop the children. They knew Mr. Baum's fancy too well, they had seen too many obstacles surmounted, to pay very serious attention to such an insignificant little difficulty as that. Until 1913, Baum went on writing some of the other stories he wanted to write. These were, of course, much less successful, and so in that year he yielded once more to the cry of the children and wrote *The Patchwork Girl of Oz*. Having invented one story to shut Oz off from the rest of the world, he was simply compelled to invent another one to open it up again, and fortunately the wireless was well enough known by 1913 so that it could afford him the necessary means of communication. *The Patchwork Girl of Oz*, one of the best of the entire series of Oz books, was such a success that Mr. Baum promised the children of America he would go on writing books about the Land of Oz as long as they cared to read them. He lived long enough to produce seven more of them, one each year, before he died in 1919. On his death the series was continued by Miss Ruth Plumly Thompson.

III

Perhaps the best key to the Oz books is found in a passage in *The Royal Book of Oz* . . . by Miss Thompson. In this book, the Scarecrow, having gone out to look for the rest of his family tree, has inadvertently slid down the bean pole and landed in a mysterious kingdom where, very uncomfortably for himself, he has come to be regarded as the incarnation of a long lost Emperor. Making the best of a bad situation, the Scarecrow gathers the fifteen little princes together and tries to amuse them. They are very literal-minded children, however, and he does not succeed very well. For example, when he tries to tell them of the wonders of the Land of Oz, the oldest prince immediately flips out a map, and not being able to find the Land of Oz located therein, at once announces serenely that he does not believe there is such a place. Well, I once knew a boy who started to read Howard Pyle's *Men of Iron* and threw it aside in disgust when he found it was a romantic story of knights and knighthood. He had expected a story of the Gary, Indiana, steel mills. Now that is the kind of child Mr. Baum did not believe in and the kind of child he did not write for. He used to say that his stories were intended for everybody whose heart was young, no matter what his physical age might be. Many years ago, in the preface to *The Magical Monarch of Mo*, he addressed the children as follows:

These stories are not true; they could not be true and be so marvelous. No one is expected to believe them; they were meant to excite laughter and to gladden the heart.

Perhaps some of those big, grownup people will poke fun at us—at you for reading these nonsense tales of the Magical Monarch, and at me for writing them. Never mind. Many of the big folk are still children—even as you and I. We can not measure a child by the standard of size or age. The big folk who are children will be our comrades; the others we need not consider at all, for they are self-exiled from our domain.

I have made much of the fact that these are *American* fairy tales. By this I do not mean that Mr. Baum has used no European materials. He was not, so far as I know, a member of the Ku Klux Klan, and he used very freely whatever suited his purpose from older literatures and from older cultures. Indeed had he not done this, his output could hardly have been recognized as wonder tales at all. The greatest villain in all the Oz books is the Nome King—the "G" is left out because the children cannot pronounce it!—the ruler of an underground nation of elves, as old as fairy lore itself. Again, we have Polychrome, the Rainbow's daughter, a character surely with nothing distinctively American about her, and in *Dorothy and the Wizard in Oz* there is a thrilling fight with the gargoyles, taken posthaste from medieval cathedrals.

These, however, are not the distinctively "Ozzy" characters. Suppose we look at the Scarecrow and the Tin Woodman. In *The Wizard of Oz*, Dorothy finds the Scarecrow, newly made, with a beanpole up his back, in the middle of a cornfield. She lifts him down and they go to the Emerald City together, where Dorothy plans to ask Oz to send her home to Kansas while the Scarecrow wants brains instead of straw in the painted sack that serves him for a head. The next addition to their party is the Tin Woodman whom they find rusted in the woods and who cannot go along with them until they oil his joints so that he may walk. The Tin Woodman was once a man of flesh and blood, one Nick Chopper, in love with a pretty Munchkin girl. But a wicked witch enchanted his ax, so that as he was working in the forest he cut himself to pieces. Fortunately Nick Chopper had among his friends a very wonderful tinsmith who, as soon as any part of Nick's body had been cut off, would replace it with tin, until at last the man was wholly tin and as good as new. Only one thing was lacking: he had no longer a heart and accordingly he did not care whether he married the pretty Munchkin girl or not. The Tin Woodman therefore goes along with Dorothy and the Scarecrow to the Emerald City in the hope that the Wizard may give him a heart. Now who but an American—in a country overrun with mechanical skill—could ever have dreamed of a creature like that?

Other, similar characters are introduced in later volumes. In *The Land of Oz*, we have Jack Pumpkinhead, the Sawhorse, the Woggle-Bug, and the Gump. "Mr H. M. Woggle-Bug, T.E." is the aristocrat of the Oz books. Once he was an ordinary bug who happened to have his dwelling place in a schoolroom. Here he drank eagerly of the font of knowledge—hence the "T.E." standing after his name: it means "Thoroughly Educated." One day, in the course of a natural science lecture, the professor noticed the bug and, by means of a magic lantern, threw him upon the screen in a highly magnified state ("H. M."). In this condition the creature managed to make his escape, and since then he has become the most learned man in the Land of Oz. Jack Pumpkinhead is a Halloween prank, a body of wood with a pumpkinhead on top of it, brought to life by means of the Magic Power of Life. At first, Mr. Baum apparently believed that when Jack's head spoiled that would be the end of him, but when fully embarked upon the Oz series, he decided that the Pumpkinhead was much too good to lose: accordingly he made a farmer of him whose business is to raise pumpkins for heads. The upper part of Jack Pumpkinhead has died and been buried several times but he is nevertheless very much alive. The Gump—(this was long before the days of Sidney Smith's cartoon creation)—is simply a crude sort of flying machine, made out of sofas, palm leaves, *et cetera*, with a stuffed head on the front of it to give it intelligence. The Sawhorse was intended originally simply for the sawing of wood, but once Tip had brought him to life by means of his Magical Powder, he was of course far better than a flesh and blood horse, for he did not need to eat and he never tired.

In *Ozma of Oz*, we meet still another amazing creature, Tik-Tok, a marvelous machine man. Unfortunately he runs down every now and then and stands helpless waiting for somebody to wind him up again. However, when he is correctly wound he is as good a man as any of them.

Later volumes introduce the Woozy, a strange animal with all square surfaces, the Ork, an ostrich-like creature who flies by means of a tail which is attached to its body like the propellor of an airplane, and a marvelous magical Teddy-bear. Again, we have rubber mountains, submarines, sinking palaces, a vegetable kingdom, a country whose inhabitants are kitchen utensils, and a city inhabited by various kinds of baker's products.

The use of machinery in the Oz books is also characteristically American. In general, magic may be said to inhere not in persons but in things. Whoever has the magical instrument can perform magic deeds. Continually, the forces of Nature, as we know them in America, are used for purposes of conveyance. In *The Wizard of Oz*, it is a Kansas cyclone which carries Dorothy and her house over the desert and deposits them in the Land of Oz. In *Ozma of Oz*, Dorothy is shipwrecked. In *Dorothy and the Wizard in Oz*, Dorothy, in California, is swallowed by an earthquake and carried down into the center of the Earth, from whence she makes her way to Oz. In *The Scarecrow of Oz*, Trot and Cap'n Bill are sucked down by a whirlpool. And in *The Road to Oz*, the Wizard sends people home from Ozma's birthday celebration in soap bubbles.

Indeed the United States is well represented in Oz. Dorothy is from Kansas; the Shaggy Man comes from Colorado; and Betsy Bobbin's home is Oklahoma. The Wizard of Oz himself is a native of Omaha. There he was connected with Bailum and Barney's Consolidated Shows, and his magic was, all of it, pure fake. He used to go up in a balloon on exhibition days to draw the crowds, and it was thus, on one occasion, when he lost control of his balloon, that he was carried to the Land of Oz. Though he was a good ruler, his pretended magic was all imposture, as Dorothy learns when she wants him to send her home to Kansas. It is not until later in his career when the Wizard becomes a pupil of the great sorceress, Glinda the Good, that he learns something about real magic.

Now what is the significance of all this? Not surely that American magic is any better than French magic or German magic. No. Simply that Mr. Baum has enlarged the resources of fairyland. He has not destroyed European magic: he has simply added to it. And he has done one thing more. He has taught American children to look for the element of wonder in the life around them, to realize that even smoke and machinery may be transformed into fairy lore if only we have sufficient energy and vision to penetrate to their significance and transform them to our use. In *Tik-Tok of Oz*, the Shaggy Man explains to Betsy Bobbin:

> "All the magic isn't in fairyland. . . . There's lots of magic in all Nature, and you may see it as well in the United States, where you and I once lived, as you can here."
>
> "I never did," she replied.
>
> "Because you were so used to it all that you didn't realize it was magic. Is anything more wonderful than to see a flower grow and blossom, or to get light out of the electricity in the air? The cows that manufacture milk for us must have machinery fully as remarkable as that in Tik-Tok's copper body. . . ."

Now this seems to me significant and important. It is not healthy—and it is not true—for children to be made to feel that romance belongs only to the past, and that everything in America today is drab, uninteresting, and businesslike. For after all we grow to resemble our dreams, and if we are dull, unimaginative children, what under the sun are we going to be as adults? Thus Mr. Baum's work is primarily significant because it has pointed in the right direction: it has helped to teach us how to find wonder in contemporary American life.

IV

I have spoken of the Land of Oz as an American utopia. By this I do not mean that the Oz books are full of social criticism. Since they were written for children, this is obviously not the case. Yet the utopia element in them is strong, and if the children do not forget it all by the time they grow up, perhaps it is not too fantastic to imagine that it may do some good. It would not be a bad thing if American lawmakers and executives were to imbibe a few of the ideals which actuate the lovely girl ruler of the Emerald City—Ozma of Oz.

Perhaps the best brief description of Oz as utopia occurs in *The Emerald City of Oz*:

The Emerald City is built all of beautiful marbles in which are set a profusion of emeralds, every one exquisitely cut and of very great size. There are other jewels used in the decorations inside the houses and palaces, such as rubies, diamonds, sapphires, amethysts, and turquoises. But in the streets and upon the outside of the buildings only emeralds appear, from which circumstance the place is named the Emerald City of Oz. It had nine thousand, six hundred and fifty-four buildings, in which lived fifty-seven thousand three hundred and eighteen people, up to the time my story opens.

All the surrounding country, extending to the borders of the desert which enclosed it upon every side, was full of pretty and comfortable farmhouses, in which resided those inhabitants of Oz who preferred country to city life.

Altogether there were more than half a million people in the Land of Oz— although some of them, as you will soon learn, were not made of flesh and blood as we are—and every inhabitant of that favored country was happy and prosperous.

No disease of any sort was ever known among the Ozites, and so no one ever died unless he met with an accident that prevented him from living. This happened very seldom, indeed. There were no poor people in the Land of Oz, because there was no such thing as money, and all property of every sort belonged to the Ruler. The people were her children, and she cared for them. Each person was given freely by his neighbors whatever he required for his use, which is as much as anyone may reasonably desire. Some tilled the lands and raised great crops of grain, which was divided equally among the entire population, so that all had enough. There were many tailors and dressmakers and shoemakers and the like, who made things that any who desired them might wear. Likewise there were jewelers who made ornaments for the person, which pleased and beautified the people, and these ornaments also were free to those who asked for them. Each man and woman, no matter what he or she produced for the good of the community, was supplied by the neighbors with food and clothing and a house and furniture and ornaments and games. If by chance the supply ever ran short, more was taken from the great storehouses of the Ruler, which were afterward filled up again when there was more of any article than the people needed.

Every one worked half the time and played half the time, and the people enjoyed the work as much as they did the play, because it is good to be occupied and to have something to do. There were no cruel overseers set to watch them, and no one to rebuke them or to find fault with them. So each one was proud to do all he could for his friends and neighbors, and was glad when they would accept the things he produced.

All in all, there is much fuller command over nature in Oz than we enjoy in any country yet known. Animals can talk and mingle with human beings on terms of equality. Even flies are considerate and kindly: if one alights on you, you do not kill it: you simply request it politely to move on, and it complies with your request. Many of the inhabitants of the country, not being made of flesh and blood, do not need food, sleep, drink, or clothes. Those who feel that misery and imperfection are necessary to interest either in literature or in life may find some comfort in the fact that around the Emerald City itself the country is so peaceful that no adventures are possible. Consequently all the Oz books take you off to some obscure corner of Oz which has not yet been cultivated and where the sway of the Queen is only nominal.

Best of all, there is no army in Oz. Ozma refuses to fight even when her kingdom seems in danger of invasion. "No one has the right to destroy any living creatures, however evil they may be, or to hurt them or make them unhappy. I will not fight—even to save my kingdom." For the safety of the world's future, the children could not well learn any more wholesome doctrine than that.

(Is it becoming clear, then, why so many of those who are well satisfied with the established order will have none of the Oz books?)

There is one element in the Oz books that the children probably do not get, and that is the element of satire. You will remember how in *The Wizard of Oz*, Dorothy, the Scarecrow, and the Tin Woodman travel to the Wizard because they want, respectively, to get home to Kansas, to receive some brains, and to be given a heart. The fourth member of the party is a Cowardly Lion, who wants courage. He is a most ferocious fighter in the jungle, but he is much concerned over the fact that whenever there is danger he is terribly afraid. He trembles desperately, pitches in to do his best, and generally comes out victorious. Nevertheless he is worried to think that the King of Beasts should be a coward. It does not seem fit somehow. So he goes to Oz to ask for courage. Mr. Baum makes the whole journey a sermon on the text: "Man does not live by bread alone but principally by catchwords." All through the journey, the Lion is the valiant protector of the party, and whenever any particularly difficult problem comes up, it is the Scarecrow who solves it. Once the Tin Woodman accidentally steps on a beetle and kills it. Greatly distressed over this act of clumsiness, he weeps bitter tears which run down his tin cheeks and rust the hinges of his jaw, so that the next time Dorothy speaks to him he is unable to answer her until she has taken the oil can out of her basket and oiled him up again. After he has a heart, he explains, he will not need to be so careful: his heart will tell him when he is doing wrong. But at present ceaseless vigilance is necessary to ensure a halfway decent life. The point is, of course, that all these creatures, except Dorothy, are already in possession of that of which they are going in search. Yet because they lack the name, the fact that they are in actual possession of the thing itself wholly eludes them.

When they arrive at the Emerald City, it is easy for the Wizard to satisfy the Scarecrow, the Lion, and the Tin Woodman. The Lion eats a dish of porridge for courage and never trembles again. A silken heart stuffed with sawdust serves the Tin Woodman a great deal better than any frail heart of flesh possibly could, and the Wizard assures him, as he puts it in his breast, that it *is* an especially kind heart. The Scarecrow's new brains are a judicious mixture of bran with needles and pins, and whenever one of these latter ingredients comes sticking through the sack covering of his head, the Scarecrow congratulates himself upon his sharpness. But Dorothy—Dorothy wants to get home to Kansas. That is a different sort of problem, and that is where the Wizard meets his downfall.

There are numerous other examples of satire also: readers of the series will recall them readily. I can refer only, very briefly, to a few of them here. The absurd conceit of the Scarecrow after he gets his brains, the outrageous sentimentality of the Tin Woodman—these are notorious and delightful. General Jinjur in *The Land of Oz* is a burlesque of the violent suffragette—(it was still safe to ridicule the suffragettes in 1904). The Donkeys of Dunkiton think that donkeys are the wisest and most beautiful of all human creatures. They do not need to go to school. The worrying fraternity are made fun of in the Flutterbudget incident of *The Emerald City of Oz*, and here Mr. Baum has skillfully chosen exactly the absurd sort of thing that nervous, imaginative children do worry about. Sometimes the satire strikes a deeper note as in the incident of the Woggle-Bug having reduced all knowledge to pills, so that the students in his college do not need to spend any of their valuable time in studying but may be free to devote it to all such important things as football and other outdoor sports. Finally, even magic itself is satirized. In *The Magic of Oz*, Mr. Baum gives the world a formula for producing magical transformations. You simply pronounce aloud the word PYRZQXGL.

V

Now I do not wish to be understood as feeling that I have written a marvelous essay on one of the great masterpieces of world literature. The Oz books are "popular" in character. That admits, of course, of no dispute. In distinction of style they are utterly lacking and often in imaginative distinction as well. Nobody could possibly write fifty volumes of fairy tales and keep the whole up to a high level of imaginative power. In this respect the series may be said to have declined notably as commercial considerations made it necessary to string it on indefinitely. How many million Oz books have really been sold, I have no idea, but that the series was immensely profitable may be inferred from the fact that not even Mr. Baum's death could put a stop to it.

As popular literature then, and along the lines indicated in this essay, I think the Oz books deserve consideration. They are an American phenomenon. It would be calamitous if children were to read them only and were therefore to stop reading Perrault and Madame D'Aulnoy and the Brothers Grimm. Nevertheless they have their place. And it is undeniable that literature conceived in terms of our own life and thought must have always a certain vividness for us which other, sometimes much finer, literature does not possess. This too has been illustrated in the experience of American children with the Oz books.

For myself, I can hardly be too grateful for the joys they brought to the child I once was. Every Christmas there was a new Oz book for me, and now, these many Christmases later, I am writing this poor essay to speak of my gratitude. So far as I know, the Oz books have never before been the object of any critical study whatever.

When I was a child, I often heard of the many letters the children wrote Mr. Baum and of his pride in them. I always intended to add one to that mighty collection, yet somehow I never did it until 1919. Then, no longer a child, I wrote to tell the magician of my childhood days what his books had once meant to me. And thus he wrote in reply, exactly two months to the day before he died:

March 6th, 1919.

Dear Mr. Wagenknecht:

Your good letter was received some time ago. I thoroughly appreciated your writing to me, and hoped to have answered it before. But with heart trouble we are inclined to be lazy, and time glides by without accomplishing all we would like to. I am very glad my books have given you pleasure, both in your childhood days and also now you are older. I have quite a few readers of mature years, who being children at heart still enjoy my tales. Received a letter from a church of England clergyman lately, telling me what a comfort my books were to him. When tired and discouraged with this war-worn world, he could let himself be taken to Oz, and for a time forget all else. It is things like your letter and his as well as the children's letters that make one feel they have done a bit to brighten up a few lives.

I am writing a little each day, and will have a new book ready for fall trade. Thanking you for writing me. It helps.

Ozily yours,
L. FRANK BAUM.

So at the end the gentle, tired magician still believed in the goodness of the world that he had made.

Our American utopia may be somewhat crude in spots but there is no denying that it is ours. It would be comparatively simple to make the history of Oz a somewhat more highly finished record, but the chances are nine out of ten that you would at the same time make it somewhat less American. Someday we may have better American fairy tales but that will not be until America is a better country.

Utopia Americana:
A Generation Afterwards

· *by Edward Wagenknecht* ·

Now that L. Frank Baum is a centenarian, it is comforting to feel that, in his own way, he is becoming a classic also. Since the copyright expired, *The Wizard of Oz* has appeared in so many versions and editions that to collect them all would be a full-time job, and if the children who are growing up now are notably different from their parents and grandparents, they do not seem to show it in their response to him. He has acquired an able biographer. His special devotees have given him a periodical of his own, which, as the years go by, finds increasingly interesting and important material to print (how many writers below the level of a Shakespeare or a Dickens can boast of such an honor?), and every summer they gather in Indiana to do homage. There has been at least one scholarly article about him in a standard journal and one perfectly crazy one in a coterie quarterly. I expect to see more of both kinds; only recently, while working on Edgar Allan Poe, I noted a possible source for Baum's General of the Isle of Phreex in Poe's story, "The Man That Was Used Up."

Baum has achieved his present position without anything in the way of "advantages" and in the face of the stupidest kind of prejudice. Having published what is regarded as the pioneer critical study of his work as far back as 1929 (thus staking out at least one field where I have some claim to be regarded as a patriarch), I ought to be able to explain the phenomenon. I am not sure that I can, completely. But perhaps I can make one or two suggestions.

I have always been suspicious of too facile explanations of Baum's (or anybody's) vogue. Because the central human figures in Baum's stories are girls, it is sometimes carelessly assumed that he appeals more to girls than he does to boys. I am not convinced that this is true. In fact, I

Reprinted from *American Book Collector*, Special Number (December 1962), pp. 12–13. Copyright © 1962 by William B. Thorsen. Reprinted by permission of William B. Thorsen and Edward Wagenknecht.

have sometimes known girls themselve to attract boys. When I was first introduced to *The Wizard of Oz*, I was at that stage in my development (it did not last long) where I imagined I did not like girls, but I cannot recall that this ever affected my devotion to Baum or to Dorothy for a moment. And most of the great Baum devotees of mature years that I happen to know are not women but men.

Of course the fact that Baum is now in his second century does give him an advantage in the way of respectability. We all still have enough of the Puritan in us so that neither fiction nor humor has become *quite* respectable in this country, and any bookseller will tell you that the increasing cost of books has hit fiction much harder than nonfiction. Just cram your pages with fact, not art (for art, too, is dangerous), and you can justify asking almost any price, because it is quite respectable to spend your money on education, but you're going to think twice before you squander it on something somebody has "made up," especially if he happens to be a new writer. One of the most learned professors I had in college published a very scholarly book on the Elizabethan jig, but I had very few teachers on any level who took any interest in contemporary films or comics or vaudeville or popular art of any kind. Yet nowadays university presses are publishing books about the dime novels that my generation had to read behind the barn and the films that we were considered frivolous for taking so seriously. While Marilyn Monroe was alive, you were expected to snicker slightly when you admitted that you liked her, and when she filmed on Lexington Avenue a perfectly innocent scene in which the wind played havoc with her skirts, she was attacked in a hysterical article in the religious press, in which she was told that she had disgraced New York (which must be used to it by now) and made herself responsible for all our sex crimes, but if you will look at the tributes paid to her after her death, you will find that "decency," "innocence," and "purity" are the words which recur most often. Every informed person knows that in her case it is the posthumous judgments which will accord with the facts, but this certainly does not make earlier stupidities and misrepresentations seem less reprehensible.

Baum was one of the few American writers who can honestly be said to have created a world, and as time goes on we do not seem to have less need of these worlds of the mind as centers of refuge from the so-called "real" world of nuclear tests, destructive insecticides and detergents, and land- and tree-eating superhighways to which we seem in our folly to have condemned ourselves. We may grant that Baum's is a minor world; nothing could be of less service to him than a determination to exalt him to a higher plane than his talents equipped him to occupy. Not so long ago a gentleman wrote me that he considered

Baum greater than Homer, to which I was obliged rudely to reply that after that it did not seem to me that any opinion of his on any literary question could possibly be of interest. But if we do not dismiss as tramps all human beings who fail to reach the level of the saints, then we ought not classify as trash all literature which does not attain classical stature. If Baum does not go deep enough to solve our problems for us, he can at times help us to forget them, which is itself a valuable service; if he brings us no new revelation of the meaning of human days, his sense of values is always sound; and if he is not a stylist in the sense in which, say, Walter de la Mare is a stylist, there is still no excuse for failing to recognize that he wrote with admirable clarity and vigor and charm.

I remember once hearing William E. Barton remark that he thought some of his generation who had been criticized for reading dime novels in their boyhood might have been better off if they had stayed with them instead of going on to the more sophisticated literature now in good odor. I have known readers who got stranded on the reef of the Oz books and never got off, which is, of course, a lamentable case of arrested development, but I am quite as distressed over those who, having responded to all Baum's sound values and fine imaginative appeal in childhood, feel called upon, in the process of growing up to put it all away and confine themselves to the "real" world. To go on to greater masters of imaginative art is one thing, but to junk imagination and suppose nothing to be real unless it is nasty and "hardboiled" is something else again. Moreover, I feel sure that those who choose the first alternative will always be able to return to Baum at intervals, and even if they do not, they will never cease to be grateful to him for the service he rendered in awakening their sense of wonder.

The Wizard of Chittenango

· by James Thurber ·

I have been for several weeks bogged in Oz books. It had seemed to me, at first, a simple matter to go back to the two I had read as a boy of ten, *The Wizard of Oz* and *The Land of Oz* (the first two published), and write down what Oz revisited was like to me now that my life, at forty, had begun again. I was amazed and disturbed to discover that there are

Reprinted from *The New Republic*, December 12, 1934, pp. 141–142. Copyright © 1934 by The New Republic, Inc. Reprinted by permission.

now twenty-eight different books about Oz (the latest one, 1934, is *Speedy in Oz*). Since the first was published nearly thirty-five years ago, about three million copies of Oz books have been sold; sales of the various books, taken together, run to almost a hundred thousand copies a year. The thing is obviously a major phenomenon in the wonderful land of books. I began my research, therefore, not by rereading the two Oz books I loved as a child (and still do, I was happy to find out later) but with an inquiry into the life and nature of the man who wrote the first fourteen of the series, Mr. L. Frank Baum.

Lyman Frank Baum was born in Chittenango, New York, in 1856. When he was about ten he became enamored of (if also a little horrified and disgusted by) the tales of the Grimm brothers and of Andersen and he determined that when he grew up he would write fairy tales with a difference. There would be, in the first place, "no love and marriage in them" (I quote the present publishers of his books, Reilly & Lee, of Chicago); furthermore, he wanted to get away from the "European background" and write tales about fairies in America (he chose Kansas as the jumping-off place for the Oz books, although he was educated in Syracuse, lived most of his life in Chicago, and spent his last years in Hollywood where he died in 1919, aged 62). There was also another significant change that he wanted to make in the old fairy tales. Let me quote from his own foreword to the first Oz book, *The Wizard*: ". . . the time has now come for a series of newer 'wonder tales' in which the stereotyped genie, dwarf and fairy are eliminated, together with all the horrible and blood-curdling incident devised by their authors to point a fearsome moral. . . . *The Wizard of Oz* aspires to be a modernized fairy tale in which the wonderment and joy are retained, and the heartaches and nightmares left out." I am glad that in spite of this high determination, Mr. Baum failed to keep them out. Children love a lot of nightmare and at least a little heartache in their books. And they get them in the Oz books. I know that I went through excruciatingly lovely nightmares and heartaches when the Scarecrow lost his straw, when the Tin Woodman was taken apart, when the Saw-Horse broke his wooden leg (it hurt for me even if it didn't for Mr. Baum).

But let me return for a moment to the story of his writings. In his late twenties he wrote two plays, *The Maid of Arran* and *The Queen of Killarney*. Under the name of Schuyler Staunton he also wrote three novels (I could not learn their titles[1]). In all he wrote about fifty books, most of them for children. He was forty-three in 1899 when he did *The*

---

1. Baum wrote two novels under the name "Schuyler Staunton," *The Fate of a Crown* (1905) and *Daughters of Destiny* (1906); Thurber may be recalling another novel *The Last Egyptian* which Baum published anonymously in 1909 [M.P.H.].

Wizard of Oz which to him was just another . . . book for children. It sold better than anything he had ever written. The next year he wrote a thing called *Dot and Tot of Merryland*. But his readers wanted more about Oz. He began to get letters from them by the thousands and he was not exactly pleased that Oz was the land they loved the best. He ignored the popular demand for four years, meanwhile writing a book called *Baum's American Fairy Tales*,[2] subtitled "Stories of Astonishing Adventures of American Boys and Girls with the Fairies of Their Native Land." He must have been hurt by its cold reception. Here he was, nearing fifty, trying to be what he had always fondly wanted to be, an American Andersen, an American Grimm, and all the while American children—and their parents—would have none of it, but screamed for more about Oz. His American fairy tales, I am sorry to tell you, are not good fairy tales. The scene of the first one is in the attic of a house "on Prairie Avenue, in Chicago." It never leaves there for any wondrous, faraway realm. Baum apparently never thoroughly understood that fatal flaw in his essential ambition, but he understood it a little. He did another collection of unconnected stories but this time he placed them, not in Illinois but in Mo. *The Magical Monarch of Mo* is not much better than the American tales; but at least one story in it, "The Strange Adventures of the King's Head," is a fine, fantastic fairy tale. The others are just so-so. On went L. Frank Baum, grimly, into . . . *The Enchanted Island of Yew*, but the girls and boys were not interested. Finally, after four years and ten thousand letters from youngsters, he wrote *The Land of Oz*. He was back where they wanted him.

I haven't space to go into even half of the Oz books, nor do I want to. The first two, *The Wizard* and *The Land*, are far and away the best. Baum wrote *The Wizard*, I am told, simply as a tour de force to see if he could animate, and make real, creatures never alive before on sea or land. He succeeded, eminently, with the Scarecrow and the Tin Woodman, and he went on to succeed in the second book with Jack Pumpkinhead, the Saw-Horse, and the Woggle-Bug. After that I do not think he was ever really successful. Admittedly he didn't want to keep doing Oz books (he wanted to get back to those American Tales). In the next six years he wrote only two,[3] and at the end of the second of these he put a tired, awkward note explaining that Oz was somehow forever cut off from communication with this world. What a heartache and a nightmare that announcement was to the children of America! But of course

---

2. Thurber is referring to the 1908 expanded edition of *American Fairy Tales* (1901) [M.P.H.].

3. Actually four: *Ozma of Oz* (1907), *Dorothy and the Wizard in Oz* (1908), *The Road to Oz* (1909), and *The Emerald City of Oz* (1910) [M.P.H.].

they didn't fall for his clumsy device: they knew he was a great wizard and could get back to Oz if he wanted to and they made him get back. From 1913 until 1919 he resignedly wrote an Oz book every year and was working on one when he died. This one was finished by Ruth Plumly Thompson,[4] a young Philadelphia woman who as a child had adored the Oz books. But she has taken them up where Mr. Baum left off, not where he began; she has never found her way into the real Oz.

I think the fatal trouble with the later books (for us aging examiners, anyway) is that they become whimsical rather than fantastic. They ramble and they preach (one is dedicated to a society in California called "The Uplifters"[5]); they lack the quick movement, the fresh suspense, the amusing dialogue, and the really funny invention of the first ones. They dawdle along like a class prophecy. None of their creatures comes to life for me. I am merely bored by the Growlywogs, the Whimsies, the Cuttenclips, the Patchwork Girl, Button-Bright, the Googly-Goo, and I am actually gagged by one Unc Nunkie. Mr. Baum himself said that he kept putting in things that children wrote and asked him to put in. He brought back the Wizard of Oz because the children pleaded and he rewrote the Scarecrow and the Woodman almost to death because the children wanted them. The children should have been told to hush up and go back to the real Wizard and the real Scarecrow and the real Woodman. They are only in the first two books.

Too much cannot be said for the drawings of Mr. John R. Neill. He began with *The Land of Oz* and his pictures were far superior to those of Mr. W. W. Denslow who illustrated *The Wizard.* After doing more than three thousand drawings (he's still at it), he keeps up beautifully.

---

4. Though the publishers said that Baum had left some unfinished notes for his successor, *The Royal Book of Oz* (1921) was written solely by Thompson [M.P.H.].

5. *The Scarecrow of Oz* (1915) [M.P.H.].

An Appreciation

· *Russel B. Nye* ·

"Years from now," *The New York Times* predicted in 1919 at the death of Lyman Frank Baum, "though the children cannot clamor for the newest Oz book, the crowding generations will plead for the old ones."

Reprinted from *The Wizard of Oz and Who He Was.* East Lansing: Michigan State University Press, 1957, pp. 1–17. Copyright © 1957 by Michigan State University Press. Reprinted by permission of Russel B. Nye.

More than a half century after Dorothy, the Wizard, and their friends were introduced to the public, their continuing popularity testifies to the accuracy of the *Times'* estimate of Baum's work. The Land of Oz has stood the test of time.

At the age of ten, so the story goes, L. Frank Baum was fascinated by the tales of the Brothers Grimm and Hans Christian Andersen, and a trifle repelled too by their undercurrents of violence and sadness. As an adult writer of children's stories, remembering his reactions as a child, he determined to construct tales of fantasy with a difference, tales that would "bear the stamp of our times and depict the progressive fairies of today." There would be in them, he said, "no love and marriage," no hate, no revenge, no attempt to intrude into a child's world the emotions of an adult society that a child could neither experience nor comprehend. He would write *American* fairy tales, using American backgrounds and materials rather than those of the European tradition familiarized by the Grimms, Perrault, Aesop, and others. In his tales, Baum wrote in the preface to *The Wizard of Oz*, "The stereotyped genie, dwarf, and fairy are eliminated, together with all the horrible and blood-curdling incident . . ." His were to be "modernized" fairy stories, "in which the wonderment and joy are retained, and the heartaches and nightmares left out." "Modern education," he wrote, "includes morality; therefore the modern child seeks only entertainment in its wonder-tales." His stories would be stripped of "fearsome" morality at least, and aimed simply to "excite laughter and gladden the heart."

Fortunately for three generations of children, Baum never fully succeeded in attaining all of his objectives. He drew freely on the past, and his books are far more derivative than possibly he realized. The Oz books conform to the accepted pattern far more often than they deviate. Elves, gnomes, wizards, beasts, dragons, princesses, witches, sorcery, all the conventional machinery of ancient folk and fairy tale appears in Oz, with Baum's own clever twists and adaptations. His strength as a storyteller for children lay in his unique ability to implement and adapt the familiar apparatus of the older tale by reworking old materials into new forms. He worked within the framework of the Grimm tradition despite his disavowal of many of its elements, constructing out of essentially traditional materials a fresh new gallery of characters and a group of delightfully varied plots. The changes he rang on the traditional fairy story, not his rejection of that tradition, account to a great extent for his effectiveness. A great part of the perennial attraction of the Oz books lies in the child's recognition of old friends in new roles and costumes.

The "horrible and blood-curdling incident" to which Baum objected in the Grimms, of course, appears nowhere in Oz. Here Baum followed his original intentions. There are excitement and danger in his stories, but violence is absent and evil under control. The witches may enchant Dorothy; they never threaten to eat her or bake her in an oven, and the bad wizards and witches who threaten Oz are frustrated creatures whom one could never imagine victorious. The Nome King, though obviously a thorough villain, is given to temper tantrums and capricious mischief much like a spoiled child, but no more dangerous and almost as easily disciplined. The Wicked Witch is defeated by a stout heart and a pail of water. The Hungry Tiger wants to eat a fat baby but his love for children won't let him—thus Baum tenderizes the tigers of folklore. Missing too are the "heartaches" of the Tin Soldier and Thumbelina, the bittersweet sentiment of Andersen, for Oz is a land of laughter, not tears, as Baum intended it to be.

In his effort to create an American *genre*, Baum had least success and more or less gave up the attempt. The tremendous popularity of *The Wizard* surprised him. He had held really higher hopes for his next book, *Baum's American Fairy Tales: Stories of Astonishing Adventures of Boys and Girls with the Fairies of their Native Land*, which appeared in 1901. These "American" tales, laid in American locales, were lost in the instant popularity of the Oz stories, and Baum's attempt to create a native *genre* simply did not come off. Clever, inventive, with a substratum of very shrewd satire, the stories fail to measure up to the standard set by the Wizard and his crew. Nor could Baum quite keep Oz out of the book; the most effective stories in the collection are those dealing with the kingdom of Quok (another version of some of the wildly wonderful realms of the later Oz books) and with the doings of the Ryls (blood brothers of Munchkins and Gillikins).

The *American Fairy Tales* were good stories, far better than most run-of-the-mill "educational" tales for children, but in the majority of them Baum failed to observe the first rule of the wonder-tale—that it must create a never-never land in which all laws of probability may be credibly contravened or suspended. When in the first story the little girl (Dorothy by another name) replies to a puzzled, lost genie, "You are on Prairie Avenue in Chicago," the heart goes out of the story. It is only in Quok, or in Baum's zany version of the African Congo, or among the Ryls, that the book captures the free spirit of Oz. The child could see Chicago (or a city much like it) with his eyes; Oz he could see much more distinctly and believably with his imagination. Baum nevertheless clung for a few years to the belief that he could make the United States an authentic fairyland. "There's lots of magic in all nature," he remarked in *Tik-Tok of Oz*, "and you may see it as well in the United

States, where you and I once lived, as you can here." But children could not. They saw magic only in Oz, which never was nor could be Chicago or Omaha or California or Kansas.

To everybody's good fortune, Baum gave up his idea of Americanizing Oz. What he had in mind, in effect, violated the basic laws of fantasy, and the Land of Oz could never have existed in defiance of them. The wonder-tale, to be successful, must assert the leadership of mind, establishing control over the novel and the strange, making order out of the new and disordered. It must appeal to the sense of wonder—that is, it must perceive and construct something which exists outside the immediate connotations of the materials at hand. Thus a child, given a few blocks, may see in and build from them a steam-shovel that will do all that a real steam-shovel may do and more. And the tale must contain, within a believable framework, the unbelievable elements of incantation and the supernatural, whereby all the rules of a child's world are nullified or suspended and by which the new and illogical may be selected, coordinated, and ordered. All these necessary elements appear in Oz. They could never appear in Chicago or Boston.

The Oz books became classics, then, not because Baum succeeded in writing a new kind of Americanized fairy story, but because he adapted the fairy tale tradition itself to twentieth-century American taste with imaginative ingenuity. There are in the Oz books a number of references to American locale, and Dorothy herself, of course, comes to Oz via a prairie twister. But beyond such casual references Oz has no real relation to the United States—it is fundamentally the out-of-time, out-of-space fairyland of tradition. Working from the midst of older materials, Baum's clever and occasionally brilliant variations on traditional themes are marks of craftsmanship and creativeness of a high order. It is not solely in their "Americanism," nor in their avoidance of the "horrible and blood-curdling," nor in their rejection of moralism (which Baum did not wholly reject), nor in their pure entertainment value (which Baum did maintain), that the power of the Oz books lies. It stems rather from Baum's success in placing his work directly in the stream of the past, in his assimilation into Oz of the ageless universals of wonder and fantasy. What Baum did was to enlarge the resources of the European inheritance by making it possible to find the old joy of wonderment in the fresh new setting of Oz, creating a bright new fairyland in the old tradition.

That this was no minor achievement is shown by what happened to Baum after *The Wizard* appeared. Its popularity required a second Oz story, and then a third, until Baum, having created Oz, could not escape it. *The Wizard* was apparently written with no intention of supplying a sequel; it is a complete unit, with nothing in it to anticipate a successor, much less thirteen of them. For almost ten years after its appearance he tried hopefully to avoid writing more Oz books, producing several stories for an older age group and even some novels for adults. He even tried to end the series in 1910 with *The Emerald City of Oz*, but he was driven back to Oz by the demands of his readers and, one suspects, his own unconscious inclinations. Finally, promising that "as long as you care to read them I shall try to write them," he resigned himself to at least one Oz story a year.

Whatever Baum's original disclaimer, the strain of moralism is strong in the Oz books. They are not simply pure entertainment, devoid of any lesson, for as Baum once admitted, he tried to hide "a wholesome lesson" behind the doings of his characters. The child (or adult, for that matter) who reads the Oz books for a second or third time can usually find its hiding place, and one of the pleasures of reading Baum lies in its discovery. Baum's "wholesome lesson" is particularly evident in his creation of characters whose function is fully as much didactic as dramatic. The lesson of the Woodman, the Scarecrow, and the Lion in *The Wizard of Oz* is clearly a moral one. The Tin Woodman, a kindly, compassionate creature who weeps at stepping on a beetle, wants a heart so that he may love. The Scarecrow, who laments his lack of a brain, shows shrewd common sense from the beginning. The Cowardly Lion, when the chips are down, is as brave as a lion can be, learning (a message of reassurance to any child) that to fear danger is normal but that the important thing is to have more courage than fear. Yet not until each possesses the symbol of what he wants is he confident and satisfied—something that Dorothy wisely recognizes. You have within you, Baum seems to say, the things you seek; the symbol is of no value while the virtue is. Jack Pumpkinhead is not very smart (for his brains are pumpkinseeds), but he is loyal, lovable, and kind—a heartening message for those at the bottom of the class.

The Wizard of Oz himself is perhaps the best example of Baum's method of indirect teaching by characterization. A gentle, inoffensive little man, the Wizard's magic is strictly of the sideshow variety. He is actually a refugee from "Bailum and Barney's" circus, where he learned a few tricks. Yet fake that he is, it is he who built Emerald City, making it a utopia out of his kindheartedness and good intent. The bluster and apparatus with which he surrounds himself hide a friendly little man; what magic he is able to work with the Woodman, the Scarecrow, and the Lion derives from his ability to capitalize on some of the foolish frailties of human nature. There is something of Colonel Sellers the salesman in the Wizard, a trace of P. T. Barnum and the "sucker born every minute" philosophy, without cruelty or intent to defraud. "How can I help being a humbug," he asks plaintively, "when all these people make me do things that everybody knows can't be done?" But there is no malice in him, and for his well-intentioned humbuggery he is rewarded by learning real sorcery from Glinda. To the child the meaning of the Wizard's story comes clear. How silly it is to turn to humbuggery to get something false, when you can have the true!

Baum had, too, a well-developed sense of satire, though satire is probably too strong a term for what Baum did. He was never zealous or intense in his attitude toward people, for his aim was amusement and not criticism. "Chaff," or "banter," describes more accurately Baum's manner of poking gently at those human frailties and foibles that the child reader could observe for himself in the world about him. The Oz stories abound with examples. The Loon People, whose King is named Bal, are inflated with self-important pretense; punctured with a thorn, they collapse as conceited people always do. The Whimsies, who have tiny heads and strong bodies, wear cardboard heads of normal size to fool observers into thinking they have brains. The China Princess, fearful that a mended crack might mar her beauty, lives a lonely, isolated life, avoiding all contact with those who might chip her perfection. The Flatheads, who had no brains at all, acted just as badly after Queen Lurline gave them some—thereby proving that it takes more than brains to make life happy and peaceful. The Foolish Owl and the Wise Donkey illustrate how false an accepted generalization can be, and the spindly Growlywogs, who are tremendously strong, show how appearances may deceive. Flutterbudgets can never be happy because they live in constant fear of what *might* happen. Only once does Baum make obvious use of current events. General Jinjur's army of girls armed with hatpins, who go to war to force men to do housework, satirizes the suffragette movement, a reference probably too sophisticated for his child readers to identify.

One of Baum's major contributions to the tradition of the fantasy tale is his recognition of the inherent wonder of the machine, his perception of the magic of *things* in themselves. In the Oz books he expanded the resources of the fairy tale to include, for the first time, the mechanical developments of the 20th century, when every child saw about him—in the automobile, the dynamo, the radio, the airplane, and the rest—the triumph of technology over distance, time, and gravity. No American child of Baum's time or after could remain unaware of the age of invention, or fail to feel the wonderment of what machines could do. The mechanical marvels of Oz fitted exactly the technological pattern of American life, its consciousness of machinery, its faith in the machine's seemingly unlimited potential. Kipling, of course, had experimented before Baum with tales of technology, but from a much more mature and sophisticated point of view. Tom Swift, the boy's version of peculiarly American Edison-Ford myth, also made machines that outstripped reality (but not by much), but Tom's creations were always presented as real, just-around-the-corner inventions, far removed from fantasy. Baum, in a burst of inspiration, moved the machine into the child's world of imagination, endowed it with life and magic, and made it the ally of all the forces of good and justice and well-being in Oz.

The machines of Oz are magician's creations, with the white magic of the sorcerer clinging to them. By transforming the talking beasts of ancient folktales into talking machines, Baum grafted twentieth-century technology to the fairy-tale tradition. The useful, friendly, companionable creatures of Oz became part of the child's family life, much as the automobile was becoming integrated into contemporary American society. The Tin Woodman, or Tik-Tok the clockwork man, the glass cats, and the robots of Oz all took on lives of their own, in the time-honored fairy-tale tradition, as friends and servants. At no time did Baum allow the machines of Oz to get out of control. They are always under orderly discipline; they never exceed their limitations; they act always in harmony with the desires of those who use them. Johnny Dooit, the obliging workman who can make anything out of anything in the best Yankee "whittling boy" tradition, never uses his skill to construct anything that might threaten the peace and security of Oz. Though Smith and Tinker built a mechanical giant for the Nome King, he is a rather ineffectual robot who is easily vanquished by the wisdom of the Scarecrow and the courage of the Lion. And there are in Oz certain limits beyond which technology cannot go, however skillful the technician and powerful his magic. Ku-Klip the Tinsmith, who built the Tin Woodman and the Tin Soldier, fails dismally when he tries to construct a flesh-and-blood creature, producing only the characterless Chopfyte, who is "always somebody else." And in the end, the most ingenious mechanics of all, Smith and Tinker, overreach themelves. One paints a lake so realistically that he drowns in it; the other builds a ladder to the moon and is so fascinated by the misty, unreal Moon Country that he refuses to leave it. Thus Baum comments on technological overdevelopment, which may undo the unwary in America as it does in Oz.

The Oz books are permeated by an authentic, persistent strain of humor that is one of Baum's most easily recognized characteristics.

They are fundamentally "funny" books from the child's point of view, for Baum was able, as few men are, to translate himself without condescension into the child's world. He put into the Oz books his own recognition of the incongruities of human nature, accurately catching and emphasizing some of the absurdities of life. Baum was no Swift or Twain, but he belonged in the same tradition and his wit is (on a lesser level) astonishingly subtle and ingenious. The pertinent but unexpected association of the apparently unrelated, the joy of novelty, the pleasure of recognition of the obvious in new form, the surprise at the perception of qualities previously unseen, the shift in an accustomed framework of values—all the classic elements of the humor tradition appear in the Oz books.

Baum's wit, though, is geared to the child's pace. It is wit a child can understand and appreciate, since it deals with concepts within the circle of his experience and those which are applicable to his own sphere of action. Baum's skill in evoking a humorous response from a child is real and expert; he locates quickly and unerringly those areas of incongruity and absurdity that are recognizable to a child and subject to his judgment. There are witty bits in the Oz books that children may miss the first time, but if adults can be prevented from explaining the joke (this is almost a crime in Oz) they can have the wonderful pleasure of finding it the second or third time.

The humor of Oz lies in the interaction of character and situation, in the genuinely humorous creations who get into equally humorous predicaments because they are what they are. Sometimes the humor is broad and obvious—such as the Kingdom of Utensia, populated by kitchenware, whose King Kleaver often makes cutting remarks to Captain Dip of the Spoon Brigade. Or Grandmother Gnit, who spends her time knitting, or gloomy old Pessim, who expects catastrophe any moment. At other times Baum's strokes are somewhat more delicate, as with Ann Soforth, the ambitious young queen who sets out to conquer the world with sixteen generals and one private, or with Diksey the jokester, who once made such a bad joke it led to war—both witty commentaries on military motivations. The Hammer-Heads refuse to allow travelers to enter their country since they are defending something precious; later it may occur to the reader that since nobody has ever seen what they are defending, possibly nobody wants it anyway. The best illustration of all, however, is probably H. M. Woggle-Bug, T.E., a masterpiece of humorous creation. A lowly field bug with no name at all, he hid in a schoolhouse and became thoroughly educated (T.E.) by eavesdropping on the lectures of Professor Nowitall. Caught in a magic lantern lens, he was projected on the classroom screen and stepped off highly magnified (H. M.), fully qualified to be Dean of the Royal College, "the most learned and important educator in the favored land of Oz." Thus H. M. Woggle-Bug, T.E., struts his way self-importantly through various adventures, the very symbol of ostentatious erudition. All this, and much more like it, is genuine humor, touched now and then with genius.

Beyond humor, or moral lessons, or adventure, the heart of the Oz books lies in the Land of Oz itself, which, as others have pointed out, is really an American Utopia. In Emerald City, as Baum described it, there was no disease, no illness, none but accidental death and that seldom. All inhabitants worked one-half the time and played one-half, a self-enforced obedience to the rule that all work or all play makes dullness or irresponsibility. Emerald City had no poor, because there was no money and no private property—everything belonged to the Ruler, who gave each what he needed. Among the people there was free and generous exchange of goods. Each person was "given freely by his neighbors whatever he required for his use, which is as much as anyone can reasonably desire." Foodstuffs were divided equally; clothes, jewels, shoes, housing, everything was there for the asking; and if the supply ran short, the Ruler's storehouses, filled with everything to make life perfect, lay open to the public. In Emerald City man lived in complete harmony with man, for "every inhabitant of that favored country was happy and prosperous." Men lived in complete harmony with nature and technology; machines and animals moved in and out of human society easily and naturally. So perfectly balanced was the relationship between man and nature in Oz that rains came for the asking, while courteous flies moved away unswatted when politely asked to do so. The only person in Oz who cannot understand animal talk or consort with them is the Ferryman, who as punishment for cruelty to an animal long ago is thus condemned to lonely isolation from the society of Emerald City.

The First Law of Baum's Utopia of Oz, the rule that inspires its harmonious order, is Love. This theme, on which Baum played constant and subtle variations, binds all the Oz books together as a moral unit. Love in Oz is kindness, selflessness, friendliness—an inner check that makes one act decently toward human beings, animals, plants, fairies, machines, and even one's enemies. A Love Magnet hangs over the gates of the City, so magnetizing all who enter that they must love and be loved, and Princess Ozma explains her kingdom's whole reason for existence by the simple remark, "The Land of Oz is Love." From love comes order, harmony, discipline, happiness, and perfection. And with love there is always happiness, its inseparable companion, represented in Oz by Glinda, Ozma's close friend and the greatest of sorceresses. Ruler of the Red Country of the Quadlings in southern Oz, Glinda has only one aim—to make people ever more happy. It is she, when selfishness threatens or unhappiness disturbs the Land of Oz, who appears, *dea-ex-machina*, to restore harmony, free the captive Ozma, and frustrate the forces of mischief.

The foils to Ozma, Glinda, and Oz are Ruggedo, the Nome King, and his subjects of the Nome Kingdom. (Baum thought *gnome* too difficult for children to pronounce.) The Nome King is the epitome of selfishness; his campaign against Oz is motivated solely by jealousy, conceit, tyranny, and all those qualities antithetical to love. But there is no war, for Ozma simply refuses to mobilize an army against him, in obedience to the law of Oz that "No one has a right to destroy any living creature, however evil they may be, or to hurt them, or make them unhappy." In the face of Ozma's faith and love, the Nome King is powerless. Beaten and frustrated, he is banished to wander homeless through the land. Kaliko, his successor, does better, but like the Nome King he too misuses his power and needs occasionally to be straightened out. Ozma's final victory over the Nomes comes not from magic, though she too is a mighty sorceress, but from the simple power of kindness and love.

The theme of selflessness as the cardinal principle of love runs through all the Oz books, forming the thread that binds them together. In Baum's world of Oz Bad=Selfishness, Good=Selflessness, Love=Happiness, Hate=Evil and Unhappiness. Those who use power for selfish ends, are Bad, and are punished in proportion to their crime. Coo-ee-oh, the vain narcissistic Queen of the Skeezers who lacks compassion and humanity, is punished by becoming a swan, capable only of admiring forever her cold reflection in a pool. Ugu and Gwig, minor magicians who misused their gifts, come to bad ends. Blinkie, a witch who froze the heart of a princess so that she could not love, had her magic powers stripped from her. First and Foremost, ruler of the Phanfasms, ally of the Nome King and the most evil creation in Oz (he always places himself first and foremost, the ultimate in selfishness) wants more than anything else to make people unhappy. Against Glinda and Ozma he has not even the remotest chance of winning. The villains of Oz have this in common—they cannot love, nor can they find or create happiness for themselves, even in trying to destroy it for others.

Oz is a family-style Utopia, phrased in terms and placed in a framework the child can understand. It is simply the perfect home, built on love, permeated by happiness, filled with a big loving family. In Oz you do enjoyable duties, live in cooperation and affection with brothers, sisters, neighbor children, and pets, find your wants satisfied from the storehouse of one's parents, and play in the happy security and harmony of the ideal home, where, as Baum remarks of Emerald City, "each one is proud to do all he could for his friends and neighbors." Dolls, dogs, cats, sawhorses, scarecrows, jack-o-lanterns, rugs, scissors, balloons, china dolls, and everything else in the house is alive, helpful, friendly, and full of fun. Ozma, the mother, rules with beneficence and justice. "The people were her children," Baum remarked of Ozma, "and she cared for them." Beyond the neighborhood lie thrillingly unknown lands of adventure in another part of town, where things and people may be bad or good, but always strange and exciting. If selfishness and unhappiness threaten to intrude on the serenity of family life, the toys and animals become allies and protectors, with Big Sister Glinda and Mother Ozma there to help. Oz is a fairyland small-town or suburban home, tailored to the pattern of a little girl's dream.

For Oz is beyond all doubt a little girl's dream-home. Its atmosphere is feminine, not masculine, with very little of the rowdy, frenetic energy of boys. There is no consistent father-image in Oz, or brother-image, to correspond to Ozma and Glinda. Dorothy brings Aunt Em and Uncle Henry from Kansas to Oz after her fourth trip, but they are merely the kindly farm relatives every little girl desires. Nowhere in Oz does Father appear. (It remained for Ruth Plumly Thompson, Baum's successor, to take a fall out of Father. In *The Hungry Tiger of Oz*, she makes Dad the cold and distant King of Down Town, a wretched place where the single rule is "Make Money.") The Land of Oz, where Dorothy is a Princess in her own right, is all that a girl could ask for in a dream home, just as Dorothy is Baum's picture of the daughter he never had. A coolly level-headed child in whom a refreshing sense of wonder is nicely balanced by healthy common sense, there is nothing fey or magic about her, nothing of the storybook princess. A solid, human child, Dorothy takes her adventure where she finds it, her reactions always generous, reasonable, and direct.

The few boys in Oz are girls' boys, drawn as little girls assume boys should be. Baum could not make Oz fit boys, nor was he capable of making boys who could fit easily and naturally into Oz society. There are no Huck Finns or Tom Sawyers in Oz, but rather a somewhat bloodless group of younger Prince Charmings. Inga, Prince of Pingaree, and Ojo, the disguised boy-prince, are little more than stuffed reproductions of traditional fairy princes. Pon, the ragged gardener's son who rises to the throne of Jinxland like an Alger hero, is not very convincing. King Bud of Noland, a merry, happy youngster, is somewhat better, though still somewhat reminiscent of a male Bobbsey twin. Zeb Hugson, Dorothy's California cousin who dropped into Oz with her in the San Francisco earthquake, is brave, kind, courteous, cheerful, and obedient, like a girl's concept of an Eagle Scout brother—but Zeb prefers his California ranch and never returns to Oz. Kiki Aru, Zeb's foil, is the prototype of the devilish younger brother. A very bad, selfish, and irritating lad, Kiki works with the Nome King to create a great deal of mischief in Oz. Cured by drinking of the Fountain of Forgetfulness (whose location many harassed sisters must have longed to find) he eventually becomes a normal boy and disappears from the story as of no further interest.

Surprisingly enough, despite the tremendous sale of Oz books during Baum's lifetime and after, neither he nor Oz received more than casual mention in contemporary surveys of children's literature, of which there were dozens published in the magazines at Christmas time. From 1900 to 1919, the years during which Baum was producing almost a book a year to the plaudits of children in the hundreds of thousands, none of his books received a review in a major journal. The lists of children's books recommended by the critics during Baum's lifetime revealed a deadly sameness—Grimm's *Fairy Tales*, Andersen, Dickens, Louisa May Alcott, Andrew Lang, Lamb's *Tales from Shakespeare*, Frances Hodgson Burnett, Miss Mulock—with an occasional daring venture into Henty, Howard Pyle, and Kenneth Grahame, or *Peter Rabbit* and *Old Mother Westwind* for the youngest.

Part of the answer lies, no doubt, in the fact that Baum set his sights (by adult critical standards) fairly low, aiming at a maximum of enjoyment with a minimum of admonition. The Oz books provided only a sketchy pattern for behavior, and in comparison to *Little Lord Fauntleroy*, for example, gave parents very little help in their job of adjusting and civilizing the young. This lack of overt moralizing bothered the educators and the critics of Baum's time. Hamilton Mabie, writing in *The Ladies' Home Journal* in 1907, remarked augustly, "The selection of books for children's reading is quite as important as the selection of food for their sustenance, but it is a duty very generally disregarded." He then proceeded to select the "best" children's books, filled with moralistic vitamins and proteins, with Baum's name conspicuously absent.

Modern critical studies of children's literature still maintain silence concerning the Oz books. The most recent and definitive study, *A Critical History of Children's Literature*, contains no mention of Baum. Entries on juvenile literature in the leading encyclopedias fail to list his name. No magazine article on Baum has ever appeared, with the exception of a short piece by James Thurber nearly twenty years ago. *Twentieth Century Authors* contains a short, inaccurate biography of Baum which includes this estimate: "The [Oz] books were lacking in style and imaginative distinction." In general, modern critics of children's literature, while admitting the appeal of the Oz books, tend to class them as popular but not worth bothering about.

It is true that the Oz books do not have the depth of Howard Pyle's retellings of the Robin Hood and King Arthur stories, or Kipling's Jungle Books, or the books of Kenneth Grahame or A. A. Milne. Baum's work, in the opinion of the critics, lacks literary quality. He tells his stories simply and directly, contributing little to the child's sense of language or to his awareness of its potentialities; they do not read aloud well, except with the youngest, for Baum is in no sense a stylist. There is in the Oz stories no more than a trace of fun with ideas nor any of the multilevelled nonsense of Lear and the logical lunacy of Lewis Carroll. And there are, however much one enjoys Baum, occasional dead spots in the action of some of the later stories.

Yet one suspects, after attempting to read Carroll or Lear to a modern American child, that Baum knew better than his critics what children enjoy and understand. The nightmarish episodes, the complex paradoxes, and the logical and mathematical implications of the *Alice* books neither fit nor satisfy the child's needs and desires, however attractive they may be to mature readers. The cloying sentimentality and obsolescent vocabulary (what child of today can identify *treacle* or a *match girl?*) of many of the nineteenth-century juvenile classics simply puzzle a modern youngster and leave him cold. The Wonderful Land of Oz, by contrast, is as real to him as his own neighborhood; the Scarecrow, the Woodman, and the Lion are old storybook acquaintances in new dress, familiar, friendly, and vividly alive.

It is manifestly unfair to Baum to criticize his work for its lack of those qualities, desirable as they may seem to adults, found in the great British writers of children's books. The votes of a million children who have read his books with fascination and enjoyment should most certainly be counted in the verdict. The Oz stories, as the critics must admit, fulfill all that a child may ask of a story—they are exciting, humorous, filled with fresh invention and swift action, sustained throughout by imaginativeness of a high order. Though he may have failed to create a specifically American fairyland quite as he wished, Baum's books have an indigenous flavor, reflecting American attitudes and ideals with as much accuracy and validity as the English classics reflected England's. The virtues of Oz are the homely American virtues of family love, friendliness for the stranger, sympathy for the underdog, practicality and common sense in facing life, reliance on one's self for solutions to one's problems. Dorothy, in the midst of strange and disconcerting events, retains a natural, direct approach that has an authentic American ring. No one has ever tried to interview the Wizard of Oz; Dorothy does, and neatly punctures the whole illusion. Throughout the Oz books the "good" characters maintain their self-integrity, finding their answers within themselves—an echo, perhaps of the Franklin tradition of self-help. There is no whisper of class consciousness in Oz (as there is in Alice's Wonderland) or any of the overtones of snobbery that nineteenth-century juvenile fiction sometimes had. The whimsicality of the British that balances on the edge of preciousness (as in A. A. Milne) is not present in Baum, nor is the insipidity of the Milne imitators. The Oz books do have their subtleties, but the whimsy is broad and the caprice is brushed in sweeping strokes.

Baum's work does not deserve the critical neglect with which it is still treated. He wrote American tales for twentieth-century American children in an American vein, and by this he should be judged. He had his weaknesses (some of them the result of fourteen Oz books), but he had his undeniable strengths. No one can accuse him of failure to provide full measure of plot, character, and action. His plots are usually exciting, humorous, imaginative, and highly inventive. The feeling of active peril and its inevitable resolution, so essential to successful children's stories, appears in all the Oz stories as Baum sensed they must; Oz is a land of persistent danger (though not very dangerous danger) in exactly the proper degree. The perils produce no nightmares, the injustices bring no tears. The solutions satisfy the child's sense of right and justice, for Baum knew that justice put aright was the clearest principle of the child's creed and the deepest into morality that the child's tale may safely go.

In the creation of character Baum displayed his greatest mastery. Here he need bow to no one. The Tin Woodman, the Scarecrow, and the Cowardly Lion, among others, have long since secured permanent places in the gallery of great creations, and are as well known to American children as Mother Goose and Reynard the Fox. After fifty years the Land of Oz is still familiar territory; its population still provides friends and playmates for millions of children. Baum could enter into the child's world on the child's terms, create and preserve its delightful atmosphere, and tell his story with the genuine sincerity of a believer. (What child can resist an attempt to pronounce Bini Aru's unpronounceable magic word, PYRZQXGL, just to see what might happen if he *did* succeed in pronouncing it correctly? Things like this are tributes to Baum's real genius for creating belief.) Baum had the child's heart, and the child's love of the strange and beautiful and good, with the ability to bring them all alive. For this gift he deserves recognition.

Concerning
The Wonderful Wizard of Oz

· *by Ruth Plumly Thompson* ·

In 1492 Christopher Columbus discovered America. In 1900 L. Frank Baum discovered Oz, the first American fairyland, a land whose characters like Mary Martin's famous song in *South Pacific* are "wholesome as blueberry pie," "corny as Kansas in August"—so utterly *us* and U.S.A., small wonder they have become a part of our language and folklore. In his odd time Baum had already turned out several successful children's books. Again seized by that irresistible writing urge, he turned to his filing cabinet which was lettered for convenience from A to Z. Baum was about to dive into one of the back folders when the letters designating the aft end caught and held his bemused attention. "O to Z, that would be 'Oz'!" murmured Baum with a chuckle. I have no doubt about the chuckle. Well, why *not?* In this homely and simple fashion, the Land of Oz came into being, the Scarecrow, the Tin Woodman, the Cowardly Lion, Dorothy, and the Little Wizard to life! For, thereupon and directly, with the precision trained mind and laconic Yankee terseness, Baum proceeded to create his *believable* unbelievable country.

This he could well do, being an imaginative realist, a distinctly American characteristic he shares with most of our boys and girls, past and present. True, they are dreamers, but active fun-loving dreamers—practical, too. In this merry plausibly plotted country, Baum gives them a land they can not only dream of but completely visualize, enter into, and enjoy. With little shrieks of laughter and vociferous cries of welcome and recognition, they have taken Oz to their collective hearts and claimed it for their own. Up to *The Wizard of Oz*, with the exception of Lewis Carroll's *Alice in Wonderland*, fairy tales began in the lazy leisurely "Once upon a time in a far country there was a certain Prince" fashion. Ho! None of this vague inconclusive stuff for Baum! With crashing suddenness he shattered the once-upon-a-time legend, ripping into his story with a terrific but perfectly probable cyclone that uproots the house of Dorothy, a small Kansas girl, and whirls it helter-skelter through the air, landing it with a *bang* in the Munchkin Country of Oz. Not only lands Dorothy in the Munchkin Country, mind you, but her house at the same bang destroys the Wicked Witch who rules the

Munchkins, making Dorothy at one stroke a most welcome deliverer and benefactor.

Drawing in our breath, clutching the book a bit tighter, we hurry after the small Kansas girl to find the Wonderful Wizard who lives in the Emerald City of Oz. This Wizard, she feels, surely will find a way to send her back to Kansas. In rapid succession, with growing excitement, often shaken by mirth, we meet the odd and strangely convincing characters who accompany Dorothy on her journey: the nonchalant Scarecrow she obligingly lifts down from his pole (the Scarecrow, being stuffed with straw, fears nothing so much as a lighted match); Nick Chopper, the Tin Woodman who was once a real woodman but met with many sad ax-idents and must now stop to oil his joints before he can proceed; and a Cowardly Lion who trembles with fright at the approach of danger but nevertheless fights with great bravery when occasion demands it. Each has a logical reason for accompanying Dorothy on her quest. The Scarecrow, whose head like his body is stuffed with straw, hopes Oz will give him real brains; the Tin Woodman yearns for a heart warm and red as the heart he used to have; and the Cowardly Lion naturally craves courage, much courage.

Quickly and concisely, Baum sketches in his geozofy as we travel along, touching briefly but with a nice attention to detail on the history and curious customs of this singular land. So deftly does he mix plausibility with implausibility, we never know where one begins and the other leaves off. In no time at all we discover that Oz is a great oblong country entirely surrounded by an impassable desert. Wavy boundary lines extending from the corners bisect Oz into four triangular kingdoms. The purple land of the Gillikins lies to the North, the blue country of the Munchkins to the East, while the yellow realm of the Winkies forms the Western triangle, the red Quadling Country the Southern. In the exact center, where all these triangles meet, rises the Emerald City, the capital built by the famous Wizard of Oz. These same boundary lines, the main countries, the characteristics and characters, the same sparkling City of Emeralds, as outlined by Baum in that first book, stand unchanged and unchanging and to the children today are as true and believable as they were fifty years ago.

Since those old Oz days, new and smaller countries have been discovered in the four principal kingdoms, new and curious tribes, celebrities, and many a lesser monarch, prince, and princess have been added. Beyond the Deadly Desert, quaint realms and dominions have been blocked in from which ambitious sovereigns have time and again issued forth to conquer Oz. Unsuccessfully, I am happy to report, for though Oz rulers on several occasions *have* changed, Oz itself *never!*

A child who may not be able to name offhand the capital of Nebraska or Montana, can tell you in a flash the capital of Oz and is often more familiar with its principal rivers, mountains, rulers, points of interest, and historical landmarks than with those of his native state—perhaps because he considers Oz his native state. In Oz, Baum actually added another state to the Union. To you it may be a state of mind, but to the boys and girls it is as definite and existent as Kansas or Maine. And woe—black woe to the author, dramatist, picture maker, or editor who dares to tamper with the cherished characters, geography, traditions, or laws of Oz!

The story of Dorothy's search for the Wizard is too well known to need repetition, but the most convincing and Baum-like touch comes when the little girl, finally face to face with Oz the Great and Terrible, discovers he is a mere mortal like herself, a former ventriloquist and circus performer who enlivened proceedings at the big shows by balloon ascensions. Blown off his course and to Oz, much as Dorothy had been, dropping from the clouds upon the astonished inhabitants, he was promptly hailed as a mighty sorcerer and proclaimed ruler of the whole country. Embarrassed no end, unable to find his way back to Omaha, the little fellow with truly American resourcefulness adapted himself to his new role by ordering and superintending the building of the Emerald City and most cleverly he governed Oz for many years. That it is a little American girl who discovers the Wizard's deep secret after all the time he has managed to fool the citizens of Oz tickles Baum's young readers as nothing else could.

"Why," exclaimed Dorothy after indignantly listening to the man's story, "I think you are a very bad man." "Oh, no, my dear, I am really a good man, but a very *bad* wizard," Oz retorts quickly; "how can I help being a humbug when all these people make me do things everybody knows are impossible?" Nothing daunted, he then proceeds to fill the Scarecrow's head with bran mixed with needles and pins, a combination that has served the straw man famously ever since, making him the sharpest man in Oz. The red emery heart filled with sawdust bestowed by the Wizard on Nick Chopper still knocks comfortably against the Tin Woodman's metal chassis. And the Cowardly Lion, already most courageous, is next dosed with an ill-tasting concoction which convinces him of his bravery. This was all that was necessary to achieve this happy result.

Tired of hiding away in his palace so his people will not find out how really harmless he is, Oz now turns to Dorothy's problem as well as his own for he is as homesick for Omaha as she is for Kansas. With the little girl's help, he constructs a great silk balloon to fly them back to

America. When it is finished, he appoints the Scarecrow ruler in his place and bids farewell to his sorrowing subjects and makes ready to leave Oz. Unfortunately the balloon escapes from its moorings before Dorothy has a chance to join the Wizard in the little basket. This, however, only adds a new interest to the story. After further travels and amazing experiences, Dorothy and her devoted friends learn from Glinda, the good sorceress of the South, that the silver shoes she is wearing are powerful enough to transport her to Kansas. These shoes, all that were left of the Wicked Witch of the East when Dorothy's house fell upon the luckless lady, Dorothy now commands to take her home. Which, of course, they do! Later, in another book, both Dorothy and the Wizard return to live in the Emerald City, Dorothy as a princess and the Wizard as a real practitioner of magic which he learns in all its branches from Glinda the Good.

The impact of the first Oz book on the ever-drowsing juvenile book industry was immediate and terrific. The instant and spontaneous welcome accorded *The Wizard*, the rapidity with which copies sold, astonished both Baum and his publishers. *The Wonderful Wizard of Oz* appeared in 1900; in 1902 a musical version of the book featuring Dave Montgomery and Fred Stone fairly took the country by storm and ran for many years on Broadway and on the road. How fortunate were those children and grown-up children of that period lucky enough to see and remember Montgomery and Stone in their unforgettable performances in that fun-filled play! As for the book, boys and girls by the thousands, bewitched by W. W. Denslow's drawings and L. Frank Baum's text, began writing the author to beg for more Oz stories. It was four years, however, before a sequel to *The Wizard* appeared.

Like all children born and growing up in the nineteen hundreds, I fell hungrily upon each new Oz book as it appeared and waited with breathless impatience for the next. All unconscious and unaware of the part Oz would play in my future and the many ways it would color and complicate my literary life, I chuckled with delicious abandon over the further adventures of the Scarecrow and his merry clan. And I assure there is many a chuckle in store. Baum not only loved and understood children, but talked to them on a comradely level with no condescension or ponderous moral in mind. Though each adventure had a gentle underlying lesson and purpose, none ever impinged on the story. Above all Baum had a sly sense of fun that delights children from six to sixty and makes the reading of Oz books to the small fry a treat, shall we say, instead of a treatment.

Librarians and Oz

This Man's World:
The Wonderful Wizard of Oz

· *by Paul Gallico* ·

It looks like a setup to tee off on a librarian in Washington by the name of Elva Van Winkle, who, according to a clipping before me, has ordered the withdrawal of the children's classic, *The Wizard of Oz*, because she thinks it is "dated and stiff" and, in extenuation, declares that only the parents are protesting.

But it could be that the moppets themselves have been pausing at the librarian's desk to complain, "Miss Van Winkle, I attempted to read this book, *The Wizard of Oz*, last night, and fell asleep half a dozen

Reprinted from *Esquire*, February 1957, pp. 32 and 34. Copyright © 1957 by Esquire Publishing Inc. Reprinted by permission.

times over it. Nobody gets slugged, stabbed, shot, or throttled; there are no space men in it, and I read page after page without finding so much as a single *biff, bang, ugh,* or *pow.* I find it stiff and dated." Perhaps Mlle Van Winkle is merely following the trend.

Naturally, the parents protest, will protest, must protest, for *The Wizard of Oz* was a part of their lives and their own childhood, and all the wonderful characters in it are still alive to them and even more so if they were so fortunate as to be taken to the musical made from it in which Fred Stone played the Scarecrow.

But all this happened half a century ago, and a half a century in this man's changing world is a long, long time.

Lyman Frank Baum, according to a very brief note on him in *The Reader's Encyclopedia,* was born in 1856 and died in 1919, and in the year 1900 published *The Wonderful Wizard of Oz* (the *Wonderful* was dropped after the first edition), and subsequently a series of tales for young folks dealing with the mythical country of Oz.

If I close my eyes, I can still see my worn copy of the book, by L. Frank Baum as he signed himself, and the illustration showing Dorothy, the little girl from Kansas, and her dog being picked up by a Kansas cyclone and blown into the Land of Oz where the capital was the magical and wonderful Emerald City.

And I see, too, in my mind's eye the figure of the Scarecrow, the Tin Woodman (the Wizard put a little door in his chest when he gave him his heart), and the pained and slightly embarrassed expression on the face of the Cowardly Lion.

I remember not much of the story, but only how I journeyed with these people, pitied and loved them. Sometimes I joined them in my dreams and, when once you have dreamed, that dream becomes a part of your existence. And so these characters were imprinted upon an entire generation, for the Oz books proved fabulously popular.

The journey through the Land of Oz was in the nature of a quest, and the Tin Woodman with his ax over his shoulder was in search of a heart, and there is another illustration that unreels before my inner eye now, the one in which the Wizard, a little, tubby, bespectacled old man, at last bestows the coveted heart upon the Woodman, holding it up by a bit of string.

What a curious thing to be questing for—a human heart. And perhaps that is why the story appears stiff and dated. One sets out to seek a vast treasure or conquer new lands, worlds, or planets, but to wish and search for nothing more than a dear and tender heart that can beat for others and be filled both with love and compassion, what kind of stuff is this to set before the child of today?

I suppose *The Water Babies* will have to be withdrawn, too, for it is only the story of how a naughty, orphaned little chimney sweep is changed by love and kindness and "cuddling"; *Alice* will have to go, and *Black Beauty* and *Hans Brinker* and all of the fairy tales of Hans Christian Andersen and the Brothers Grimm. And will there still be a copy of *Little Men* on library shelves? Or are there still little minds and hearts that can be reached by these?

How can one look into the child of today to see or understand what it thinks or feels and by what it is stirred? One can remember one's own emotions when one was young and the impression made upon one by books, the wonderful experience of discovering, reading, and acquiring samples of the treasures from the great storehouse that lay open to one.

To me, when I was young, the world of the imagination where magical things happened in defiance of the natural laws by which I was bound was a better and more exciting one than that in which I physically dwelt. I never wholly quit that fantasy world, and it has left its marks upon my writing, and my thinking, too. The stories I read I felt deeply; I identified myself with the characters and lived their lives.

Does watching television have the same effect? Does the child transmute what he sees into his dreams and thus into a part of his personality and character? And what about the sweet individuals in comic books? Have they all contributed to making the children's books of my generation "stiff and dated"?

Mind you, I am neither deploring nor viewing with alarm, though it's a close thing, and if someone were to drop a hat I might easily give way to a nostalgic sadness that the child of the second half of the century is to be denied delights that were opened to me.

But each generation succeeds most marvelously in growing up in its own way in spite of the rampant old-fogyism it encounters on the way. Looking at the world which my generation raised on the old classics and without the distractions of radio and television to contend with, it does not strike me as a conspicuous success, what with two World Wars since the turn of the century and the diplomats whose youth was contemporaneous with mine busy organizing what may well be the final one.

Perhaps this new generation, raised on *wham, pow, bam, ugh, biff,* and *oof,* which ranges in its mind behind the moon and to the stars, or learns its morality in the simple black-and-white terms of the western, will save us. They may grow up far more realistically than we did, without too much faith in magic or miracles, which can be a dangerous drug. It seems to me that our home-grown diplomats are always acting, in the face of patent disaster, as though in the last moment they expect the good fairy to materialize, wave her wand, and cause all the wicked men to disappear.

As for me, I am afraid I am too old to change. I think I shall order me a copy of *The Wizard of Oz* and read it again.

A Defense of the Oz Books

· *by Bernard M. Golumb* ·

I can no longer bear in silence the profession-wide disdain for the Oz books. . . . What is wrong with the Oz books? Well, they are "negative." Of the terms evasive of exact meaning, negative seems to me to be one of the foremost. They are negative to what "positive"? Perhaps to that wonderful series of watered-down biography "The Childhood of Famous Americans." They circulate wildly, providing satisfactory statistics. Yet they are frankly remedial, at best fourth-grade level but read avidly by sixth-graders. Time and time again the school child, in requesting a biography from me, had been told by his teacher that the "little orange books" were not acceptable.

But the Oz books are unrealistic fantasy. We live in a practical age and fantasy should not be encouraged. For that reason most libraries stock the realistic *Freddie the Pig*. From these books twentieth-century minds learn how our pig friend learns to fly or how he acts in conjunction with the "baseball team from Mars." Since few of our little ones see pigs in their urban lives, this presentation of the noble animal cannot be considered amiss.

The chief professional criticism, taught in our seminaries, the library schools, is that all series are bad. Oz books are undoubtedly a series. The only good series was the Perkins "Twins" series and it was too bad they were so good. . . .

Perhaps the most popular juvenile author today is Walter Farley, whose "Black Stallion" is the hero of countless junior horse lovers. The Black Stallion holds the attributes found in most horses, intelligence, honor, integrity, loyalty, honesty, fellowship, bravery, in fact the whole Boy Scout oath.

We buy Farley's books in multiple copies. The kiddies clamor for them, reread them. . . . Finally when they have read them all many

Reprinted from *Library Journal*, October 15, 1957, pp. 137–138. Published by R. R. Bowker (a Xerox company). Copyright © 1957 by Xerox Corporation. Reprinted by permission.

times, and are growing out of them, the girls will switch to "Joan Foster" books, the boys will probably quit reading. . . .

These [Farley] books are written in unimpeachable literary style, veritable Miltonian prose. They present accurate material on the nature of horses. We don't mind that they seem to be a series. Maybe books, like "The Black Stallion" and "Joan Foster," are only collections of sequels. . . . Why should the Oz books be singled out as unacceptable? Who says one has to have all of them if one has any? . . . How many of our children's librarians or their little evaluation groups have taken the opportunity to judge each title on its own merits?

I have read and reread the Oz books at least five times each. That is those by Thompson and Baum. The others have no charm for me. I read almost nothing else from the age of seven to ten. I read Oz books periodically until I entered the army. That my reading for three years was so limited is not the fault of the books, but of the library and the librarians. I could have been better directed perhaps.

Nevertheless, I was the best reader in the class. I developed the literary habit. My vocabulary was better than most of my classmates, my grades as good. I continued by series through Edgar Rice Burroughs, Sabatini, Rohmer, Altsheler, Cooper, and finally "good books." During the time that my playmates found other things to do, including car-stealing, the pleasure that I had gotten from the Oz books persistently drew me back to the library. I find that I am as well read and frequently better read than my fellow professional librarians. Having read the Oz books did not harm me. I submit that they probably did me a world of good. I shall read them to my children who I think will enjoy them immensely. Then I shall donate them to some good public library.

Why Librarians Dislike Oz

· by Martin Gardner ·

Longtime admirers of L. Frank Baum have the satisfaction these days of watching the librarians and critics develop a slow, creeping awareness of the fact that a Hans Christian Andersen once lived in the United States. Children, of course, have known this since 1900. But among

Reprinted from *American Book Collector*, Special Number (December 1962), pp. 14–16. Copyright © 1962 by William B. Thorsen. Reprinted by permission of William B. Thorsen and Martin Gardner.

librarians and self-styled experts on juvenile literature, a strange myth has developed: Baum was just another hack author of series books and the sooner the youngsters forget about him the better. In 1953 Cornelia L. Meigs edited for Macmillan a 624-page *Critical History of Children's Literature;* not a single mention in it of Baum. To this day there are thousands of children's librarians around the nation—kindly, bespectacled, gray-minded ladies—who will tell you with pride that they do not permit a single Oz book to sully their shelves.

Now here indeed is a most curious paradox. At the moment there are a dozen or so editions of *The Wizard of Oz* in print. It obviously is the best-loved fairy tale ever written by an American author. "I can still read *The Wizard of Oz* with as much enjoyment as I found in it fifty years ago," writes Edward Wagenknecht in his afterword to a new Reilly and Lee edition. (Professor Wagenknecht is a distinguished author who teaches English literature at Boston University. His booklet *Utopia Americana,* 1929, was the first critical appreciation of Baum and is now much prized by collectors.) MGM's musical extravaganza, starring Judy Garland as Dorothy, has become a staple TV feature. Articles on Baum are turning up in the literary quarterlies (e.g., "The Utopia of Oz" by S. J. Sackett, *The Georgia Review,* Fall, 1960; "The Oddness of Oz," by Osmond Beckwith, *Kulchur 4,* 1961).

"I have never known a child," writes Clifton Fadiman in a new Macmillan edition of *The Wizard,* "who didn't scoot through it at supersonic speed, enjoying every word and making fast friends at once with those Three Musketeers of Oz—the Cowardly Lion, the Scarecrow and the Tin Woodman. . . . I can remember reading them [Oz books] aloud, hour after hour after hour, to our two children Anne and Kim. . . . Our ancient, dog-eared, thumb-marked tattered Oz volumes still occupy a place of honor on the shelf."

On Mr. Fadiman's shelf, yes; but not on the shelves of the children's section in thousands of public libraries. Nevertheless, the growing popularity of Oz is having its impact on the librarians. Ten years ago they reacted to any mention of Oz with cold, blank stares. Today they will tell you that *The Wizard* is not really a bad book, but of course everybody knows (by "everybody" they mean all the other librarians) that it is the only good book Baum ever wrote.

Well, Baum wrote a lot of other good books; in fact many of his other fantasies are better than *The Wizard.* But why this curious, persistent resistance to Baum? Why this allergy to Oz? After giving the matter some thought I have concluded that seven principal factors are involved.

1. Baum's Oz books, with the exception of *The Wizard,* were pub-

lished by Reilly and Britton (later Reilly and Lee), a small Chicago firm that lacked the prestige of the large eastern houses. To make matters worse, Reilly and Britton specialized in series books by hacks: the Boy Scouts of the Air series, the Boys Big Game series, the Airship Boys series, and so on. Baum himself, using the pseudonym of Edith Van Dyne, wrote ten novels in the Aunt Jane's Nieces series, five in the Mary Louise series, and two books about Orissa Kane, girl aviator. (Ten years ago one could still find Edith Van Dyne books on twenty-five-cent tables; now the dealers are wised up and likely to ask several dollars per volume.) Without exception, these nonfantasy series books issued by Reilly and Britton are without merit. It was easy to suppose that the Oz books, also issued in series, were equally poor; as poor as, say, the Raggedy Ann fantasy series which became popular in the decade following Baum's death in 1919.

2. Even if series books *have* a certain merit, they annoy librarians. A child reads one book, his interest is hooked, he demands another. Stock one, you must stock them all. Librarians found it expedient to avoid series books altogether, and of course this included the Oz books.

3. Baum's books were oversize volumes, lacking the side-stitching and reinforced hinges necessary to withstand strenuous handling. And strenuous handling they got. Librarians do not like to keep replacing shaky volumes or going to the expense of rebinding.

4. The illustrations in Baum's books (with the exception of Maxfield Parrish's pictures for *Mother Goose in Prose*) are not first rate; certainly not to compare with Tenniel's illustrations for *Alice*, Ernest Shepard's drawings for the *Pooh* books and *The Wind in the Willows*, Garth Williams's drawings for *Charlotte's Web*, or Arthur Rackham's many superb illustrations for various children's classics. William Wallace Denslow, who illustrated *The Wizard of Oz* and one other Baum fantasy, *Dot and Tot of Merryland*, was a Chicago newspaper cartoonist of no great shakes. John R. Neill, who illustrated all of Baum's other Oz books and most of his non-Oz fantasies, was a Pennsylvania artist of so-so talents.

Not that Neill's pictures are not just right for a child! They have color, detail, realism; they enter happily into the spirit of Baum's imagination. But adult taste (and adults, remember, buy the books) has moved steadily in the modern direction, toward semi-abstract, distorted pictures, beside which Neill's art has a quaint, old-fashioned look. I have not the slightest doubt that if a careful test were made to determine what sort of pictures young children, free of parental nudging, do in fact prefer, they would choose Neill over most of the modern illustrators who win prizes for their work. (I once showed a prize-winning illustration—it purported to be a picture of a cat—to a small child. He turned it upside down trying to puzzle it out.) But the trend in art has moved steadily away from Neill,* who was not great to begin with. Surely this has been another factor in the development of the Oz allergy.

5. Baum's books received little editing. Even the best of writers often need heavy editing (witness Thomas Wolfe!), but Reilly and Britton simply did not have the staff for it. I have no direct proof of this, but I suspect that Baum's copy was printed pretty much in the form received. As a result, there is a carelessness and roughness in many of his paragraphs that could easily have been polished out by a skillful editor.

It is tiresome to hear critics of Baum call attention to these spots of careless writing; the overall worth of a work of fiction is seldom affected by such trivia. Especially its worth for a child. You can give a child a book written with great stylistic elegance and drenched with poetic phrasing, but if the child is not interested in what happens to the characters in the next chapter he will quite sensibly put down the book and turn on the TV. Baum was a great story teller; he was not a great stylist. This too has played a role in prejudicing the librarians.

6. Many later Oz books, by writers other than Baum, are not up to the level of Baum's books. The best, in my opinion, are some of the Oz books by Ruth Plumly Thompson, who has done nineteen of them, and the two Oz books by Jack Snow. But three Oz books by Neill, the artist, are very poor. Many critics of Oz fail to distinguish between Baum and the various authors who carried on after his death; indeed, I am sure that many of them never read an Oz book by Baum other than *The Wizard.*

7. Fantasy is not for everybody. Even at the eight-to-ten age level, an ideal age for starting on Oz, there is no question that children divide rather sharply into two classes: those who enjoy far-out fantasy and those who don't. It is a division that tends to last throughout their lives. I know of no studies by professional psychologists on this matter, but I hazard the guess that an eight-year-old's liking for fantasy reflects the strength of his imagination; his ability to call up familiar images from daily life and put them together in strange, unexpected, Ozzy ways. I suspect also that it is from the ranks of such children, when grown, that come our most creative individuals. Frank D. Drake, the radio astronomer who named and now directs Project Ozma, the program of listening in on radio waves from outer space in the hope of hearing messages from other planets, is (not unexpectedly) an Ozma-

---

* Since I wrote this in 1962, the trend in children's book illustration has swung back to realism.

politan. I have yet to meet an American writer of fantasy or science fiction, from Ray Bradbury down, who did not enjoy the Oz books as a child. And I know of many professional philosophers, scientists, artists, and professors of English literature who will not hesitate to pay tribute to Baum's genius.

Consider, now, the poor librarian. What sort of mind is most attracted to such a profession? You see at once that for the most part (there are of course exceptions) it would attract a prosaic, matter-of-fact mind. An individual with a soaring imagination is not likely to be happy shuffling file cards and carrying on a librarian's routine chores. As a result, a strong selective factor establishes a built-in prejudice among librarians against wilder forms of fantasy. I sometimes suspect that all children's librarians come from Abilone, Arizona; admirers of *The Circus of Dr. Lao* will know what I mean. The good citizens of Abilone attended Dr. Lao's circus, but its colossal marvels left them unimpressed. The man with the long neck and green necktie, in G. K. Chesterton's essay "The Dragon's Grandmother," surely was a librarian. This essay is the greatest defense ever written of the fairy tale; it can be found in *Tremendous Trifles*, and every juvenile librarian should be forced to read it.

Lord Dunsany wrote a poem called "A Word in Season" that I cannot read without thinking of Baum and his critics. I will quote only the middle stanza:

> Their watchers looked for a wind to blow;
>   And the new wind sang, and they could not hear it.
> It slipped at dusk by the mean dull row
> Of their narrow houses, from fields of snow
>   In a magical land: they were very near it
> For wonderful moments, and did not know.
>   The new wind sang and they could not hear it.

But there are happy signs that at least the librarians are beginning to take the cotton out of their ears. Perhaps the age of space, with its Ozzy prospect of finding intelligent life elsewhere in the universe, has something to do with it. Perhaps it is the great need for creative, bold, imaginative thought in the sciences, especially in the social and political fields. Whatever it is, fantasy for children seems to be coming back into its own. Coming back, that is, among the parents who buy the books. The youngsters have never changed.

Oz and the Fifth Criterion

· by C. Warren Hollister ·

A few years ago Martin Gardner made the provocative statement, "America's greatest writer of children's fantasy was, as everyone knows except librarians and critics of juvenile literature, L. Frank Baum." Whatever one may think of Mr. Gardner's judgment of Baum, he is on the mark in suggesting that few librarians and children's literature critics are Oz enthusiasts. What do they have against the Oz books?

Martin Gardner suggests several possibilities: that the Oz books are too popular and librarians get tired of checking them in and out, that the books are poorly bound, that they are illustrated in an unfashionably realistic style. I can't believe that these are the reasons.

I think the answer is perfectly straightforward: The fourteen Oz books of L. Frank Baum fall short of many other children's fantasies when measured by the four criteria which critics usually apply to children's fiction: *theme, characterization, plot,* and *style.* "We have nothing against Baum," the critics would say. "It's only that there are so many *better* writers of fantasy—Carol Kendall, Lloyd Alexander, Alan Garner, Tove Janson, P. L. Travers, Mary Norton, Lucy Boston, Kenneth Grahame, on and on." Read the pedestrian opening of *The Wizard of Oz:*

Dorothy lived in the midst of the great Kansas prairies, with Uncle Henry, who was a farmer, and Aunt Em, who was the farmer's wife. Their house was small, for the lumber to build it had to be carried by wagon many miles. There were four walls, a floor and a roof, which made one room; and this room contained a rusty-looking cooking stove, a cupboard for the dishes, a table, three or four chairs, and the beds.

Now compare the stylish beginning of a widely praised fantasy of 1968, with an oddly similar title to Baum's: *A Wizard of Earthsea,* by one of my favorite authors, Ursula K. Le Guin:

The island of Gont, a single mountain that lifts its peak a mile above the storm-racked Northeast Sea, is a land famous for wizards. From the towns in its high valleys and the ports on its dark narrow bays many a Gontishman has gone forth to serve the Lords of the Archipelago in their cities as wizard or mage, or, looking for adventure, to wander working magic from isle to isle of all Earthsea.

Reprinted from *The Baum Bugle,* Christmas 1971, pp. 5–8. Reprinted by permission of C. Warren Hollister.

Of these some say the greatest, and surely the greatest voyager, wa a man called Sparrowhawk, who in his day became both dragonlord and Archmage.

The difference between the two books is striking. Le Guin's *Wizard of Earthsea* is a deeply intelligent, sensitive, imaginative fantasy that excels in all four criteria: it has a great underlying theme (coming of age), rich characterization, a tight plot, and a lean, rhythmic style. Baum's *Wizard of Oz* doesn't measure up. It appears to have no underlying theme—no unity of conception. Its characterizations seem shallow. Dorothy has no inner problems, doesn't develop, doesn't grow. Oz never really changes. As for plot, it rambles. There is a pointless story within a story in Chapter 14, and the last seven chapters, involving a long journey to the Quadling country, are anticlimactic. The style, which has been described, unfairly, as "sentimental" is, in fact, straightforward but undistinguished, lacking in sparkle and in witty, surprising turns of phrase.

So much for *The Wizard of Oz*. Baum's other Oz books yield to much the same criticisms. Why bother with them at all?

The difficulty is, we can't really avoid them. For the past seventy years children have persisted in loving Oz. *The Wizard* has sold something over 7,000,000 copies, is now available in dozens of different editions and imprints, and has been translated into twenty-seven languages—including Dutch, Hungarian, Portuguese, Japanese, and Russian. The Russian translator of *The Wizard of Oz*, Alexander Volkov, suppressed Baum's name and claimed credit for authorship himself. Volkov has now written a series of original Oz stories for Russian children, plagiarizing heavily from Baum, but making plots of his own.

All fourteen of Baum's Oz books have remained constantly in print since the time of their original publication between 1900 and 1920. Recently they were all republished in an attractive new format (strongly bound!) and they are now selling more briskly than ever. The 1939 MGM movie *The Wizard of Oz*, the leading television attraction of all time, was described at its 1970 showing as having perhaps been seen by more people than any other theatrical production in the history of mankind.

Obviously Oz has mass appeal. It has also made its impact on the American intelligentsia. I am constantly hearing comments from professors and writers who, coming to my home and happening to see some Baum first editions, tell me—often at length—how much they loved Oz stories as children. The first effort of American astronomers to scan the heavens for signals of intelligent life from the stars was named "Project Ozma." And Ozma, Baum's queen of Oz, doesn't even appear in *The Wizard.* Those scientists had been reading the later Oz books, too. A number of important creative writers have testified to the impact of Oz on their childhood: James Thurber, Ray Bradbury, John Dickson Carr, Paul Gallico, many others—even the Newbery Award–winning fantasy writer, Lloyd Alexander. Scholarly essays on Oz have appeared in *Georgia Review, American Quarterly, Chicago Review,* the *Saturday Review, Psychology Today,* and a number of smaller journals. M.A. and Ph.D. dissertations have been devoted to aspects of Baum and Oz. And there are major collections of rare Baum books at such libraries as Yale, New York Public, Syracuse University, and the University of Texas. A few years ago Harvard purchased a $1500 Baum-Denslow presentation copy of *The Wizard.*

Oz is uniquely popular, intellectually influential, and seemingly timeless—yet medicore with respect to theme, characterization, plot, and style. Obviously something is badly out of focus. The critics would argue that popularity is irrelevant, standards are everything. Julia Sauer, of the Rochester, New York, Public Library, wrote that it is "absurd to say that the best children's books are necessarily those which are most popular with the children. . . . A child's opinion should not be misconstrued by those who make or by those who buy books. It is not the final test."

These words appeared in *The Horn Book* in 1949. Since then we have witnessed the great drift to TV and Marshall McLuhan's prediction of the demise of all libraries and all books. We hope he is exaggerating, yet we ought not to be complacent. In continuing to insist on uncompromising, adult-imposed library norms, we may lose much of what remains of our child audience. This may well be the cost of paying too much attention to good but narrow standards, too little to what children love. There is danger today in insisting that children's book rooms be educational rather than recreational, that children's stories bring edification rather than joy. There is danger in always seeking so-called "literary" children's books as against books that beguile and entrance. There is, indeed, something terribly musty, emasculated, and phoney in deliberately writing a "literary" children's book—which is all too often (to quote a recent writer) a matter of "pleasing adults rather than children, for these are the ones who buy and judge, award and recommend."

My plea, then, is not to redeem L. Frank Baum (who hardly needs it) but to achieve something much more basic: a long-needed critical reexamination of the four criteria. One children's literary critic, looking at Baum's seventy-year record of mass acceptance among children, conceded recently that she would now admit the Baum Oz books, despite all their faults, into our libraries. That won't suffice! What critics must do, for their own good health and professional credibility, is to stop telling us why Oz is bad and start figuring out why Oz is great; not "Down with Oz—it fails to meet our criteria," but "Where have our criteria gone wrong?" This is their job—their profound obligation to the field of children's literature and to themselves.

As a beginning, I offer this suggestion. I propose the addition of a fifth criterion—the most important of them all for children's fantasy—*three-dimensionality.* By three-dimensionality I don't mean simply the old cliché, "willing suspension of disbelief." That negative, vapid phrase would far better be expressed positively: "the compulsion to believe." But three-dimensionality means still more. It is the magical tugging of the child-reader through the page into the story—into the other world. You not only suspend disbelief in Oz; you not only positively, ardently believe in Oz; you are there!

Three-dimensionality is, I suggest, the secret of Oz's astonishing popularity, just as it is the secret of the more recent popularity of C. S. Lewis's Narnia stories, particularly among English children, and of Tolkien's adult fantasy, *The Lord of the Rings.* By comparison, Ursula Le Guin's *Wizard of Earthsea,* Lloyd Alexander's *High King,* and most other distinguished modern fantasies are two-dimensional. Beautifully plotted, written, charactered, and themed, they lack the special magic of Oz. They lack that beguilement, utterly transcending the four criteria, which brings joyous intoxication to the child-reader and, afterward, a memory that never passes—a recollection of the taste of joy, the three-dimensional experience of going into another universe where everything is brighter and more fragrant, more dangerous, and more alive—a world of intensely satisfying unexpectedness—a real journey—a "trip" akin to the now fashionable chemical "trips," yet more real and entrancing than LSD—and with a happy ending always.

This longing for a journey into elsewhere runs deep in the human psyche. It is usually called "escapism," a term which was rescued from ill-repute and permanently ennobled by J. R. R. Tolkien in his essay, *On Fairy-Stories.* "Why should a man be scorned," Tolkien asks, "if, finding himself in prison, he tries to get out and go home? Or, if, when he cannot do so, he thinks and talks about other topics than jailers and prison walls?" Leonard Wibberley has suggested that some of the more exotic behavior of young people today is a direct result of their parents and educators and librarians having deprived them of fantasy during childhood. Now, with their imaginations stunted and starved, they act out their need by wearing bizarre clothes or achieve it artificially with drugs. They know no other way to escape.

Many children's critics—puritans at heart—suspect a book such as

The Wizard of Oz that does nothing for the child but give him joy. It teaches him very little, doesn't preach, doesn't improve his literary taste. But joy has its uses, too. No child can make the journey to Oz without acquiring in the process a fascination for books, a realization that reading needn't always be the sour, educative, edifying medicine it sometimes seems in school. Reading becomes an exciting quest for other books touched with the same enchantment as the Oz books.

What a pity that this touch of enchantment, so real to children, is invisible to so many adult critics. Perhaps it is because adult critics were themselves invisible to Baum, who wrote exclusively for children. His stories draw the child in, carrying him to Oz as effectively as did Ozma's magic belt. But the critic is usually left behind. To him, the pages of the Oz books are opaque—two-dimensional. The critic reads what is on the page, but can't see through the page—or pass through the page—to Oz. So he is bewildered: he wonders what it's all about—weak plot, shallow characters, no theme, pedestrian style. Dorothy is superficial? Rather she is broadly sketched so that children can *become* Dorothy for a time, ride the cyclone with her, walk in her silver shoes down the Yellow Brick Road as they could not if Dorothy had hated her father or been astigmatic or had an I.Q. of 156, or were tormented by oncoming puberty. The critic asks, why don't Oz characters ever develop and mature? Every child knows the answer: nobody grows older in Oz. Why aren't the Oz plots more unified? Real adventures in magical lands are, as children know, tantalizingly open-ended. Why isn't Baum's style more glittering? Because glitter gets in the way. To pass through the page into the other world, the words must be as nearly *invisible* as possible. They should merely carry the story, as Baum's words do effectively, unpretentiously. Where is the theme? The theme is Oz.

If critics recognized this fifth criterion—three-dimensionality—Oz would enter our libraries not begrudged but warmly welcomed. The critics and librarians who have given their lives—and their love—to children's books would at last discover the very books that American children have always loved most of all. More than that, critics and librarians would learn the secret that three-dimensionality is more than a mere criterion. It is a kind of magic that carries one between worlds— that has transported countless children to Glinda's castle, the Nome King's caverns, the Emerald City. It might carry librarians and critics there too, if only they understood what so many of our children know— that there really is a way to Oz.

Current Criticism

The Land of Oz:
America's Great Good Place

· *by Marius Bewley* ·

The considerable imaginative achievement represented by the fourteen Oz books has been ignored for well over half a century. Even those critics who have recognized their classic status have hesitated to approve their style; but Baum was always a satisfactory writer, and at his best his prose reflects themes and tensions that characterize the central tradition of American literature. Since he wished to create in Oz a specifically American fairyland, or Utopia, it is not particularly surprising that at first his writing was influenced by the comparatively new

Reprinted from *Masks and Mirrors: Essays and Criticism*, pp. 255–267. Copyright © 1970 Marius Bewley. Reprinted with the permission of Atheneum Publishers.

school of realists and naturalists. The description of the grimly impoverished Kansas farm of Dorothy Gale's aunt and uncle with which *The Wonderful Wizard of Oz* (1900) begins is a very good example of writing in this genre:

When Dorothy stood in the doorway and looked around, she could see nothing but the great gray prairie on every side. Not a tree nor a house broke the broad sweep of flat country that reached the edge of the sky in all directions. The sun had baked the plowed land into a gray mass, with little cracks running through it. Even the grass was not green, for the sun had burned the tops of the long blades until they were the same gray color to be seen everywhere. Once the house had been painted, but the sun blistered the paint and the rains washed it away, and now the house was as dull and gray as everything else.

Whe Aunt Em came there to live she was a young, pretty wife. The sun and wind had changed her, too. They had taken the sparkle from her eyes and left them a sober gray; they had taken the red from her cheeks and lips, and they were gray also. She was thin and gaunt, and never smiled, now. When Dorothy, who was an orphan, first came to her, Aunt Em had been so startled by the child's laughter that she would scream and press her hand upon her heart whenever Dorothy's merry voice reached her ears; and she still looked at the little girl with wonder that she could find anything to laugh at.

But Baum soon moved on to more distinguished models in the same mode, and in at least one instance, surprising as it may seem, he appears to have been strongly influenced by Stephen Crane.

Stephen Crane is a writer of great ability, but during the past fifteen or twenty years extravagant claims have been made for his work. His short story "The Open Boat," published in 1897, has been described by more than one eminent critic as the best short story in English up to the time of its publication, which is nonsense of course. In 1907 Baum published his third Oz book, *Ozma of Oz*. The opening chapter of this book, "The Girl in the Chicken-Coop," is so close to Crane's story in theme, imagery, and technique that it is impossible to imagine, on comparing the two in detail, that the similarity is wholly, or even largely, accidental. Baum's narrative of how Dorothy, during a storm at sea, is blown from the ship's deck in a chicken-coop and rides out the gale is developed through images and themes that correspond closely with those employed by Crane in his account of how four men battle the elements in a ten-foot dinghy after their ship has foundered. Considerations of space make it impossible to demonstrate this similarity in a brief essay by parallel quotations, but as most readers who will have an edition of Stephen Crane on their shelves are not likely to have *Ozma of Oz* as conveniently to hand, here are a few excerpts from the opening chapter:

Dorothy decided she must go to him; so she made a dash forward, during a lull in the storm, to where a big square chicken-coop had been lashed to the deck with ropes. She reached this place in safety, but no sooner had she seized fast hold of the slats of the big box in which the chickens were kept than the wind . . . suddenly redoubled its fury. With a scream like that of an angry giant it tore away the ropes that held the coop and lifted it high into the air, with Dorothy still clinging to the slats. Around and around it whirled, this way and that, and a few moments later the chicken-coop dropped far away into the sea, where the big waves caught it and slid it up-hill to a foaming crest and then down-hill into a steep valley, as if it were nothing more than a plaything to keep them amused. . . .

She kept tight hold of the stout slats and as soon as she could get the water out of her eyes she saw that the wind had ripped the cover from the coop, and the poor chickens were fluttering away in every direction, being blown by the wind until they looked like feather dusters without handles. The bottom of the coop was made of thick boards, so Dorothy found she was clinging to a sort of raft, with sides of slats, which readily bore up her weight. After coughing the water out of her throat and getting her breath again, she managed to climb over the slats and stand upon the firm wooden bottom of the coop, which supported her easily enough. . . .

Down into a valley between the waves the coop swept her, and when she climbed another crest the ship looked like a toy boat, it was such a long way off. Soon it had entirely disappeared in the gloom. . . .

She was tossing on the bosom of a big ocean, with nothing to keep her afloat but a miserable wooden hen-coop that had a plank bottom and slatted sides, through which the water constantly splashed and wetted her through to the skin! And there was nothing to eat when she became hungry—as she was sure to do before long—and no fresh water to drink and no dry clothes to put on. . . .

As if to add to her troubles, the night was now creeping on, and the gray clouds overhead changed to inky blackness. But the wind, as if satisfied at last with its mischievous pranks, stopped blowing. . . .

By and by the black clouds rolled away and showed a blue sky overhead, with a silver moon shining sweetly in the middle of it and little stars winking merrily at Dorothy when she looked their way. The coop did not toss around any more, but rode the waves more gently—almost like a cradle rocking—so that the floor upon which Dorothy stood was no longer wet by water coming through the slats. Seeing this, and being quite exhausted by the excitement of the past few hours, the little girl decided that sleep would be the best thing to restore her strength and the easiest way in which she could pass the time. The floor was damp and she was herself wringing wet, but fortunately this was a warm climate, and she did not feel at all cold.

The similarities between Crane's story and Baum's chapter are not merely superficial, and it is both amusing and enlightening to read critical articles such as " 'The Open Boat,' an Existentialist Fiction," by Peter Buitenhuis in *Modern Fiction Studies* (Autumn, 1959), or Caroline Gordon's essay on "The Open Boat" in *The House of Fiction*, as if they were also an analysis of "The Girl in the Chicken-Coop." The double application, which works out remarkably well, might have the salutary effect of recalling children's librarians and partisan literary critics back into a balanced and sanative perspective in which measured justice could be done to both authors.

Perhaps it was the nature of the land whose history he was writing that drew Baum's style away from literary realism. At any rate, after several more books, one becomes aware of allegorical themes and attitudes that put one in mind of Hawthorne's short stories. In *The Scarecrow of Oz* Baum tells the story of a Princess whose heart was frozen by witchcraft so that she could no longer love:

Trot saw the body of the Princess become transparent, so that her beating heart showed plainly. But now the heart turned from a vivid red to gray, and then to white. A layer of frost formed about it and tiny icicles clung to its surface. Then slowly the body of the girl became visible again and the heart was hidden from view.

It is possible that Jack Pumpkinhead was suggested to Baum by Hawthorne's "Feathertop: A Moralized Legend," but he draws nearest to Hawthorne in his treatment of certain themes that, without breaking the frame of a children's story, explore the heart and personality with a good deal of subtlety. In *The Tin Woodman of Oz* (1918) Baum searches into the ambiguities of identity and one's relation to one's own past in a remarkable episode. The Tin Woodman, whose man's body was gradually replaced by tin parts as his limbs, torso, and head were successively severed by an enchanted ax, sets out in this book to recover his past and to rectify certain sins of omission of which he had been guilty in his youth. In a remote part of the Munchkin country he comes face to face with his severed but still living head:

The Tin Woodman had just noticed the cupboards and was curious to know what they contained, so he went to one of them and opened the door. There were shelves inside, and upon one of the shelves which was about on a level with his tin chin the Emperor discovered a Head—it looked like a doll's head, only it was larger, and he soon saw it was the Head of some person. It was facing the Tin Woodman and as the cupboard door swung back, the eyes of the Head slowly opened and looked at him. . . .

"Dear me!" said the Tin Woodman, staring hard. "It seems as if I had met you somewhere, before. Good morning, sir!"

"You have the advantage of me," replied the Head. "I never saw you before in my life."

A pilgrim in search of his own past, its recovery proves impossible for the Tin Woodman, and he and his former head remain strangers without a common ground of meeting. The pilgrimage back through time to one's origins and source was a favorite theme of many American writers—for example, of Hawthorne in his last fragmentary novels, or of James in *The Sense of the Past* or "A Passionate Pilgrim." Baum, who handles the theme expertly enough on his own level, also finds that the past cannot be repeated, or even rediscovered in any satisfying way.

Probably Baum never tried to incorporate a consistent meaning or set of values in his books, yet a significant pattern of values does exist in them. We know, for example, that General Jinjur, who captures the Emerald City with her army of girls in *The Land of Oz* (1904), is an extended satire on the suffragette movement; and Baum's deep affection for the monarchy and the trappings of royalty that runs through all the books reflects a facet of sensibility shared by many nineteenth-century Americans. Baum created a land so rich in palaces, crowns, costume, heraldry, and pomp that he had no grounds for complaining, as James had done, of the poverty of the American environment in supplying the writer with material. Yet Oz remains unmistakably an *American* fairyland. In nothing is this more apparent than in the way Baum transforms magic into a glamorized version of technology and applied science.

A few years ago, in a book called *The Machine in the Garden*, Leo Marx analyzed nineteenth-century American literature in relation to technology. American society evolved under the stimulus and energy provided by a new age of industrialization and technical discoveries. The new attitudes characteristic of this era were superimposed on a largely pastoral ideal inherited from the eighteenth century and from Jeffersonian agrarianism. "Within the lifetime of a single generation," Marx writes, "a rustic and in large part wild landscape was transformed into the site of the world's most productive industrial machine." This process of transformation really began in earnest with the widespread application of steam power. In an incredibly short space of time, "this fresh, green breast of the new world" had been replaced by a man-made landscape. Describing the painting *American Landscape*, by Charles Sheeler, Marx writes:

No trace of nature remains. Not a tree or a blade of grass in view. The water is enclosed by man-made banks, and the sky is filling with smoke. Like the reflection upon the water, every natural object represents some aspect of the collective enterprise. Technological power overwhelms the solitary man; the landscape convention calls for his presence to provide scale, but here the traditional figure acquires new meaning: in this mechanical environment he seems forlorn and powerless.

The second half of *The Machine in the Garden* is concerned with showing us just how the dialectic between the pastoral vision and technology, which is the destructive element, is a central theme in nineteenth-century American literature. Marx equates the pastoral dream with "the kingdom of love," and technology with "the kingdom of power," and he asserts that they have waged war in American literature end-lessly since Hawthorne. Now, the tension between pastoralism and technology is one of the things the Oz books are about, whether Baum was conscious of it or not. In the American literature of which Marx writes, technology seems to triumph despite the resistance the authors offer to it. The locomotive turns the garden into a desert. It is a distinguishing mark of the Oz books that a satisfactory resolution of the tension is achieved in them, and the Munchkins on their small farms in the East continue down to the time that Baum wrote of them to exemplify an agrarian ideal.

The best description of the economic, social, and political conditions that go to make up the Oz way of life is to be found in Baum's sixth book on Oz, *The Emerald City of Oz* (1910):

[The Emerald City] has nine thousand, six hundred and fifty-four buildings, in which lived fifty-seven thousand, three hundred and eighteen people, up to the time my story opens.

All the surrounding country, extending to the borders of the desert which enclosed it upon every side, was full of pretty and comfortable farmhouses, in which resided those inhabitants of Oz who preferred country to city life.

Altogether there were more than half a million people in the Land of Oz . . . and every inhabitant of the country was happy and prosperous.

No disease of any sort was ever known among the Ozites, and so no one ever died unless he met with an accident that prevented him from living. This happened very seldom indeed. There were no poor people in the Land of Oz, because there was no such thing as money, and all property of every sort belonged to the Ruler. The people were her children, and she cared for them. Each person was given freely by his neighbors whatever he required for his use, which is as much as anyone may reasonably desire. Some tilled the land and raised great crops of grain, which was divided equally among the entire population, so that all had enough. There were many tailors and dressmakers and shoemakers and the like, who made things that anyone who desired them might wear. Likewise there were jewelers who made ornaments for the person, which pleased and beautified the people, and these ornaments were also free to those who asked for them. Each man and woman, no matter what he or she produced for the good of the community, was supplied by the neighbors with food and clothing and a house and furniture and ornaments and games. If by chance the supply ever ran short, more was taken from the great storehouses of the Ruler, which were afterwards filled up again when there was more of any article than the people needed.

Everyone worked half the time and played half the time, and the people enjoyed the work as much as they did the play, because it is good to be occupied and to have something to do. There were no cruel overseers set to watch them, and no one to rebuke them or to find fault with them. So each one was proud to do all he could for his friends and neighbors, and was glad when they would accept the things he produced.

At first this seems a garden into which no machine is likely to intrude. But we have to remember that magic is the science or technology of Oz. In *Magic, Science, and Religion* Malinowski wrote:

> Magic is akin to science in that it always has a definite aim associated with human instincts, needs, and pursuits. . . . The magic art is directed towards the attainment of practical aims. Like the other arts and crafts, it is also governed by a theory of principles which dictate the manner in which the act has to be performed in order to be effective. . . . Thus both magic and science show certain similarities, and with Sir James Frazer, we can appropriately called magic a pseudo-science.

The Ozites were much aware of the scientific character of magic. Glinda the Good, who, subject to Princess Ozma, ruled the Quadling Country in the south, always retired to her laboratory to perform her magical experiments, and the Wizard of Oz carried a small black bag filled with his magical instruments in very much the fashion of a nineteenth-century country doctor. In *The Patchwork Girl of Oz* (1913) the Shaggy Man explicitly says in some verses that he recites: "I'll sing a song of Ozland . . . where magic is a science." In *Glinda of Oz* (1920) we are told of the island of the Skeezers, enclosed in a glass dome, which could be submerged for defensive purposes. The method by which this was accomplished clearly reveals the "scientific" character of Oz magic:

> "I now remember," returned Aujah, "that one of the arts we taught Coo-ee-oh was the way to expand steel, and I think that explains how the island is raised and lowered. I noticed in the basement a big steel pillar that passed through the floor and extended upward to this palace. . . . If the lower end of the steel pillar is firmly embedded in the bottom of the lake, Coo-ee-oh could utter a magic word that would make the pillar expand, and so lift the entire island to the level of the water.

But there is no need to multiply instances of this magical technology. The Ozites understood the necessity of bringing this source of energy and power under the control of the central government, and only Glinda the Good, the Wizard, and Ozma herself were entitled to practice magic legally. By this prohibition, which placed government restrictions on promiscuous and uncontrolled "technological" experimentation, Oz remained her pastoral landscape and guaranteed her people's happiness. There were of course criminal practitioners of magic—particularly in the still wild Gillikin Country in the north—but one of the principal functions of government in Oz was to keep these enemies of order under control. There were machines in Oz, but as with Tik-Tok, the clockwork man, they tended to be thoroughly humanized. And where the Powder of Life could be used as a source of power and energy, the steam engine and the dynamo could scarcely be considered a serious threat to human happiness.

Marx writes that American literature has been concerned with the endless warfare between "the kingdom of love" and "the kingdom of power." For love, technology is a destructive element because it is dehumanizing. So far from liberating man's humanity by giving him control over nature, as the nineteenth century often believed, technology tends to approximate man to the level of the machine he creates. It is perhaps an awareness of this threat that led so many American writers in the nineteenth century to accept the ideal of a selfless love as the central value of their work. Fenimore Cooper's Natty Bumppo embodies this ideal of selflessness and service to others; virtually all of Hawthorne's stories and novels revolve around the theme of "the magnetic chain of humanity," by which he means unselfish and disinterested love of humanity, and this is also one of the principal subjects of Henry James's fictions. Selflessness and loving kindness constitute the very air of Oz. It is the only American territory in which the magnetic chain of humanity is rarely broken, and in which the selfless generosity of James's "American Princess," Milly Theale, would appear little more than normal behavior. In an introductory essay to *The Wonderful Wizard of Oz*, Russel B. Nye wrote in 1957:

The First Law of Baum's Utopia of Oz, the rule that inspires its harmonious order, is Love. This theme, on which Baum played constant variations, binds all the Oz books together as a moral unit. Love in Oz is kindness, selflessness, friendliness—an inner check that makes one act decently toward human beings, animals, plants, machines, and even one's enemies.

One has to bear in mind that love in Oz is a value actively present in the stories, dramatized in the action, and realized in the characters. There is nothing self-conscious, sentimental, or priggish about it. It is the imaginative element in which Dorothy, Ozma, Glinda, the Tin Woodman, the Scarecrow, the Cowardly Lion, and all the rest exist and have their meaning. As Nye points out, the most evil character in all the Oz books is the ruler of the Phanfasms, whose title is the First and Foremost. That beautifully sinister title sums up the final meaning of Oz history. The aggrandizement of the individual and private self at the expense of others is the root of all evil.

Marx speaks of a "design of the classic American fables" which embodies "the idea of a redemptive journey away from society in the direction of nature." A number of Americans managed to make their way to Oz—from Kansas, Nebraska, Oklahoma, and, of course, California. To do so they had to cross the Deadly Desert. The way was arduous and the dangers great; but when these happy few arrived in Oz they were confronted by a pastoral world as unspoiled as that which once greeted the eyes of those Dutch sailors whom Scott Fitzgerald invokes at the close of *The Great Gatsby*. It was a world in which magical technology was strictly controlled, and in which perfect selflessness and love were the element of life. It was, in short, the Great Good Place.

The Utopia of Oz

· by S. J. Sackett ·

Now that the third generation of American children is being raised on the Oz books, by L. Frank Baum, it is perhaps time to look over the series and see what can be found in it. There are many qualities that can be found in these stories and many approaches that can be made to them. They can be considered purely as literature; they can be examined as exercises in morality; they can be explored to discover why their appeal has endured.

I choose here rather to consider the Oz books as examples of Utopian fiction. Certainly they represent an ideal country, even though their creator never indicates how it would be possible to bring the ideal conditions to actual existence, or even whether it would be desirable so to do. Certainly they have influenced the generations of children who have read them in certain attitudes toward government and society.

The Land of Oz, after Princess Ozma came to the throne, was a confederation of four separate kingdoms. That of the Winkies, to the west, was ruled over by Nick Chopper, the Tin Woodman; that of the Munchkins, to the east, by a mysterious king who was never a figure in the stories about Oz; that of the Gillikins, to the north, by the good witch whom Dorothy Gale met when she first came to Oz but who had

Reprinted from *The Georgia Review*, Volume XIV (1960), pp. 275–290. Copyright © 1960 by the University of Georgia. Reprinted by permission of *The Georgia Review* and S. J. Sackett.

no further role in the history of Oz; that of the Quadlings, to the south, by the benign sorceress Glinda the Good. Over them all ruled Ozma.

Oz was never a thoroughly civilized and mapped country; it always had a permanent frontier in the form of vast unexplored areas where no one ever traveled and where all sorts of strange beings might (and did) live. To a certain extent this condition was owing to a philosophy of *laissez-faire* on the part of Ozma and the other administrative officials. "That government is best which governs least"—such a motto might have been inscribed over the façade of Ozma's palace. Neither Ozma nor anyone else wanted to meddle in the affairs of the citizenry, who were free, within extraordinarily broad limits, to do anything they wanted to.

That the individual citizen was so free as this is more surprising in view of the tremendous power which Ozma herself, to say nothing of her counselors Glinda the Good and the Wizard of Oz, could wield. As one reads the chronicles of Oz, however, one is struck by the fact that Ozma seems almost deliberately to have refrained from exercising her vast powers. She came to the throne, it is true, only in 1904; and the last book by the first Royal Historian of Oz appeared in 1921. From this it might be argued that Ozma had had by that time only seventeen years to function effectively as a ruler. On the other hand, she was an absolute monarch with unlimited power and no restraint except self-restraint; and viewed from that standpoint, in those seventeen years she had done remarkably little. A few bridges are mentioned in later books over streams which had had no bridges in earlier books, and presumably Ozma had wished these into existence with her magic belt; yet even by 1921 many of the main thoroughfares of Oz were broken by unbridged rivers. Apparently one of the earliest acts was the abolition of money, for the use of money is referred to in the first two books and is not mentioned, except occasionally as something that the inhabitants of Oz knew about, after 1904. Aside from these two matters, Ozma's reign has been, by the standards of the outside world, a do-nothing reign. It may be that Ozma fears to meddle in her subjects' lives so much that she leans over backward to avoid taking action; it may be, as indeed is hinted in the books themselves, that she is an adherent of Frederick Jackson Turner's theory that the challenge of the frontier was important in developing the strengths of the American character and thus attempts to maintain primitive conditions as a deliberate policy. Life, one gathers from the Oz books, isn't much fun unless you can have adventures, and you can't have adventures when things are too civilized, orderly, and expected. But whatever the reason for her unwillingness to take action,

Ozma's powers are so great that she must be highly complimented on her restraint in not using them.

The limits imposed on the broad freedom enjoyed by the citizens of Oz were really only two. First, individual communities, which had by our standards a startling degree of independence from the central government, were not to fight each other, as the Flatheads and Skeezers once did (*Glinda of Oz*) and as the Horners and Hoppers seemed to do almost perennially (e.g., in *The Patchwork Girl of Oz*). Second, no unauthorized person could make use of magic. Violations of this rule were recounted in *The Patchwork Girl of Oz, The Lost Princess of Oz*, and *The Magic of Oz*. Aside from these two restrictions, everything else was legal.

People in Oz were suspicious of laws. The Tin Woodman once remarked, ". . . laws were never meant to be understood, and it is foolish to make the attempt" (*The Land of Oz*, p. 174). But if Oz had had a constitution, it probably would have been expressed in one sentence: Do what you like, unless it hurts somebody else. (The reason why magic was prohibited was that so many people, like Ugu the Shoemaker, used magic for evil instead of for good.)

The reason for so much freedom is that life is more fun if you are free to do whatever you want. Absolute freedom, however, has its drawbacks, as the King of Bunnybury discovered in *The Emerald City of Oz* (pp. 210–24). The King was weary of taking responsibility and wanted to be free of it; but he learned that responsibility brings with it so many privileges that it is far wiser to live with responsibility than to live in the irresponsibility of anarchy. If freedom is essential, but absolute freedom is disastrous, then the solution to the problem of government must be in a *via media* of voluntary acceptance of responsibility. And this, in effect, is the principle which underlies government in Oz. It is voluntary cooperation that turns the trick; and in Oz voluntary cooperation can perform wonders, even as thousands of mice, working together, can pull a cart carrying a lion (*The Wizard of Oz*, pp. 72–79).

Oz is a monarchy; there is no question about that. Obviously what is needed is a vigorous command to maintain freedom under these conditions; and under these conditions the nature of the commander is all important. Absolute power in the hands of Jinjur is tyranny; absolute power in the hands of Ozma is benevolence. The character of the political leader is of the highest consequence. And too often in less ideal places than Oz, political leadership is of low quality. In *The Wizard of Oz*, after the Scarecrow had been made ruler of the Emerald City, the people boasted, ". . . there is not another city in all the world that is ruled by a stuffed man." "And," commented the Royal Historian with a dry irony which undoubtedly escaped the youngest of his readers, "so far as they knew, they were quite right" (p. 169).

While royalty was necessary for the maintenance of authority—and, one suspects, because Baum was working in the tradition of the European fairy tale—it was a highly democratic royalty. Even the aristocratic Princess Langwidere of Ev darned her own socks (*Ozma of Oz*, p. 95); and Ozma, the supreme ruler of Oz, was really a merry little girl who enjoyed playing with her commoner girlfriends.

Under Ozma's beneficent rule, based as it was on as much absence of law as possible, there were of course very few criminals. How can you break a law when there are no laws to break? For this reason crime and delinquency were not problems in the Oz state. But when laws were broken, the inhabitants of Oz had a philosophy ready to meet the problem. In this respect, it is worthy quoting at some length from the scene in which Ojo, the first lawbreaker after Ozma came to the throne, found himself in prison.

Ojo was imprisoned for having picked a six-leaved clover, contrary to the law of Oz, which forbade unauthorized magic. (Six-leaved clovers were used by magicians.) His jailer, a motherly lady named Tollydiggle, welcomed him to the prison and then asked him what dinner he would prefer. After he made his choice, she left him alone while she prepared it.

Ojo was much astonished, for not only was this unlike any prison he had ever heard of, but he was being treated more as a guest than a criminal. There were three doors to the room and none were bolted. He cautiously opened one of the doors and found it led into a hallway. But he had no intention of trying to escape. If his jailor was willing to trust him in this way he would not betray her trust, and moreover a hot supper was being prepared for him and his prison was very pleasant and comfortable. So he took a book from the case and sat down in a big chair to look at the pictures.

This amused him until the woman came in with a large tray and spread a cloth on one of the tables. Then she arranged his supper, which proved the most varied and delicious meal Ojo had ever eaten in his life.

Tollydiggle sat near him while he ate, sewing on some fancy work she held in her lap. When he had finished she cleared the table and then read to him a story from one of the books.

"Is this really a prison?" he asked, when she had finished reading.

"Indeed it is," she replied. "It is the only prison in the land of Oz."

"And am I a prisoner?"

"Bless the child! Of course."

"Then why is the prison so fine, and why are you so kind to me?" he earnestly asked.

Tollydiggle seemed surprised by the question, but she presently answered:

"We consider a prisoner unfortunate. He is unfortunate in two ways—because he has done something wrong and because he is deprived of his liberty. Therefore we should treat him kindly, because of his misfortune, for otherwise he would become hard and bitter and would not be sorry he had done wrong. Ozma thinks that one who has committed a fault did so because he was not strong and brave; therefore she puts him in prison to make him strong and brave. When that is accomplished he is no longer a prisoner, but a good and loyal citizen and everyone is glad that he is now strong enough to resist doing wrong. You see, it is kindness that makes one strong and brave; and so we are kind to our prisoners."

Ojo thought this over very carefully. "I had an idea," said he, "that prisoners were always treated harshly, to punish them."

"That would be dreadful!" cried Tollydiggle. "Isn't one punished enough in knowing he has done wrong? Don't you wish, Ojo, with all your heart, that you had not been disobedient and broken a Law of Oz?"

"I—I hate to be different from other people," he admitted.

"Yes; one likes to be respected as highly as his neighbors are," said the woman. "When you are tried and found guilty, you will be obliged to make amends in some way. . . . But now we have talked enough, so let us play a game until bedtime." [*Patchwork Girl of Oz*, pp. 198–201].

This makes it clear that the dominant philosophy of penology in the Land of Oz is that progressive one which holds that it is more important to rehabilitate the criminal and restore him to a productive place in society than it is to inflict on him society's vengeance for his act.

One of the reasons why there is no crime in the Land of Oz is that there is no money and therefore no temptation to rob anyone. The trouble with money, as the Shaggy Man once remarked, is that it "makes people proud and haughty; I don't want to be proud and haughty. All I want is to have people love me . . ." (*The Road to Oz*, pp. 22–24). And fittingly the medium of exchange in the Land of Oz is love. The Tin Woodman once explained the system as follows: "If we used money to buy things with, instead of love and kindness and the desire to please one another, then we should be no better off than the rest of the world. . . . Fortunately money is not known in the Land of Oz at all. We have no rich, and no poor; for what one wishes the others all try to give him, in order to make him happy, and no one in all Oz cares to have more than he can use" (*The Road to Oz*, pp. 164–165). The only way to acquire goods or services, then, is to be so lovable that other people want to give them to you. True, you might steal goods (though you cannot under this system compel services); but there is no need to steal goods when one has only to be loved and they will be given to him. Why give of your goods to someone else? Because you love him and find pleasure in helping him.

It is true that Oz was not a heavily industrialized nation. It was chiefly agricultural, with only one city (its capital, the Emerald City); there were a few towns and villages scattered over the countryside, but the bulk of the land—that of it at least that was not wilderness—was under cultivation, and the bulk of the inhabitants were farmers. Most of them were self-sufficient; they raised their own food, spun their own cloth and made their own garments, and built their own houses. In a society like this there is little need for money anyway.

Yet, surprisingly enough, there was conspicuous consumption. There were palaces, for example; and there were servants. Palaces, however, could be built by magic and thus required no manpower; and only those had servants who were so beloved that there were people who wished to do nothing but serve them, as for instance the Scarecrow. And we must confess that this kind of hero-worship is a common human trait.

Most Utopias imply a wish to implement them in the real world; and while there is no doubt that L. Frank Baum would have agreed to the general proposition that the real world would be a better place if it were more like his agrarian paradise, there is real reason to doubt that he ever seriously thought that the world could ever be made more Oz-like except perhaps in small details like the adoption of progressive prison reform. And, in truth, one might well scoff that the Utopia of Oz was made possible by the existence of magic and that human nature is too corrupt for so perfect a fairyland.

On the other hand, however, we have ourselves more magic than we well know what to do with. We have what Baum himself considered the magic of electricity. We have magic that even Baum at his most inventive never dreamed of—the magic of atomic energy, the magic of solar power. Our mastery of such magic is already so complete that there is nothing—literally nothing—that the human race might want to do in the way of rearranging its physical environment that would be impossible of accomplishment. All that is wanted is the will to do it. Surely even Oz never had such power as this.

And so far as the unchangeability of human nature is concerned, Baum has provided us with an answer for that, too. The key to the problem is epistemology. You must assume with Locke that the mind at birth is a *tabula rasa*, an empty page; that there are no innate ideas, no Jungian archetypes or other inherited memories. According to this theory the individual's environment will completely mold his personality, for he has no inherited psychological characteristics. Each experience that he has will form his personality, little by little. If his environment is Utopian, if he experiences nothing but love, his personality will be molded in the direction that this environment and these experiences indicate to him. He becomes, then, a person who is at home and at ease in the Utopian society. The only reason, according to this theory, that human nature is what it is is that the Utopian environment has never been tried. By establishing a Utopian environment, you change human nature.

It is not far-fetched to say that in the Oz books Baum subscribed to this theory. The problem of language aside, it would be difficult to imagine a better description of the awakening of a new mind, the first initial marks made upon the *tabula rasa*, than the following account, told by the Scarecrow to Dorothy, of his early moments:

My life has been so short that I really know nothing whatever. I was only made day before yesterday. What happened in the world before that time is all unknown to me. Luckily, when the farmer made my head, one of the first things he did was to paint my ears, so that I heard what was going on. There was another Munchkin with him, and the first thing I heard was the farmer saying,

"How do you like those ears?"

"They aren't straight," answered the other.

"Never mind," said the farmer; "they are ears just the same," which was true enough.

"Now I'll make the eyes," said the farmer. So he painted my right eye, and as soon as it was finished I found myself looking at him and at everything around me with a great deal of curiosity, for this was my first glimpse of the world.

"That's a rather pretty eye," remarked the Munchkin who was watching the farmer; "blue paint is just the color for eyes."

"I think I'll make the other a little bigger," said the farmer; and when the second eye was done I could see much better than before. Then he made my nose and my mouth; but I did not speak, because at the time I didn't know what my mouth was for. I had the fun of watching them make my body and my arms and legs; and when they fastened on my head, at last, I felt very proud, for I thought I was just as good a man as anyone.

"This fellow will scare the crows fast enough," said the farmer; "he looks just like a man."

"Why, he is a man," said the other, and I quite agreed with him. The farmer carried me under his arm to the cornfield, and set me up on a tall stick, where you found me. He and his friend soon after walked away and left me alone.

I did not like to be deserted in this way; so I tried to walk after them, but my feet would not touch the ground, and I was forced to stay up on that pole. It was a lonely life to lead, for I had nothing to think of, having been made such a little while before. [*The Wizard of Oz*, pp. 30–33].

Even more detailed is the description of the bringing of the Saw-Horse to life. It is too lengthy for extensive quotation; but it is well worth reading as an account of the way one sensation after another marks the empty page of the mind at birth (*The Land of Oz*, pp. 47–51).

If this process does really accurately describe the way the human mind is formed, then it is perfectly feasible to change human nature by changing the environment in which human nature exists. This is, after all, the method used by the Soviet Union. And while we may feel that the environment of the Soviet Union is far from Utopian, the Soviet outlook on some things is so different from our own, and we find it so difficult to understand the so-called "Russian mentality," that perhaps the creation of a Communist environment actually has effected some changes in human nature. Even so basic a drive as sex has been altered and suppressed by the Soviet government. If this can be done, then perhaps a more perfect society could create more perfect human beings.

Two more points need to be made here concerning the reasons why the social structure of Oz worked as well as it did. The first is that the inhabitants subscribed to a philosophy given verse form by Johnny Dooit:

> *The only way to do a thing,*
> *Is do it when you can,*
> *And do it cheerfully, and sing*
> *And work and think and plan.*
> *The only real unhappy one*
> *Is he who dares to shirk;*
> *The only really happy one*
> *Is he who cares to work.*
>
> [*The Road to Oz*, p. 134]

There is no question that there is a deep psychological satisfaction in work well done. Our own society faces some of its current problems because the proletarians—whether they were serfs or industrial laborers—have always seen as the principal distinction between themselves and the more wealthy orders of society that the poor work and the rich are idle. Therefore they have adopted as the ruling principle of the proletarian Utopia—the Land of Cockayne—that it is a land where no one works. But this, if it could ever be accomplished, would be an unsatisfying country in which to live; if they could ever attain it, they would miss work because they would miss the satisfactions, the pride in accomplishments and even the pleasure in muscular action, that work gives. Work becomes degrading and stultifying only when you are doing someone else's work, especially when you are doing it under conditions where you cannot feel proud of the finished product, and you cannot feel proud of the finished product unless you have participated in all stages of the job from design to completion. The truth of this assertion can be seen in the success of the do-it-yourself movement in the United States today, in which thousands of men are performing tasks for fun that they would find onerous if they had to perform them at someone else's direction. We are living in an industrial society where work is often degrading because it must be done at an employer's command; thus our industrial workers have fought for a five-day week, now a four-day week, soon a three-day week, and one of the problems of our society has been to find things for people to do in their spare time. Oz, on the other hand, was an agricultural society where nearly everyone was nearly self-sufficient, and its inhabitants had learned from joyful experience that "The only really happy one/Is he who cares to work." Perhaps when automation has made leisure the possession of nearly all our people, we can begin again to discover the satisfactions in work.

The last point that should be made about the success of the unique socioeconomical system of Oz is that it was based upon a set of values which are totally foreign to us. We measure success—sometimes we try to claim that we don't, but without conviction—in money. Ozma, however, very early in her reign established a whole new standard: "the only riches worth having," she said, are "the riches of content" (*The Land of Oz*, p. 287). That man who is contented is most wealthy. If that is their measure of success, it is no wonder that the inhabitants of Oz have done well in their Utopia.

Thus far we have been discussing the general principles upon which the Utopia of Oz was founded. It is time now to take up a few of the specific principles of the Utopia.

To begin with, nonconformity was prized, as might be expected in so free a society. As the Scarecrow remarked on one occasion, ". . . I am convinced that the only people worthy of consideration in this world are the unusual ones. For the common folks are like the leaves of a tree, and live and die unnoticed" (*The Land of Oz*, p. 188). While the Scarecrow, who was unusual himself, might have exercised some pardonable pride in framing this statement, still we must take it as the considered judgment of the wisest man in all Oz.

Another issue taken up in Oz was the relationship between the human (or quasi-human) and the mechanical. At one point, for instance, the Tin Woodman and Tik-Tok, both made of metal but the first alive while the second was mechanical, discussed which was the superior. Tik-Tok was quick to concede defeat: "I can-not help be-ing your in-fe-ri-or," he confessed, "for I am a mere ma-chine. When I am wound up I do my du-ty by go-ing just as my ma-chin-er-y is made to go" (*Ozma of Oz*, p. 115). It is the fact that the machine cannot initiate policy, then, according to this line of reasoning, which makes man superior to his creations, however ingenious the latter may be.

The status of women was at one time at least, prior to Ozma's accession to the throne, a major issue. Jinjur's successful rebellion, recounted in *The Land of Oz*, was a rebellion of the women against the men. While there is no question that the Royal Historian deprecated the act of rebellion, it is also clear that he sympathized with the impulse behind the revolutionaries, that of bettering woman's lot—though he felt that Jinjur had gone too far. The effect of Jinjur's feminist revolution can be observed in the following scene, describing what the Scarecrow and his party saw as they reentered the Emerald City in a counterrevolutionary move:

> As they passed the rows of houses they saw through the open doors that men were sweeping and dusting and washing dishes, while the women sat around in groups, gossiping and laughing.
>
> "What has happened?" the Scarecrow asked a sad-looking man with a bushy beard, who wore an apron and was wheeling a baby-carriage along the sidewalk.
>
> "Why, we've had a revolution, your Majesty—as you ought to know very well," replied the man; "and since you went away the women have been running things to suit themselves. I'm glad you have decided to come back and restore order, for doing housework and minding the children is wearing out the strength of every man in the Emerald City."
>
> "Hm!" said the Scarecrow, thoughtfully. "If it is such hard work as you say, how did the women manage it so easily?"
>
> "I really do not know," replied the man, with a deep sigh. "Perhaps the women are made of cast-iron" [pp. 170–171].

Such a scene indicates that perhaps there was really a problem in the relationships between the sexes in the Land of Oz. The accession of Ozma seems to have settled the difficulty, however, for there was no sign of it in any of the narratives dealing with events after she came to the throne.

War was never much of a problem in Oz, and there was not a military tradition. The customary pattern for military organization, however, was to have several officers and only one private; this was the pattern followed both in the Royal Army of Oz itself (*Ozma of Oz*) and in the Army of Oogaboo (*Tik-Tok of Oz*). Part of the reason was that, because of the freedom of the entire society, the individuals who entered these armies were free to select their own rank. Since the privates did the actual fighting, there were very few who were willing to accept a private's job; the titles and uniforms of the officers' ranks, however, as well as their comparative safety, attracted many to the upper echelons of military life. This suggests that if, in the outside world, those who are in a position to cause a war were also under the obligation of fighting it, there would be many fewer wars; whereas the attractions of militarism are such that men can always be found to embrace it so long as they are under no necessity to face the unpleasant realities of warfare.

Oz was free from many of the fads which have attracted much attention in the outside world. At one time, however, Dorothy was taken by an idea which was rather close to vegetarianism. She was shocked by discovering that Billina, the yellow hen, ate "horrid bugs and crawly ants," but, as Billina pointed out, human beings eat the chickens that ate the bugs. Thinking this over "almost took away her appetite for breakfast," the Royal Historian reported (*Ozma of Oz*, pp. 32–35). The word "almost" is significant here, and there is no sign that Dorothy ever thought further along this line; but I feel certain that at that point she rather inclined toward vegetarianism.

Perhaps the greatest problem in the Land of Oz was education. Some there were, including Ozma herself, who doubted the value of education at all, suspecting that the search for education was only an excuse used by those who wished to evade responsibility outside the academy. "You see," Ozma once explained to Dorothy, who had asked her about Professor Woggle-Bug's College, "in this country are a number of youths who do not like to work, and the college is an excellent place for them" (*Ozma of Oz*, p. 258).

On the other hand, it is notable and significant that the character who boasted that "the only school we need is the school of experience. Books are only fit for those who know nothing, and so are obliged to learn things from other people" (*The Road to Oz*, pp. 78–79) was a gray donkey. And one wonders whether the Royal Historian did not intend some irony when he chronicled Professor Woggle-Bug's explanation of his famous School Pills in the following words: ". . . You see, until these School Pills were invented we wasted a lot of time in study that may now be better employed in practising athletics. . . . They give us an advantage over all other colleges, because at no loss of time our boys become thoroughly conversant with Greek and Latin, Mathematics and Geography, Grammar and Literature. You see they are never obliged to interrupt their games to acquire the lesser branches of learning" (*The Emerald City of Oz*, p. 98). This is so devastating a self-indictment, in fact, that one suspects that the Royal Historian felt that such branches of study as mathematics and literature had some value which had escaped not only the Woggle-Bug but also Princess Ozma. Or perhaps—to clear the Princess from an ungallant imputation of obtuseness—her tart remark was directed not against colleges as colleges but against colleges where the students waste time on frivolous pursuits.

It is probable that the low repute of learning in Oz, in some circles at least, was owing to the excessive pedantry and incomprehensibility of the members of the learned professions. The Shaggy Man on one occasion even suggested that college lecturers and ministers were much like the long-winded and verbose inhabitants of Rigmarole Town (*The Emerald City of Oz*, pp. 235–236). And the Royal Historian himself once let slip a comment which perhaps indicated his agreement: "All donkeys love big words" (*The Road to Oz*, p. 70) perhaps may be taken to mean that all who love big words are donkeys.

So much concern was shown for the problems of training the intellect, in fact, that it should not surprise us to learn that perhaps the central philosophical problem in the Land of Oz was whether the intellect or the emotions were more desirable attributes. Certainly it was the many long disagreements which they had over this issue, some of the most interesting of which were reported in *The Wizard of Oz*, which paradoxically made the Scarecrow and the Tin Woodman such firm friends. (Their friendship, by the way, may suggest that the Royal Historian felt that the best answer to the problem was the uniting of the intellect and the emotions in a harmonious relationship.) And on one occasion Dorothy confessed that she did not "know which of her two friends was right" (p. 44).

The Scarecrow's problem really was that he confused knowledge with intellect. Knowledge is an accumulation of facts; intellect is the ability to accumulate facts and to use them to solve problems. The Wizard of Oz himself explained this distinction to the Scarecrow: "A baby has brains," Oz said, "but it doesn't know much. Experience is the only thing that brings knowledge, and the longer you are on earth the more experience you are sure to get" (*The Wizard of Oz*, p. 153). Thus the Scarecrow, even before the Wizard supplied him with brains, was intelligent; he merely lacked knowledge.

Once we have clarified this matter, we can determine the nature of intelligence, as it was viewed in Oz, by examining the Scarecrow's actions as those of a person in whom the intellect is dominant. Viewed from this standpoint, it is clear that intelligence is valuable. As the Scarecrow himself once remarked, ". . . I consider brains far superior to money, in every way. You may have noticed that if one has money without brains, he cannot use it to advantage; but if one has brains without money, they will enable him to live comfortably to the end of all his days" (*The Land of Oz*, p. 206).

Certain it is that on Dorothy's first trip to the Emerald City the Scarecrow's intelligence was invaluable for solving problems which the travelers met. Time and again he applied the cool force of logic to the situations with which they were confronted, and in nearly every case his suggestions were successfully adopted (*The Wizard of Oz*, e.g., pp. 55, 58–61).

The disadvantage of intellectuality is that it makes its possessor cold and unfeeling. Thus the Scarecrow once remarked to Dorothy, "I cannot understand why you should wish to leave this beautiful country and go back to the dry, gray place you call Kansas." Dorothy replied, in her innocence, "That is because you have no brains." Ironically, it was really because the Scarecrow had nothing but brains, as Dorothy's explanation makes clear: "No matter how dreary and gray our homes are, we people of flesh and blood would rather live there than in any other country, be it ever so beautiful. There is no place like home" (*The Wizard of Oz*, pp. 29–30). This is clearly an emotional appeal. The important result of the Scarecrow's adventures with Dorothy was not that he got brains from the Wizard; the important result for him was that he developed his affections.

It was because he felt that he had no brains that the Scarecrow directed all his attention to intellectuality and was on the verge of becoming an unemotional thinking machine. Similarly, the Tin Woodman, who felt he had no heart, directed all of his attention to the life of the emotions and was on the verge of becoming excessively sentimental. Thus "he walked very carefully, with his eyes on the road, and when he saw a tiny ant toiling by he would step over it, so as not to harm it. The Tin Woodman knew very well he had no heart, and therefore he took great care never to be cruel or unkind to anything" (*The Wizard of Oz*, p. 52).

That emotions are desirable things to have we learn from the Scarecrow's case as well as the Tin Woodman's. The latter's own argument for benevolence and kindheartedness actually is weak: "you must acknowledge that a good heart is a thing that brains cannot create, and that money cannot buy" (*The Land of Oz*, p. 286). While this is true, it still does not establish benevolence as a desirable characteristic. This is done rather by the whole moral tendency of the Oz stories, which are set in a benevolistic framework much like that found in the sermons of the seventeenth-century English latitudinarians, Barrow, South, and Tillotson, whose philosophy remained popular well into the nineteenth century.

The disadvantage of emotionalism is that it leads sometimes to excessive sentimentality (which the Royal Historian uniformly treats with ridicule) and to sorrow, as the Wizard of Oz once tells the Tin Woodman (*The Wizard of Oz*, p. 154). On many occasions the Tin Woodman weeps so much that he rusts his jaws and cannot speak.

If a great deal of attention was paid in Oz to the problems of the intellect versus emotion, very little was given to artistic problems. In the preface to *The Wizard of Oz* the Royal Historian pointed out the superiority of fairy tales which are not gory to fairy tales which are; and that was the extent of the literary interests shown in the Oz books. None of the little girls who are the heroines of most of the Oz stories— Ozma, Dorothy, Betsy Bobbin, and Trot—spend much time reading;

their favorite recreations are listening to stories, talking with each other, going to parties, and playing games.

We have rather more information on the state of music in the Land of Oz, particularly in various conversations with a live phonograph which the Royal Historian recounted in *The Patchwork Girl of Oz*. In the course of these conversations various judgments are stated or implied. Classical music, according to the phonograph, "is considered the best and most puzzling ever manufactured. You're supposed to like it, whether you do or not, and if you don't, the proper thing is to look as if you did." The Royal Historian used the term "dreary" to describe the classical music which the phonograph played (p. 88). Rag-time, on the other hand, was described by the Royal Historian as "a jerky jumble of sounds" and as "bewildering." Scraps commented, "That's the other extreme. It's extremely bad!" while Ojo exclaimed, "It is, indeed, dreadful" (pp. 88–90). Popular music, according to the Royal Historian, was "a strain of odd, jerky sounds"; the phonograph itself defined a popular song as follows: "One that the feeble-minded can remember the words of and those ignorant of music can whistle or sing" (p. 136). That there was music in Oz we have the Royal Historian's word; yet if it was not classical, rag-time, or popular, one wonders what it was. Probably it was composed principally of two-steps and waltzes and closely resembled such songs as "By the Light of the Silvery Moon" and "Down by the Old Mill Stream." A few light classical numbers, much like those written by Victor Herbert in this country, might also have found favor.

But these are minor matters, serving only to round out our picture of life in the Utopia of Oz. The important thing, the matter which I set out to consider, is how American young people would have been affected by their exposure to the chronicles of this Utopia. I leave aside matters of morality; the morality of Oz was a conventional one with no startling innovations to offer, the general tendencies of which were benevolent, and we can say simply that children who read the Oz books would be influenced to be good children in the conventional sense of the word, with an especial disposition toward charitable or benevolent actions. But we can say also that they would have been influenced to believe in the freedom of the individual, in the voluntary acceptance of responsibility, in progressive prison reform, in the proposition that money is relatively unimportant in life, in the possibility of making a better world, in the pleasures of work, in the significance of contentment, in nonconformity, in the superiority of man to machine, in the need for permitting both sexes to share equally in the good life, in the folly of war, in reverence for life, in a truly substantial education, and in the need for the intellect and the emotions to be brought into harmony.

If we had enough people who believed in these things, our world would be almost as good for us as the Land of Oz was for its inhabitants. The attitudes listed above are all positive ones, and among them you can find practically the complete roll call of the attitudes desirable to ensure the continuance of democracy, of civilization, of life—of everything that we in the United States hold valuable. A third generation of American children is now having the Oz books read to it or is reading them for itself. We can all say, "Thank God."

The Wizard of Oz: Parable on Populism

· by Henry M. Littlefield ·

On the deserts of North Africa in 1941 two tough Australian brigades went to battle singing,

> *Have you heard of the wonderful wizard,*
> *The wonderful Wizard of Oz,*
> *And he is a wonderful wizard,*
> *If ever a wizard there was.*

It was a song they had brought with them from Australia and would soon spread to England. Forever afterward it reminded Winston Churchill of those "buoyant days."[1] Churchill's nostalgia is only one symptom of the worldwide delight found in an American fairy tale about a little girl and her odyssey in the strange land of Oz. The song he reflects upon came from a classic 1939 Hollywood production of the story, which introduced millions of people not only to the land of Oz, but to a talented young lady named Judy Garland as well.

Ever since its publication in 1900 Lyman Frank Baum's *The Wonderful Wizard of Oz* has been immensely popular, providing the basis for a profitable musical comedy, three movies, and a number of plays. It is an indigenous creation, curiously warm and touching, although no one really knows why. For despite wholehearted acceptance by generations of readers, Baum's tale has been accorded neither critical acclaim, nor extended critical examination. Interested scholars, such as Russel B.

---

1. Winston S. Churchill, *Their Finest Hour* (Cambridge, 1949), pp. 615–616.

Reprinted from *The American Culture*, edited by Hennig Cohen. Boston: Houghton Mifflin, 1968, pp. 370–382. Copyright © 1968 by the Trustees of the University of Pennsylvania. Reprinted by permission of Henry M. Littlefield.

Nye and Martin Gardner, look upon *The Wizard of Oz* as the first in a long and delightful series of Oz stories, and understandably base their appreciation of Baum's talent on the totality of his works.[2]

The Wizard of Oz is an entity unto itself, however, and was not originally written with a sequel in mind. Baum informed his readers in 1904 that he had produced *The Marvelous Land of Oz* reluctantly and only in answer to well over a thousand letters demanding that he create another Oz tale.[3] His original effort remains unique and to some degree separate from the books which follow. But its uniqueness does not rest alone on its peculiar and transcendent popularity.

Professor Nye finds a "strain of moralism" in the Oz books, as well as "a well-developed sense of satire," and Baum stories often include searching parodies on the contradictions in human nature. The second book in the series, *The Marvelous Land of Oz*, is a blatant satire on feminism and the suffragette movement.[4] In it Baum attempted to duplicate the format used so successfully in *The Wizard*, yet no one has noted a similar play on contemporary movements in the latter work. Nevertheless, one does exist, and it reflects to an astonishing degree the world of political reality which surrounded Baum in 1900. In order to understand the relationship of *The Wizard* to turn-of-the-century America, it is necessary first to know something of Baum's background.

Born near Syracuse in 1856, Baum was brought up in a wealthy home and early became interested in the theater. He wrote some plays which enjoyed brief success and then, with his wife and two sons, journeyed to Aberdeen, South Dakota, in 1888. Aberdeen was a little prairie town and there Baum edited the local weekly until it failed in 1891.[5]

For many years western farmers had been in a state of loud, though unsuccessful revolt. While Baum was living in South Dakota not only was the frontier a thing of the past, but the Romantic view of benign nature had disappeared as well. The stark reality of the dry, open plains and the acceptance of man's Darwinian subservience to his environment served to crush Romantic idealism.[6]

Hamlin Garland's visit to Iowa and South Dakota coincided with Baum's arrival. Henry Nash Smith observes,

2. Martin Gardner and Russel B. Nye, *The Wizard of Oz and Who He Was* (East Lansing, Mich., 1957), pp. 7 ff, 14–16, 19. Professor Nye's "Appreciation" and Martin Gardner's "The Royal Historian of Oz," totaling some forty-five pages, present as definitive an analysis of Baum and his works as is available today.

3. L. Frank Baum, *The Marvelous Land of Oz* (Chicago, 1904), p. 3 (Author's Note).

4. Gardner and Nye, *Wizard*, pp. 5–7, 23.

5. Ibid., pp. 20–22.

6. See Calton F. Culmsee, *Malign Nature and the Frontier* (Logan, Utah, 1959), 7:5, 11, 14. The classic work in the field of symbolism in western literature is Henry Nash Smith, *Virgin Land* (New York, 1961), pp. 225–226, 261, 284–290.

Garland's success as a portrayer of hardship and suffering on northwestern farms was due in part to the fact that his personal experience happened to parallel the shock which the entire West received in the later 1880's from the combined effects of low prices, . . . grasshoppers, drought, the terrible blizzards of the winter of 1886–1887, and the juggling of freight rates. . . .[7]

As we shall see, Baum's prairie experience was no less deeply etched, although he did not employ naturalism to express it.

Baum's stay in South Dakota also covered the period of the formation of the Populist party, which Professor Nye likens to a fanatic "crusade." Western farmers had for a long time sought governmental aid in the form of economic panaceas, but to no avail. The Populist movement symbolized a desperate attempt to use the power of the ballot.[8] In 1891 Baum moved to Chicago where he was surrounded by those dynamic elements of reform which made the city so notable during the 1890s.[9]

In Chicago Baum certainly saw the results of the frightful depression which had closed down upon the nation in 1893. Moreover, he took part in the pivotal election of 1896, marching in "torch-light parades for William Jennings Bryan." Martin Gardner notes besides, that he "consistently voted as a democrat . . . and his sympathies seem always to have been on the side of the laboring classes."[10] No one who marched in even a few such parades could have been unaffected by Bryan's campaign. Putting all the farmers' hopes in a basket labeled "free coinage of silver," Bryan's platform rested mainly on the issue of adding silver to the nation's gold standard. Though he lost, he did at least bring the plight of the little man into national focus.[11]

Between 1896 and 1900, while Baum worked and wrote in Chicago, the great depression faded away and the war with Spain thrust the United States into world prominence. Bryan maintained midwestern control over the Democratic party, and often spoke out against American policies toward Cuba and the Philippines. By 1900 it was evident that Bryan would run again, although now imperialism and not silver seemed the issue of primary concern. In order to promote greater enthusiasm, however, Bryan felt compelled once more to sound the silver

7. Smith, *Virgin Land*, p. 287.
8. Russel B. Nye, *Midwestern Progressive Politics* (East Lansing, Mich., 1959), pp. 63, 56–58, 75, 105. See also John D. Hicks, *The Populist Revolt* (Minneapolis, 1931), pp. 82, 93–95, 264–268.
9. See Ray Ginger, *Altgeld's America* (New York, 1958).
10. Gardner and Nye, *Wizard*, p. 29.
11. See William Jennings Bryan, *The First Battle* (Lincoln, Nebr., 1897), pp. 612–629. Two recent studies are notable: Harold U. Faulkner, *Politics, Reform and Expansion* (New York, 1959), pp. 187–211 and Nye, *Politics*, pp. 105–120.

leitmotif in his campaign.[12] Bryan's second futile attempt at the presidency culminated in November 1900. The previous winter Baum had attempted unsuccessfully to sell a rather original volume of children's fantasy, but that April, George M. Hill, a small Chicago publisher, finally agreed to print *The Wonderful Wizard of Oz*.

Baum's allegiance to the cause of Democratic Populism must be balanced against the fact that he was not a political activist. Martin Gardner finds through all of his writings "a theme of tolerance, with many episodes that poke fun at narrow nationalism and ethnocentrism." Nevertheless, Professor Nye quotes Baum as having a desire to write stories that would "bear the stamp of our times and depict the progressive fairies of today."[13]

The Wizard of Oz has neither the mature religious appeal of a *Pilgrim's Progress*, nor the philosophic depth of a *Candide*. Baum's most thoughtful devotees see in it only a warm, cleverly written fairy tale. Yet the original Oz book conceals an unsuspected depth, and it is the purpose of this study to demonstrate that Baum's immortal American fantasy encompasses more than heretofore believed. For Baum created a children's story with a symbolic allegory implicit within its story line and characterizations. The allegory always remains in a minor key, subordinated to the major theme and readily abandoned whenever it threatens to distort the appeal of the fantasy. But through it, in the form of a subtle parable, Baum delineated a midwesterner's vibrant and ironic portrait of this country as it entered the twentieth century.

We are introduced to both Dorothy and Kansas at the same time:

Dorothy lived in the midst of the great Kansas prairies, with Uncle Henry, who was a farmer, and Aunt Em, who was the farmer's wife. Their house was small, for the lumber to build it had to be carried by wagon many miles. There were four walls, a floor and a roof, which made one room; and this room contained a rusty-looking cooking stove, a cupboard for the dishes, a table, three or four chairs, and the beds. . . .

When Dorothy stood in the doorway and looked around, she could see nothing but the great gray prairie on every side. Not a tree nor a house broke the broad sweep of flat country that reached to the edge of the sky in all directions. The sun had baked the plowed land into a gray mass, with little cracks running through it. Even the grass was not green, for the sun had burned the tops of the long blades until they were the same gray color to be seen everywhere. Once the house had been painted, but the sun blistered the paint and the rains washed it away, and now the house was as dull and gray as everything else.

When Aunt Em came there to live she was a young, pretty wife. The sun and

---

12. See Richard Hofstadter's shattering essay on Bryan in *The American Political Tradition* (New York, 1960), pp. 186–205. See also Nye, *Politics*, pp. 121–122; Faulkner, *Reform*, pp. 272–275.

13. Gardner and Nye, *Wizard*, pp. 1, 30.

wind had changed her, too. They had taken the sparkle from her eyes and left them a sober gray; they had taken the red from her cheeks and lips, and they were gray also. She was thin and gaunt, and never smiled now. When Dorothy, who was an orphan, first came to her, Aunt Em had been so startled by the child's laughter that she would scream and press her hand upon her heart whenever Dorothy's merry voice reached her ears; and she still looked at the little girl with wonder that she could find anything to laugh at.

Uncle Henry never laughed. He worked hard from morning till night and did not know what joy was. He was gray also, from his long beard to his rough boots, and he looked stern and solemn, and rarely spoke.

It was Toto that made Dorothy laugh, and saved her from growing as gray as her other surroundings. Toto was not gray; he was a little black dog, with long silky hair and small black eyes that twinkled merrily on either side of his funny, wee nose. Toto played all day long, and Dorothy played with him, and loved him dearly.[14]

Hector St. John de Crèvecoeur would not have recognized Uncle Henry's farm; it is straight out of Hamlin Garland.[15] On it a deadly environment dominates everyone and everything except Dorothy and her pet. The setting is Old Testament and nature seems grayly impersonal and even angry. Yet it is a fearsome cyclone that lifts Dorothy and Toto in their house and deposits them "very gently—for a cyclone—in the midst of a country of marvelous beauty." We immediately sense the contrast between Oz and Kansas. Here there are "stately trees bearing rich and luscious fruits . . . gorgeous flowers . . . and birds with . . . brilliant plumage" sing in the trees. In Oz "a small brook rushing and sparkling along" murmurs "in a voice very grateful to a little girl who had lived so long on the dry, gray prairies" (p. 20).

Trouble intrudes. Dorothy's house has come down on the Wicked Witch of the East, killing her. Nature, by sheer accident, can provide benefits, for indirectly the cyclone has disposed of one of the two truly bad influences in the Land of Oz. Notice that evil ruled in both the East and the West; after Dorothy's coming it rules only in the West.

The Wicked Witch of the East had kept the little Munchkin people "in bondage for many years, making them slave for her night and day" (pp. 22–23). Just what this slavery entailed is not immediately clear, but Baum later gives us a specific example. The Tin Woodman, whom Dorothy meets on her way to the Emerald City, had been put under a spell by the Witch of the East. Once an independent and hardworking human being, the Woodman found that each time he swung his axe it

14. L. Frank Baum, *The Wonderful Wizard of Oz*, pp. 11–13. All quotations cited in the text are from the inexpensive but accurate Dover paperback edition (New York, 1960).

15. Henry Nash Smith says of Garland's works in the 1890s, "It had at last become possible to deal with the Western farmer in literature as a human being instead of seeing him through a veil of literary convention, class prejudice or social theory" (*Virgin Land*, p. 290).

chopped off a different part of his body. Knowing no other trade he "worked harder than ever," for luckily in Oz tinsmiths can repair such things. Soon the Woodman was all tin (p. 59). In this way eastern witch-craft dehumanized a simple laborer so that the faster and better he worked the more quickly he became a kind of machine. Here is a Populist view of evil eastern influences on honest labor which could hardly be more pointed.[16]

There is one thing seriously wrong with being made of tin; when it rains rust sets in. Tin Woodman had been standing in the same position for a year without moving before Dorothy came along and oiled his joints. The Tin Woodman's situation has an obvious parallel in the condition of many eastern workers after the depression of 1893.[17] While Tin Woodman is standing still, rusted, solid, he deludes himself into thinking he is no longer capable of that most human of sentiments, love. Hate does not fill the void, a constant lesson in the Oz books, and Tin Woodman feels that only a heart will make him sensitive again. So he accompanies Dorothy to see if the Wizard will give him one.

Oz itself is a magic oasis surrounded by impassable deserts, and the country is divided in a very orderly fashion. In the North and South the people are ruled by good witches, who are not quite as powerful as the wicked ones of the East and West. In the center of the land rises the magnificent Emerald City ruled by the Wizard of Oz, a successful hum-bug whom even the witches mistakenly feel "is more powerful than all the rest of us together" (p. 24). Despite these forces, the mark of good-ness, placed on Dorothy's forehead by the Witch of the North, serves as a protection for Dorothy throughout her travels. Goodness and inno-cence prevail even over the powers of evil and delusion in Oz. Perhaps it is this basic and beautiful optimism that makes Baum's tale so char-acteristically American—and midwestern.

Dorothy is Baum's Miss Everyman. She is one of us, levelheaded and human, and she has a real problem. Young readers can understand her quandary as readily as can adults. She is good, not precious, and she thinks quite naturally about others. For all of the attractions of Oz Doro-thy desires only to return to the gray plains and Aunt Em and Uncle Henry. She is directed toward the Emerald City by the good Witch of the North, since the Wizard will surely be able to solve the problem of the impassable deserts. Dorothy sets out on the Yellow Brick Road wearing

16. Hicks declares that from the start "The Alliance and Populist platforms championed boldly the cause of labor . . ." (*Revolt*, p. 324). See also Bryan's Labor Day speech, *Battle*, pp. 375–383.

17. Faulkner, *Reform*, pp. 142–143.

the Witch of the East's magic Silver Shoes. Silver Shoes walking on a golden road; henceforth Dorothy becomes the innocent agent of Baum's ironic view of the silver issue. Remember, neither Dorothy, nor the good Witch of the North, nor the Munchkins understand the power of these shoes. The allegory is abundantly clear. On the next to last page of the book Baum has Glinda, Witch of the South, tell Dorothy, "Your Silver Shoes will carry you over the desert. . . . If you had known their power you could have gone back to your Aunt Em the very first day you came to this country." Glinda explains, "All you have to do is to knock the heels together three times and command the shoes to carry you wherever you wish to go" (p. 257). William Jennings Bryan never outlined the advantages of the silver standard any more effectively.

Not understanding the magic of the Silver Shoes, Dorothy walks the mundane—and dangerous—Yellow Brick Road. The first person she meets is a Scarecrow. After escaping from his wooden perch, the Scarecrow displays a terrible sense of inferiority and self-doubt, for he has determined that he needs real brains to replace the common straw in his head. William Allen White wrote an article in 1896 entitled "What's the Matter With Kansas?" In it he accused Kansas farmers of ignorance, irrationality and general muddle-headedness. What's wrong with Kansas are the people, said Mr. White.[18] Baum's character seems to have read White's angry characterization. But Baum never takes White seriously and so the Scarecrow soon emerges as innately a very shrewd and very capable individual.

The Scarecrow and the Tin Woodman accompany Dorothy along the Yellow Brick Road, one seeking brains, the other a heart. They meet next the Cowardly Lion. As King of Beasts he explains, "I learned that if I roared very loudly every living thing was frightened and got out of my way." Born a coward, he sobs, "Whenever there is danger my heart begins to beat fast." "Perhaps you have heart disease," suggests Tin Woodman, who always worries about hearts. But the Lion desires only courage and so he joins the party to ask help from the Wizard (pp. 65–72).

The Lion represents Bryan himself. In the election of 1896 Bryan lost the vote of eastern labor, though he tried hard to gain their support. In Baum's story the Lion, on meeting the little group, "struck at the Tin Woodman with his sharp claws." But, to his surprise, "he could make no impression on the tin, although the Woodman fell over in the road and lay still." Baum here refers to the fact that in 1896 workers were

18. Richard Hofstadter (ed.), *Great Issues in American History* (New York, 1960), 2:147–153.

often pressured into voting for McKinley and gold by their employers.[19] Amazed, the Lion says, "he nearly blunted my claws," and he adds even more appropriately, "When they scratched against the tin it made a cold shiver run down my back" (pp. 67–68). The King of Beasts is not after all very cowardly, and Bryan, although a pacifist and an anti-imperialist in a time of national expansion, is not either.[20] The magic Silver Shoes belong to Dorothy, however. Silver's potent charm, which had come to mean so much to so many in the Midwest, could not be entrusted to a political symbol. Baum delivers Dorothy from the world of adventure and fantasy to the real world of heartbreak and desolation through the power of silver. It represents a real force in a land of illusion, and neither the Cowardly Lion nor Bryan truly needs or understands its use.

All together now the small party moves toward the Emerald City. Coxey's Army of tramps and indigents, marching to ask President Cleveland for work in 1894, appears no more naively innocent than this group of four characters going to see a humbug Wizard, to request favors that only the little girl among them deserves.

Those who enter the Emerald City must wear green glasses. Dorothy later discovers that the greenness of dresses and ribbons disappears on leaving, and everything becomes a bland white. Perhaps the magic of any city is thus self-imposed. But the Wizard dwells here and so the Emerald City represents the national capital. The Wizard, a little bumbling old man, hiding behind a facade of papier-mâché and noise, might be any president from Grant to McKinley. He comes straight from the fairgrounds in Omaha, Nebraska, and he symbolizes the American criterion for leadership—he is able to be everything to everybody.

As each of our heroes enters the throne room to ask a favor the Wizard assumes different shapes, representing different views toward national leadership. To Dorothy, he appears as an enormous head, "bigger than the head of the biggest giant." An apt image for a naive and innocent little citizen. To the Scarecrow he appears to be a lovely, gossamer fairy, a most appropriate form for an idealistic Kansas farmer. The Woodman sees a horrible beast, as would any exploited eastern laborer after the trouble of the 1890s. But the Cowardly Lion, like W. J. Bryan, sees a "Ball of Fire, so fierce and glowing he could scarcely bear to gaze upon it." Baum then provides an additional analogy, for when the Lion "tried to go nearer he singed his whiskers and he crept back tremblingly to a spot nearer the door" (p. 134).

19. Bryan, *Battle*, pp. 617–618. "During the campaign I ran across various evidences of coercion, direct and indirect." See Hicks, *Revolt*, p. 325, who notes that "For some reason labor remained singularly unimpressed" by Bryan. Faulkner finds overt pressure as well (*Reform* pp. 208–29).

20. Faulkner, *Reform*, pp. 257–258.

The Wizard has asked them all to kill the Witch of the West. The golden road does not go in that direction and so they must follow the sun, as have many pioneers in the past. The land they now pass through is "rougher and hillier, for there were no farms nor houses in the country of the West and the ground was untilled" (p. 140). The Witch of the West uses natural forces to achieve her ends; she is Baum's version of sentient and malign nature.

Finding Dorothy and her friends in the West, the Witch sends forty wolves against them, then forty vicious crows, and finally a great swarm of black bees. But it is through the power of a magic golden cap that she summons the flying monkeys. They capture the little girl and dispose of her companions. Baum makes these Winged Monkeys into an Oz substitute for the plains Indians. Their leader says, "Once . . . we were a free people, living happily in the great forest, flying from tree to tree, eating nuts and fruit, and doing just as we pleased without calling anybody master." "This," he explains, "was many years ago, long before Oz came out of the clouds to rule over this land" (p. 172). But like many Indian tribes Baum's monkeys are not inherently bad; their actions depend wholly upon the bidding of others. Under the control of an evil influence, they do evil. Under the control of goodness and innocence, as personified by Dorothy, the monkeys are helpful and kind, although unable to take her to Kansas. Says the Monkey King, "We belong to this country alone, and cannot leave it" (p. 213). The same could be said with equal truth of the first Americans.

Dorothy presents a special problem to the Witch. Seeing the mark on Dorothy's forehead and the Silver Shoes on her feet, the Witch begins "to tremble with fear, for she knew what a powerful charm belonged to them." Then "she happened to look into the child's eyes and saw how simple the soul behind them was, and that the little girl did not know of the wonderful power the Silver Shoes gave her" (p. 150). Here Baum again uses the silver allegory to state the blunt homily that while goodness affords a people ultimate protection against evil, ignorance of their capabilities allows evil to impose itself upon them. The Witch assumes the proportions of a kind of western Mark Hanna or Banker Boss, who, through natural malevolence, manipulates the people and holds them prisoner by cynically taking advantage of their innate innocence.

Enslaved in the West, "Dorothy went to work meekly, with her mind made up to work as hard as she could; for she was glad the Wicked Witch had decided not to kill her" (p. 150). Many western farmers have held these same grim thoughts in less mystical terms. If the Witch of the West is a diabolical force of Darwinian or Spencerian nature, then another contravening force may be counted upon to dispose of her.

Dorothy destroys the evil Witch by angrily dousing her with a bucket of water. Water, that precious commodity which the drought-ridden farmers on the great plains needed so badly, and which if correctly used could create an agricultural paradise, or at least dissolve a wicked witch. Plain water brings an end to malign nature in the West.

When Dorothy and her companions return to the Emerald City they soon discover that the Wizard is really nothing more than "a little, old man, with a bald head and a wrinkled face." Can this be the ruler of the land?

Our friends looked at him in surprise and dismay.

"I thought Oz was a great Head," said Dorothy. . . . "And I thought Oz was a terrible Beast," said the Tin Woodman. "And I thought Oz was a Ball of Fire," exclaimed the Lion. "No; you are all wrong," said the little man meekly. "I have been making believe."

Dorothy asks if he is truly a great Wizard. He confides, "Not a bit of it, my dear; I'm just a common man." Scarecrow adds, "You're more than that . . . you're a humbug" (p. 184).

The Wizard's deception is of long standing in Oz and even the Witches were taken in. How was it accomplished? "It was a great mistake my ever letting you into the Throne Room," the Wizard complains. "Usually I will not see even my subjects, and so they believe I am something terrible" (p. 185). What a wonderful lesson for youngsters of the decade when Benjamin Harrison, Grover Cleveland, and William McKinley were hiding in the White House. Formerly the Wizard was a mimic, a ventriloquist, and a circus balloonist. The latter trade involved going "up in a balloon on circus day, so as to draw a crowd of people together and get them to pay to see the circus" (pp. 186–87). Such skills are as admirably adapted to success in late-nineteenth-century politics as they are to the humbug wizardry of Baum's story. A pointed comment on midwestern political ideals is the fact that our little Wizard comes from Omaha, Nebraska, a center of Populist agitation.[21] "Why that isn't very far from Kansas," cries Dorothy. Nor, indeed, are any of the characters in the wonderful land of Oz.

The Wizard, of course, can provide the objects of self-delusion desired by Tin Woodman, Scarecrow, and Lion. But Dorothy's hope of going home fades when the Wizard's balloon leaves too soon. Understand

21. Professor Nye observes that during 1890 (while Baum was editing his Aberdeen weekly) the Nebraska Farmers' Alliance "launched the wildest campaign in Nebraska history" (*Politics*, pp. 64–65). Bryan was a senator from Nebraska and it was in Omaha that the Populist party ratified its platform on July 4, 1892. See Henry Steele Commager (ed.), *Documents of American History* (New York, 1958), 2:143–146.

this: Dorothy wishes to leave a green and fabulous land, from which all evil has disappeared, to go back to the gray desolation of the Kansas prairies. Dorothy is an orphan; Aunt Em and Uncle Henry are her only family. Reality is never far from Dorothy's consciousness and in the most heartrending terms she explains her reasoning to the good Witch Glinda,

Aunt Em will surely think something dreadful has happened to me, and that will make her put on mourning; and unless the crops are better this year than they were last I am sure Uncle Henry cannot afford it [p. 254].

The Silver Shoes furnish Dorothy with a magic means of travel. But when she arrives back in Kansas she finds, "The Silver Shoes had fallen off in her flight through the air, and were lost forever in the desert" (p. 259). Were the "her" to refer to America in 1900, Baum's statement could hardly be contradicted.

Current historiography tends to criticize the Populist movement for its "delusions, myths, and foibles," Professor C. Vann Woodward observed recently.[22] Yet *The Wonderful Wizard of Oz* has provided unknowing generations with a gentle and friendly midwestern critique of the Populist rationale on these very same grounds. Led by naive innocence and protected by goodwill, the farmer, the laborer, and the politician approach the mystic holder of national power to ask for personal fulfillment. Their desires, as well as the Wizard's cleverness in answering them, are all self-delusion. Each of these characters carries within him the solution to his own problem, were he only to view himself objectively. The fearsome Wizard turns out to be nothing more than a common man, capable of shrewd but mundane answers to these self-induced needs. Like any good politican he gives the people what they want. Throughout the story Baum poses a central thought; the American desire for symbols of fulfillment is illusory. Real needs lie elsewhere.

Thus the Wizard cannot help Dorothy, for of all the characters only she has a wish that is selfless, and only she has a direct connection to honest, hopeless human beings. Dorothy supplies real fulfillment when she returns to her aunt and uncle, using the Silver Shoes, and cures some of their misery and heartache. In this way Baum tells us that the silver crusade at least brought back Dorothy's lovely spirit to the disconsolate plains farmer. Her laughter, love, and goodwill are no small addition to that gray land, although the magic of silver has been lost forever as a result.

22. C. Vann Woodward, "Our Past Isn't What It Used To Be," *The New York Times Book Review* (July 28, 1963), p. 1; Hofstadter, *Tradition,* pp. 186–205.

Noteworthy too is Baum's prophetic placement of leadership in Oz after Dorothy's departure. The Scarecrow reigns over the Emerald City, the Tin Woodman rules in the West, and the Lion protects smaller beasts in "a grand old forest." Thereby farm interests achieve national importance, industrialism moves West, and Bryan commands only a forest full of lesser politicians.

Baum's fantasy succeeds in bridging the gap between what children want and what they should have. It is an admirable example of the way in which an imaginative writer can teach goodness and morality without producing the almost inevitable side effect of nausea. Today's children's books are either saccharine and empty, or boring and pedantic. Baum's first Oz tale—and those which succeed it—are immortal not so much because the "heart-aches and nightmares are left out" as that "the wonderment and joy" are retained (p. 1).

Baum declares, "The story of 'The Wonderful Wizard of Oz' was written solely to pleasure children of today" (p. 1). In 1963 there are very few children who have never heard of the Scarecrow, the Tin Woodman, or the Cowardly Lion, and whether they know W. W. Denslow's original illustrations of Dorothy, or Judy Garland's whimsical characterization, is immaterial. *The Wizard* has become a genuine piece of American folklore because, knowing his audience, Baum never allowed the consistency of the allegory to take precedence over the theme of youthful entertainment. Yet once discovered, the author's allegorical intent seems clear, and it gives depth and lasting interest even to children who only sense something else beneath the surface of the story. Consider the fun in picturing turn-of-the-century America, a difficult era at best, using these ready-made symbols provided by Baum. The relationships and analogies outlined above are admittedly theoretical, but they are far too consistent to be coincidental, and they furnish a teaching mechanism which is guaranteed to reach any level of student.

The Wizard of Oz says so much about so many things that it is hard not to imagine a satisfied and mischievous gleam in Lyman Frank Baum's eye as he had Dorothy say, "And oh, Aunt Em! I'm so glad to be at home again!"

Afternote

Following the publication of this article a number of letters pointed out the interesting compositon of southern Oz. The writers claim that brittle little people made of Dresden china, bogs, marshes, brooding monster-ridden forests, hammer-headed folk who prey on travelers in the hills, combined with the rich, red Quadling farm country, render that part of Oz a Tennessee Williams treasury of social and geographic stereotypes. Perhaps and perhaps not; I'm unconvinced. However, all correspondents agree that students thoroughly enjoy following and adding to this blueprint left us by L. Frank Baum.

Because so many of his children's stories contain strong social commentary, they remain interesting to a variety of readers. I look forward to the time when major libraries will accept Baum as the genuine and subtle craftsman he was.

The Oddness of Oz

· by Osmond Beckwith ·

Twenty Years After

In 1950, a father wanting to read to a young daughter, I bought with other "children's classics" *The Wonderful Wizard of Oz* by L. Frank Baum. Later, drawn by curiosity, I also bought most of the remaining Oz titles by Baum (for this series so popular with children had not been allowed to die with the author's death in 1919). In my own childhood I had known Baum only from his *Ozma of Oz*, a book I seem to remember having found in our school library: odd if true, for schools consistently denied shelf space to Oz as to most ephemeral or "fad" books which children read to the exclusion of anything else.

In my fatherly reading and rereading I discovered—if what seemed so obvious could be a discovery—the material for an article on the unconscious in children's literature like that of an earlier study by an English novelist on *Elsie Dinsmore*. (If now known only to specialists, in their day the "Elsie books" were a juvenile series as frantically popular and endlessly extended as Oz. Of all such series, Oz seems the only one to please successive younger generations.)

I researched Baum in the New York Public Library, discovering nothing about Oz of the kind I feared; more oddly, since Dorothy, the Scarecrow, the Tin Woodman, and the Cowardly Lion were apparently firmly fixed in American public imagination, almost nothing in print about their creator. Of the few brief adult Oz-appreciations then extant, the best and longest—itself brief enough—was still the earliest,

Reprinted from *Children's Literature*, Vol. 5. Philadelphia: Temple University Press, 1976, pp. 74–91. Copyright © 1976 by Francelia Butler. Reprinted by permission of Francelia Butler.

that of American editor and anthologist Edward Wagenknecht in a 1929 chapbook.

I intended my Baum article for *Neurotica* (1948–1951), a little magazine edited by G. Legman, author also of the magazine's most sensational and influential article, "The Psychopathology of the Comics," also in its way a study of children's literature. It was Legman who made the rather mortifying suggestion that my interest in Baum was a name-fatality: "Oz," that is, because of Osmond or "Ozzie." (For whatever such name-fatalities may be worth, my daughter's as well is a variant of Dorothy.)

Later Legman told me, "If you're going to write about Baum there's a man you ought to meet." And so to Oz I owe my introduction to Martin Gardner, who needs no introduction as a writer and critic of children's literature. Among his numerous avocations at that time, he was, I think, contributing editor of *Humpty Dumpty Magazine.*

My Baum knowledge shrank when faced with Martin Gardner's, his collection of Oziana and rarer Baum titles, his friendships and correspondence with other Oz-buffs. Martin prophesied truly that the forthcoming expiration of the *Wonderful Wizard's* copyright (in 1956) would spark new interest in Baum. In anticipation he was then trying to place his own Baum-biography, "The Royal Historian of Oz," with a large-circulation magazine such as the *Ladies' Home Journal.* He showed me the manuscript, which I examined nervously, expecting on every page to find myself anticipated. But to my relief it was straightforward biography in his usual lucid style.

In turn I showed my manuscript, which Mrs. Gardner began reading. Then and later its first two sentences ran: *"The Wonderful Wizard of Oz,* America's most popular juvenile fantasy, originally appeared in 1900, a little more than ten years after the death of Louisa May Alcott. Like Miss Alcott, Oz-author L. Frank Baum made his appeal especially to young girls." At which point Mrs. Gardner stopped reading and demanded immediately, "Martin, is that true?" "I'm afraid it is," he replied. In our subsequent discussion I don't remember that we read any more of my manuscript.

Time passed. "The Royal Historian" did not appear in a magazine of large circulation, but in two 1955 issues of the *Magazine of Fantasy & Science Fiction. Neurotica* was long defunct before I finished the thirty-second revision (a conservative estimate) of my article. That saw print finally (1961) in *Kulchur,* another little magazine, as "The Oddness of Oz."

Twenty years later Baum needs much less introduction than my article gave him. Beside Martin Gardner's, he has been the subject of another full-length biography and several respectful critical articles, while the *Wonderful Wizard* has reached publishing apotheosis in a 1973 coffee-table-sized *annotated* edition. Yet it is still questionable whether all this later research has better answered my article's theme-question: What made (makes) Oz so popular?

Explanations of Oz's vitality are generally in terms of the books' "native" or "indigenous" subject matter—which is merely to repeat Edward Wagenknecht's earlier definition of Oz as "the first distinctive attempt to construct a fairyland out of American materials." Wagenknecht had even insisted that only an American—in a country overrun with mechanical influences—could have conceived the robots and automata which are so characteristic a part of Ozian fantasy.

Creating robots and automata would seem automatically to place Baum as a forerunner in the United States' growing concern with science-fiction and scientific fantasy (a concern as great today as twenty years ago). Yet, to an unprejudiced adult, rereading the Oz books will disclose little likeness to modern science-fiction. Rather the resemblance is to those English Christmas pantomimes in which the role of "principal boy" is traditionally played by a girl (in Oz, however, the principal boy always wears skirts). The question of the indigenous quality of the books deserves to be taken up in more detail.

The Oddness of Oz

There are strong similarities between *The Wonderful Wizard of Oz*, the prototype of the series, and another more universally acknowledged children's classic: Lewis Carroll's *Alice in Wonderland* (published in 1865, when Baum was nine).

Both *Alice* and *The Wonderful Wizard* are fables of innocence and experience. Both have as "hero" a little girl. Both are packed as full as puddings of unconscious distortions and symbolizations. The differences between them, including basic differences in literary ability, are biographical or, if you like, indigenous.

Carroll's Alice drops down the rabbit hole unharmed and unharming; she even replaces the crockery examined on her way, so as not to hurt anybody, but Baum's Dorothy enters Oz with a death, her cyclone-carried house killing an old woman. Though an atmosphere of delicacy, of social contretemps, embarrassing situations, tiffs, and misunderstandings accompanies Alice throughout her long dream—which is always identified as a dream—the only situation that seems likely to become serious is ended by her awakening. It is quite different with Dorothy. Her adventures not only include attacks by mythical beasts but by lions, wolves, bees, monkeys, and creatures who snap their heads like hammers. She is overcome by poison gas, and almost by chapter threatened with death in various forms.

The motivating force in both books is a search, but while Alice looks for the lovely garden she has glimpsed in her first hour in Wonderland, Dorothy, surrounded by all the beauty of a fairy kingdom, only wants to go home. Alice travels alone; Dorothy makes friends, but what sort of friends?—a straw-stuffed scarecrow, a woodchopper who having chopped himself to bits is now completely artificial, and a lion afraid of his own roar (three different ways of writing eunuch). Searching for the wonderful wizard who is to heal them, and give each his heart's desire, the friends reach the Emerald City of Oz, but must be blinkered in order to enter. Aloof and terrifying, the Wizard refuses his help unless Dorothy kills off still another old woman, the powerful witch of whom he lives in constant fear. In attempting this exploit, the Scarecrow is eviscerated, the Tin Man scrapped, the Lion captured, and the girl enslaved.

Carroll tells his tale by puns, parodies, and witty transubstantiations of harsh reality. The word "death," if I am not mistaken, occurs only once in his entire book. But Baum's approach throughout is literal and matter-of-fact. He doesn't suggest that his horrors might not exist; he spares no detail to increase their vividness. The climactic episode of the book is Dorothy's "melting" of the Wicked Witch, who, in Baum's words, "fell down in a brown, melted, shapeless mass and began to spread over the clean boards of the kitchen floor. Seeing that she had really melted away to nothing, Dorothy drew another bucket of water and threw it over the mess. She then swept it all out the door."

The story resumes as Dorothy's revivified friends return to claim the Wizard's promise. But the Wizard proves a fraud, an old balloon-ascensionist in Oz by accident, like Dorothy. For the three citizens of fairyland he is able to improvise placebos, not for the human being. He constructs a balloon, but bungles the take-off and leaves Dorothy behind, so the travelers renew their journey, this time to the palace of Glinda the Good Witch of the South, eternally young and beautiful. From her Dorothy learns that a pair of magic slippers—loot of that first accident with the cyclone—has been on her feet all the time. She wishes herself home, following a distribution of thrones: to the Scarecrow the missing Wizard's, to the Tin Woodman the melted Witch's, and to the Lion (who in a side excursion has knocked off the technical claimant) that of Beasts.

The Marvelous Land of Oz, Baum's second Oz book, offers no points of comparison with Carroll's sequel but is a fable of sex warfare, in which a palace revolt led by a strong-minded girl calling herself General Jinjur unseats King Scarecrow. It is more than a revolt, it is a revolution. As a "sad-looking man with a bushy beard, who wore an apron and was wheeling a baby-carriage," informs the Scarecrow: "Since you went away the women have been running things to suit themselves. I'm glad you have decided to come back and restore order, for doing housework and minding the children is wearing out the strength of every man in the Emerald City."

Most of the book's action is taken up, not so much by the Scarecrow's efforts to regain the throne as by his difficulties, aided by the Tin Woodman and other newly introduced manikins, in keeping out of harm's way. Tip, a boy brought up by the old witch Mombi, is the creator, thanks to the old woman's Powder of Life, of such contraptions as Jack Pumpkinhead, the Saw-Horse, and the "Gump." The Woggle-Bug, a ridiculous pedant, completes the party. These half-crippled makeshifts stumble through a series of flights and escapes, appealing finally to Glinda. The sorceress has her own army of young girls, which recaptures Oz and throws Jinjur into chains. Glinda overpowers the hag Mombi, who admits that the real heir to the throne of Oz, the missing princess Ozma, was committed to her care years ago and transformed by her *into a boy!* (italics in the original). All eyes turn to the boy Tip. Glinda orders Mombi to reverse her incantations, with this result:

From the couch arose the form of a young girl, fresh and beautiful as a May morning. . . . [She] cast one look into Glinda's bright face, which glowed with pleasure and satisfaction, and then turned upon the others. Speaking the words with sweet diffidence, she said:
"I hope none of you will care less for me than you did before. I'm just the same Tip, you know; only—only—"
"Only you're different!" said the Pumpkinhead; and everyone thought it was the wisest speech he had ever made.

Ozma of Oz, third in the series, reintroduces Dorothy, washed ashore in a floating chicken coop with a talking yellow hen, on the beach of the land of Ev (perhaps Eve?). The hen insists her name is Bill, though Dorothy prefers to call her Billina. Ev turns out to be the familiar Baum matriarchal fairyland, its temporary ruler the Princess Langwidere, who has thirty different heads, one for each day of the month.

Ev's late king has sold his wife and children to the Nome King before committing suicide. Dorothy rescues his faithful servant, Tik-Tok; he (Baum's automatons are always male) rescues her from the terrifying Wheelers, although his clockwork fails when it is a question of braving Langwidere, who has insisted on an exchange of heads with Dorothy.

Coming to rescue the Queen of Ev, Ozma with her army of twenty-six officers and one private (this is not an efficient girl-army like Glinda's or Jinjur's) crosses the burning desert which separates Ev from Oz. Dorothy and Ozma love each other immediately. Dorothy frees Billina from Langwidere's hen-yard after watching her lick the rooster.

Ozma's expedition enters the underground Nome Kingdom by passing between the legs of a mechanical colossus. The Nome King, a fat and smiling villain, has transformed the Evians into bric-a-brac which he invites the Ozians to identify; if they guess wrong they become bric-a-brac themselves. All fail except Dorothy, until Billina, nesting under the throne, overhears the King's secret codes and disenchants everyone. The King summons his army, but, blinded and poisoned by two of Billina's eggs smashed in his face, he is unable to prevent the theft of his magic belt and the loss of all his prisoners.

The fourth book is the first to introduce a boy—that is, a boy who stays boy. Whether or not he is responsible, *Dorothy and the Wizard in Oz* is one of the most gloomy and depressing of the series. Most of the action takes place underground, and a steady succession of horrible characterizations expresses the most implacable hatred of anything fertile or human.

Dorothy and her companion Zeb (for which read Zed) are dropped by an earthquake into the kingdom of the Mangaboos (three syllables of fright, disgust, and horror), who are vegetables, reproducing asexually from a parent tree. The Wizard appears and slices up the Mangaboos' magician for disputing authority with him. Dorothy picks the Mangaboo Princess to restore, as usual, woman's rule.

This princess not remaining friendly, the earth people with their cat and horse are driven into the Black Pit. Beyond, in open country, they meet a normal family of two children with father and mother, but *invisible:* seemingly endurable in this form. They have a bloody encounter with invisible Bears, and take to the hole in the mountain again. Passing the Braided Man, who sells an appropriate brand of Baum comic-relief, they climb to the land of the Wooden Gargoyles. Earth, grass, leaves are wooden; nothing grows or flows; and the Wooden Gargoyles never speak; they hate sound. Inevitably the earth people are captured, and escape death only by stealing the Gargoyles' detachable wings. After touching a match to this firetrap, they plunge into another hole in the mountain, which seems, like Dante's Malebolge, to grow up through the middle of the earth.

Again they fall into a worse danger, the den of the Dragonettes. Since the half-grown monsters cannot eat them, having been secured by a careful mother before going out on her hunting, they engage in a "whimsical" conversation parodying the reactions of well-educated and dutiful children of a mother who happens to be a dragon.

Rescued through Ozma's magic intervention, the party is transported to Oz, and the remainder of the book is devoted to the humiliation of Jim, the flesh-and-blood Cab-Horse, by the mechanical Saw-Horse: and a trial for murder of Eureka, the cat, whose continual threats to eat one of the Wizard's pet piglets have furnished a cannibalistic commentary to the action.

These first four books contain the meat of Baum's message. The later stories merely dilute and conventionalize this strong original flavor.

In these books Baum has found a surprising number of ways to vary his message; or, as a psychoanalyst might say, his neurosis has found a variety of outlets. In the analyst's terminology again, everything is "over-determined." Nothing is ever simply demonstrated once.

Very particularly in *The Wonderful Wizard of Oz*, the most artistic as it is the most honest of the series—for only there are we occasionally allowed to glimpse the pathos of his condition—has Baum set out, almost as a real artist might, to personalize all his anxieties.

He is by autobiographical definition Dorothy, an innocent child, who through no fault of her own (but very luckily, nevertheless) kills her mother as she is born. It is all for the best, everyone assures her, but still she is guiltily anxious to get out of a world where such things happen. She goes to look for her father, who can, perhaps *send her back.* Her innocence is complemented and balanced by the innocence of the Scarecrow (Baum again), who has just been born and is therefore of the same age as Dorothy. A love affair is indicated, and of course Dorothy does love the Scarecrow best of all, but after all he is only a man stuffed with straw, an intellectual who only wants brains. As might be expected, the Scarecrow is never of any use to Dorothy in physical difficulties: he gives good advice, but is always getting knocked over or punched flat when the fighting begins. So the Woodchopper is required. He has *once* been a real man who has loved a woman, but an older woman has been jealous—not of him but of his beloved who lives with her, in just what relationship is not explained—and by magic the Woodchopper's axe has repeatedly slipped until he is cut to pieces, a friendly tinsmith supplying prostheses. The Woodman still loves until his heart is cut through; but then he ceases to love. He means to ask Oz for a heart and afterward to return and ask the girl to marry him, when he can love her again. (He forgets all about this, incidentally, after he gets the heart, but maybe that is because it is really a heart that Oz gives him. The Woodman is a very delicate person and would be unlikely to call things by their proper names.)

There is a great deal of fine characterization in the Woodman, who of course is Baum again at a more advanced stage. He is depressed, weeps easily, avoids stepping on insects and hurting people's feelings, and is pathetically grateful for Dorothy's ministrations. He is of tin—the ridiculous metal. The terrible "chopper who chops off your head" is armed with a gleaming axe which he uses for nothing except to cut down trees (until later—Baum's characterizations do not hold very long). He is a nightmare deglamorized. All good so far.

The Lion is Baum again in man's conventional sexual role. What is the point of being king of beasts, he seems to be saying, and come roaring out of the forest, if I am full of inward doubts and fears and can be stopped by a slap on the nose? What is the use of a thick beard and big teeth and loud voice, if they cannot even get me a mate (as they apparently have not)? Better if I turned into a little dog and ran at the girl's heels—because that's what I want to do, if the truth were known. And so another nightmare is tamed.

It should not pass unnoticed that Baum, while satisfying himself, has also satisfied the canons of conventional romance by surrounding his heroine not only with protectors but with guardians. What was usually accomplished by relationship or senescence—and the nineteenth century made great play with uncles and grandfathers—he accomplishes by emasculation, not only once but three times.

However, the attitude so far (and Baum is one-third through his book) is not unhealthy. Three objects of greater fear to a child than a Lion, a Scarecrow, and a Chopper (who is also a Cripple) could not easily be named, and yet Baum has kept them all gentle and touching. He has pumped them full of himself, and since he is a harmless and pathetic fellow, he is saying in substance to the child, "And so are your fears!"

But he has gone as far as he can go on that line. Ten pages after the fake-Lion he introduces the Kalidahs, terrifying invented animals. The childish reader invariably trembles at this point, puzzling the adult, to whom the Kalidahs do not seem that terrible. But the child is right. There are other terrors in the world, then, besides "men," he feels; the Kalidahs are *real*. They are all the more real because they are made up. There is no chance of their ever turning back into Daddy. We are in the world of nightmare, of fever dreams, where a pet grows the "body of a bear and the head of a tiger."

Baum is now definitely committed to a tale of adventure, and little more healthy can occur. The Emerald City ought by right to be a vast fake, since its people are compelled to wear green glasses, but actually it is a fake-fake and the emeralds are real. The Wizard plays out all over again the Baum "appearances": he is a Head, a beautiful Lady, and a horrible Beast. His ultimate exposure is long deferred. For the story he is a father-figure, who instead of being tender or loving, or even weak and pathetic, is suspicious and implacable. Instead of consoling and comforting his daughter, he ridicules her fears, and tells her she can only win his love by killing again. Even in the conventional story-book sense the Wizard is a horrible man. He insists that the witch is evil, but admits she has never harmed him; it is only because she *might* that he wishes Dorothy to kill her; he is too cowardly to do so himself. He is Baal or Moloch, immolating children to placate the elements; and this aspect of his character is suggested by his fourth appearance, as a flaming ball of fire.

No one could ever possibly like the Wizard after this self-indictment; and yet his subsequent devaluation is only used to humanize him, even to justify him: fear makes us do anything! "I think you are a very bad man," Dorothy says. "Oh, no, my dear," he replies, safely complaisant now that his archenemy is liquidated, "I'm really a very good man; but I'm a very bad Wizard, I must admit." Dorothy is not quite reassured. When he satisfies her friends, however (which is not very hard to do), she allows herself to be appeased. Poor Dorothy! Her history is that of a gradual reconciliation.

Glinda, the Good Witch, must not be taken as a mother-symbol. The mothers are all ugly old women, who get it in the neck deservedly. Glinda is eternally young and eternally beautiful. She has never married; she could hardly be a mother! Glinda, in boarding-school terminology, is Dorothy's *ideal*. There is no man good enough for her. To emphasize this point, a long story is told about an earlier sorceress, possibly one of Glinda's remote ancestresses, and her difficulties in choosing a husband. True love, in Oz, is love between girls, when one is a little older than the other, innocent, sterile, and uncompetitive. Glinda thinks only of what Dorothy wants. She puts only one kiss on her forehead. She assists Dorothy's friends, who in her presence uneasily remember their rags, their scars, their crude beastliness. Kindliness repays adoration, for Glinda. The sixth form puts the third form on to the ropes, and all ends happily at Prize-Day.

Oz revenges as many old injuries as it invents fantastic fulfillments: the chief resentment apparently, next to having been brought into the world in the wrong form, is for having been brought into the world at all. Though "mothers" are worse than "fathers" in the Oz world, both are preferably extinct altogether. In no other American children's books, even Horatio Alger's, do there seem to be so many orphans. No human Oz-star in our four-book canon ever has both parents at once. Only the supers have a normal and usually comic family life. The animals fare no better: there are no records of the parentage of the Cowardly Lion, the Hungry Tiger, or Jim the Cab-Horse. Eureka the cat is a foundling. Billina is presumably immaculately hatched and brought up by a farmer boy who (to make the double point) never knew until too late whether she was a hen or a rooster. But the horrible Dragonettes have a horrible mother.

Baum's fondness for automata and magically created beings can be safely attributed to this same rejection or exclusion of natural begetting. Only the Tin Woodman, whom we already know to be the most honest and touching of the Ozian creatures, is allowed mention of a real father and mother, though both are long dead. The Scarecrow is the contrivance of two farmers (male), and Tik-Tok the invention of two inventors (male). Tip by himself, while still male, gives life to the Gump and the Saw-Horse, but these are very lumpish productions, almost stillbirths; it would seem, in Oz as in the real world, that two progenitors are really necessary. Mombi and Tip's creation of Jack Pumpkinhead seems to be an uglified travesty of birth (as Tip's later transformation is a sweetened travesty of emasculation). After the boy has laboriously worked to make his man, the old woman comes along and sprinkles it with the powder of life, quickening it for her own nefarious purposes. And even this powder she had originally stolen from a male magician. The solemn Jack Pumpkinhead insists on addressing Tip as "Father"; and since Tip is a little boy who is really a little girl, the confusions and insults appear deliberately multiplied.

The drama of decapitation (in the psychoanalytic vocabulary, decapitation and castration are synonymous) is played over and over and again as entr'acte. The Tin Woodman, who has once chopped off his own head, chops off the head of a hunting Wildcat. Oz first appears as an enormous Head, hairless, armless, and legless. The Lion kills his opponent, the spider-monster, by striking off its head. The Scarecrow twists the necks of the Crows. The Scarecrow's head is also removable (he tells Oz: "You are quite welcome to take my head off, as long as it will be a better one when you put it on again"); and this is only one of a selection of demountable, retractable, and replaceable heads that culminate in Langwidere's gallery of thirty. The Hammer-Heads use their heads like battering rams; the Scoodlers use theirs as missiles. The Gump is all head. Jack Pumpkinhead deserves his name: he is in continual fear lest his head rot off. And so on. The conversations about decapitation recall that other humorous work, *The Mikado*.

Billina the hen is Oz's final topsy-turvy insult to injury. On the surface a "sensible" young female, she will have nothing to do with love, which like the suffragettes of Jinjur's army she sees only as mas-culine presumption ("Do you think I'd let that speckled villain of a rooster lord it over *me!*"). She lays eggs and has, apparently, hatched them, but she never mentions the offspring of this incubation; the barnyard role of the mother-hen is not for her. She speaks of "thirteen" as a suitable clutch to illustrate, presumably, her real feelings about this unlucky necessity. Laying to her is a sanitary habit ("I feel better since I laid my morning egg"), and she is only concerned with the freshness (infertility) of her product. She connives in the use of her eggs as poisonous weapons, in fact suggests it. Though she frees the Queen-mother of Ev and her children, it is not out of maternal concern; she derides the Queen's anxiety and tells her sarcastically, "Don't worry. Just at present they [the lifeless children] are out of mischief and per-fectly safe, for they can't even wiggle. Come with me, if you please, and I'll show you how pretty they look." Billana's reward, "a beautiful necklace of pearls and sapphires," is, like Ozma's new clothes, the typical material reward of the spoilt-child gold-digger—and should be contrasted with the merely appetitive fudge and chocolates awarded Jinjur and her suffragettes.

Sociologically viewed, the Oz myth as Baum created it can be con-sidered a vast transvaluation of juvenile romantic values. Boys' adven-tures become girls' adventures; girls' humiliations become boys' humil-iations; boys' affairs with older boys become girls' affairs with older girls; and the mother is the villain instead of the father. It is a transval-uation because the values remain the same: traveling, fighting, and killing achieve the rewards, and the punishments are subordination and domesticity. (It should be remembered that the Wicked Witch "tor-tures" Dorothy by making her do housework!) The arena is no longer the social one of Louisa May Alcott but the transvestite one of a boy-turned-girl. Baum has kissed his elbow; Tip has put on women's clothes; but it is only to breed more girls-turned-boys. (In this connec-tion it may not be insignificant to note that the *L.* in L. Frank Baum stood for "Lyman.") A determination to expunge the "man" from his name might seem to explain this amputation of his signature, so impor-tant to a writer. But both his name's syllables would have quickly grown hateful to a young fantasist continually addressed as "LIE MAN!"

Baum's frantic popularity with young girl readers really requires no further explanation. This audience, if not completely understanding, could appreciate his idolization of an immature and impubescent femi-ninity. The combination of innocence with authority that produced all these girlish brows wrinkling over problems of finance and policy, these girlish arms driving chariots of state or extended imperiously, these girlish feet in the silver of safety or the satin of luxury, had the attraction, to them, of a mirror of Narcissus.

What young boy readers saw in Oz is not so clear, though clearly it was not the image of themselves they found in boys' books. But the boys Oz did strike were struck deep (all or most of the adults who find Oz unforgettable seem to be men). In psychoanalytic language, the boyish girls of Oz are *phallic,* and thus deeply reassuring to boys (or men) with castration anxieties. The reassurance is against their unconscious fear that girlish girls are what they seem to be, castrated boys.

Coda

Apart from Oz, many of Baum's other fantasies offer examples of his obsession for those who care to look. Even *Father Goose, His Book* (of which more later), Baum's first big "hit" as a children's author, has a title whose obvious commercial transposition (a father goose is a gander) also hints at a transposition of traditional authority-roles. *The Enchanted Island of Yew* (published a year before *The Marvelous Land of Oz*) has a fairy heroine who—reversing Tip's sex-change—becomes a knight. The idea of ambivalent (interchangeable) sex is further emphasized in that book by the chapter on Twi land, where everything exists in double form. *John Dough and the Cherub* was Baum's try at purely equivocal sex: Chick the Cherub is an incubator baby, and his or her sex is never disclosed. The "Trot" books, *The Sea Fairies* and *Sky Island* (which Baum hoped would replace Oz), star another boyish little girl and her crippled (one-legged) male companion, with more queens and feminine warfare.

Of all Baum's unconscious embodiments, in or out of Oz, Billina the hen must be the one based on actual experience. Baum had begun breeding and raising chickens in adolescence, a hobby—his family was wealthy—he still took seriously enough at the age of thirty to treat technically in his first published book, *The Book of the Hamburgs.* The previous portrait of Billina is too brief, chiefly because psychoanalytically she is an embarrassment of riches. Almost everything she does cries out for interpretation.

Note that Billina comes to her audience already equipped with the fascination young children find in domestic fowl such as chickens (or geese). They lay eggs, and from these fascinating eggs hatch apparently sexless, or sexually identical, babies. With admirable simplicity, as children see it, both eggs and droppings emerge from the mother fowl's single body opening or *cloaca.* Kept ignorant of the reproductive pur-

pose of the second female opening in humans, young children com-
monly surmise that they too were born through the human *cloaca* or
anus, like eggs. This belief is forgotten or repressed with growing
knowledge but retains much unconscious strength.

Poultry-breeders must also consciously recognize—what many adult
human males often resist recognizing—that male fowl do the work of
fatherhood without a penis or intromittent organ. This characteristic in
itself could explain young Baum's engrossing interest in chickens as
well as his later overdetermination, after the success of *Father Goose,
His Book*, to decorate his newly purchased house everywhere, on porch,
walls, furniture, even to the extent of a specially made stained-glass
living room window, with pictured geese.

Throughout the book which should be named after her, Billina is
characterized by her regular laying. She is indifferently casual about the
results, inviting Dorothy for example to eat her first egg (though indignantly rejecting Dorothy's "cannibalistic" suggestion that she eat it
herself) and assenting silently when the Hungry Tiger is offered her
second. Baum the poultry-fancier knows these eggs are infertile and
takes pains to excuse Billina's indifference by telling us so through
Billina's beak. But his point is beyond his childish readers, to whom
Billina's eggs are her *babies*. (Consciously Baum may not know this but
his unconscious creature the Tiger knows, and four times in one speech
warns us that it is babies, "fat babies," who are in danger.)

The Hungry Tiger, by the way, has a previous record: another Oz-
critic has already seen in his hangup between appetite and conscience
the psychoanalytic concept of id and superego. Alas, this admission
only conceals a deeper admission which is not made. The Tiger, a
traditional glutton, is also a eunuch. Like the Cowardly Lion, with
whom he has everything in common (both are now slaves, happily
yoked to Ozma's chariot), he has resigned completely his too-demand-
ing masculine role in the jungle. (Indeed, conceptually the Tiger is just
another and weaker form of Lion, as Tik-Tok is another and weaker
form of the Tin Woodman.)

To return to Billina: while no eggs or babies actually suffer before the
final climactic sacrifice (but in a good cause!) of her two egg-babies at
once smashed on the Nome King's face, it is Billina's hard-headed acceptance of the risk that intensifies—for childish readers; adults hardly
notice—the growing suspense as to when heaven's wrath (perhaps the
mechanical giant's retributive hammer?) will fall on this unnatural
mother.

Eggs or no eggs, Billina is a hen, and therefore a mother. But not a
good mother. (Noticeable throughout the book is her repeated morning

"kut, kut, ka-daw!" coming in place of the "cock-a-doodle-do!" which is never heard. Quite literally and as the proverb says, Billina is a "crowing hen." But her feminist scorn of frivolous male animals—the two Ozians, with ribbons tied to their tails—or her rooster-licking revenge on bossy brothers and fathers, should not disguise that she is also a living reminder that mothers are hens.) To know she is a bad mother is not even necessary to hear her mock a good mother (the Queen of Ev), though it helps. Since there is no other in this Oz book, Billina herself must be the mother-villain—as in a very real sense she is.

She is not only a bad mother but a bad child. Couched under the King's throne (hens more naturally roost somewhere higher, but let it pass), she is the primal guilty eavesdropper on the parents' secrets. (Everything is there, even to being awakened from sleep by their noise! The Nome King's nagging Chief Steward takes the part of wife.)

In her next-morning's bargaining with the King, Billina uses as counter her latest casual egg—for which, contrarily, the King shows the most frightened respect. In his womanless underground world women's alarming fertility is "poisonous," unsafe except as lifeless ornament (explaining his transformation of the Queen of Ev). His anxious fib about "surface" things could not deceive us: of the thirty-odd surface creatures invading the King's domain, only one has this quality he fears.

Billina is now revealed as the book's heroine, to the joy and confusion of the youthful reader. Joy because of the coming comeuppance of that wicked *man*, the King; confusion because this is going to be done, and can only be done, by a *mother*. (Mothers don't *do* these things in Oz. There is also here a very deep and troubling confusion between good and evil, which the childish reader—and probably also the author—feels but cannot resolve, and so must put out of mind by violent action.)

Billina must necessarily change her identification-role, which she does, aptly enough, in the transformation scene, where for the first time she acts alone and we see only through her eyes. She turns now into the girlish *ideal* (Glinda the Good again), though this time more down-to-earth: the swaggering, scoffing (but kindly) older girl, whom the younger girl watches with frightened awe as she breaks all of Mama's rules unharmed.

This scene also supplies the point, which few children—or mothers—will miss, of the Queen of Ev turned into a footstool. But the kindly transformations are not the climax of the book, which is of course the King's humiliation. In that violent hurly-burly the child reader is completely satisfied, put beyond good and evil. The chapter ends in a complete denial of fertility-value, with eggs being created wholesale and scattered by the hundreds on the ground.

Billina's portrait has been objected to on the ground that she appears in the fifth book, *The Road to Oz*, with baby chicks. Giving a whimsical answer to a whimsical objection, the explanation might be that in the interim she has matured, met the rooster of her dreams, married and settled down. But no father chicken is brought on the scene and Billina retains enough maternal indifference to announce she has given all her chicks the same name. We adults, who know what happens when a cock and a hen appear to be fighting, might consider these chicks the natural result of Billina's "fight" with the Evian rooster in Langwidere's hen-yard. But the right answer is that Billina's character is no more consistent than any other Ozian's from book to book.

As to the overall span of Oz books: not only their internal evidence but the demands of the commercial "series" they became (demands with which Baum was thoroughly familiar from his other potboiling work) must contradict the sentimental idea that Oz was extended as a planned Utopia, coherent legend, or "labor of love." As a recognized brand-name, Oz was continued for MONEY. The plain evidence is that Baum was reluctant to go on repeating himself. Though not carrying his reluctance as far as Arthur Conan Doyle, for example—who grew to detest the very mention of *his* unconscious creation—Baum did announce in his fifth book and confirm in his sixth that he had had it with Oz. (Making our four-book canon even more reasonable.) But Baum was a gentle, unaggressive man, in debt, the support of his family, a semi-invalid during his last years, and he can hardly be blamed for doing what so many other more healthy (and wealthy) writers do as a way of life.

Because, Because, Because, Because of the Wonderful Things He Does

· *by Ray Bradbury* ·

Let us consider two authors whose books were burned in our American society during the past seventy years. Librarians and teachers did the burning very subtly by not buying. And not buying is as good as burning. Yet, the authors survived.

Reprinted from *Wonderful Wizard, Marvelous Land* by Raylyn Moore. Bowling Green, Ohio: Bowling Green University Popular Press, 1974, pp. xi–xviii. Copyright © 1974 by Raylyn Moore. Reprinted by permission of Bowling Green University Popular Press.

Two gentlemen of no talent whatsoever.

Two mysteries of literature, if you can call their work literature.

Two men who changed the world somewhat more than they ever dreamed, once they were in it, once their books came to be published and moved in the minds and blood of eight-year-olds, ten-year-olds, twelve-year-olds.

One of them changed the future of the entire world and that Universe which waited for Earthmen to birth themselves in space with rockets.

His name: Edgar Rice Burroughs. His John Carter grew to maturity two generations of astronomers, geologists, biochemists, and astronauts who cut their teeth on his Barsoomian beasts and Martian fighting men and decided to grow up and grow out away from Earth.

The second man, also a "mediocre" talent, if you can believe the teachers and librarians of some seventy years, created a country, Oz, and peopled it with not one influence, but several dozens.

His name: L. Frank Baum.

And once you begin to name his people in his country, it is hard to stop: Dorothy, Toto (indeed a very real person), the Tin Man, the Scarecrow, Tik-Tok, Ozma, Polychrome, the Patchwork Girl, Ruggedo, Prof. Woggle-Bug, Aunty Em, the Wicked Witch of the ———. You see how easily the names pop out, without having to go look them up!

Two mysteries, then. One the mystery of growing boys to men by romanticizing their taffy bones so the damn things *rise* toward the sun, no, toward Mars. Now, let us set Mr. Burroughs aside.

Let us get on with the mystery of L. Frank Baum, that faintly old-maidish man who grew boys inward to their most delightful interiors, kept them home, and romanced them with wonders between their ears.

And this book is, of course, about the latter mystery, the mystery of that strange dear little Wizard Himself. The man who wanted to work magic but, oh dear, not *hurt* anyone along the way. He is that rare chef who would never dream to yell at his cooks, yet got results anyway: a bakery-kitchen full of valentines, sweet-meats, dragons without teeth, robots with feelings, Tin Men who were once real (to reverse the Pinocchio myth), and girls who are so toothsome and innocent that if you nibble them at all, it would only be their toes, ears, and elbows.

It is a book about a man compelled to money, but saved by his secret self, his hidden creative person.

It is a book about a man who set out, unknowingly, to slaughter his own best talents, but was saved by a mob of strange creatures from another land who knew better than he that they needed to be born. And in birthing themselves ensured the miraculous fact that if we all went to the nearest travel agency tomorrow and were asked if we wanted to go to Alice's Wonderland or the Emerald City, it would be that Green Place, and the Munchkins and the Quadlings and all the rest, every time!

It is fascinating to compare memories of Dorothy and Oz and Baum with Alice and the Looking Glass and the Rabbit Hole and Lewis Carroll, who made out better with librarians and teachers.

When we think of Oz a whole mob of incredibly lovely if strange people falls across our minds.

When we think of Alice's encounters we think of mean, waspish, small, carping, bad-mannered children ranting against *going* to bed, refusing to get *out* of bed, not liking the food, hating the temperature, minding the weather out of mind.

If Love is the lubricant that runs Oz to glory, Hate is the mud in which all sink to ruin inside the mirror where poor Alice is trapped.

If everyone goes around democratically accepting each other's foibles in the four lands surrounding the Emerald City, and feeling nothing but amiable wonder toward such eccentrics as pop up, the reverse is true when Alice meets a Caterpillar or Tweedledum and Tweedledee or assorted knights, Queens, and Old Women. Theirs is an aristocracy of snobs, no one is good enough for them. They themselves are crazy eccentrics, but eccentricity in anyone else is beyond comprehension and should best be guillotined or grown small and stepped on.

Both books, both authors, stay in our minds, for mirror-reversed reasons. We float and fly through Oz on grand winds that make us beautiful kites. We trudge and fight our way through Wonderland, amazed that we survive at all.

Wonderland, for all its fantasy, is most practically real, that world where people have conniption fits and knock you out of line on your way onto a bus.

Oz is that place, ten minutes before sleep, where we bind up our wounds, soak our feet, dream ourselves better, snooze poetry on our lips, and decide that mankind, for all it's snide and mean and dumb, must be given another chance come dawn and a hearty breakfast.

Oz is muffins and honey, summer vacations, and all the easy green time in the world.

Wonderland is cold gruel and arithmetic at six A.M., icy showers, long schools.

It is not surprising that Wonderland is the darling of the intellectuals.

It is similarly not surprising that dreamers and intuitionists would reject the cold mirror of Carroll and take their chances on hotfooting it over the forbidden desert which at least promises utter destruction for purely inanimate reasons (the desert, after all, is not alive and doesn't know whom it is destroying), heading for Oz. Because in Oz of course reside amiable villains who are really not villains at all. Ruggedo is a fraud and a sham, for all his shouts and leaping about and uttering curses. Whereas Wonderland's Queen of Hearts really *does* chop off heads and children are beaten if they sneeze.

Wonderland is what we Are.

Oz is what we would hope and like to be.

The distance between raw animal and improved human can be measured by pegging a line between Alice's Rabbit Hole and Dorothy's Yellow Brick Road.

One need not polarize oneself by picking one country, one heroine, one set of characters. It is not either-or, or this or that. It can be both.

It is the sad/happy state of mankind always to be making such measurements: where we are as against where we would like to be.

I hope that the lovers of Wonderland and the lovers of Oz do not break up into permanent warring camps. That would be foolish and fruitless, for growing humanity needs proper doses of reality and proper doses of dreaming. I would like to believe Alice puts antibodies in our blood to help us survive Reality by showing us as the fickle, reckless, abrupt, and alarming children we are. Children, of course, recognize themselves in the mostly bad-mannered grotesques that amble, stalk, and wander up to Alice.

But mean and loud and dreadful make for high tea lacking vitamins. Reality is an unsubstantial meal. Children also recognize a good dream when they see it, and so turn to Mr. Baum for the richer cake rather than the swamp gruel, for the mean-spirit that is really Santa Claus pretending at horrible. Children are willing to risk being smothered in true marmalade and saccharine. Mr. Baum provides both, with some narrow escapes from the maudlin and the thing we damn as sentimentality.

No matter if Mr. Baum was his own worst enemy. . . . The more he tried to be commercial, the more his intuitive self seemed to pop to the surface saying, finally, "To hell with you, I'm going *my* way!" And away it went, dragging Mr. Baum screaming after it, he yelling for money, his Muse settling for warm creations. Ironically if Mr. B. had relaxed more, and let the Muse drag him, he would probably have wound up wiser, happier, richer.

I suddenly realize . . . that a funny thing happened on my way into this Introduction: Mr. Carroll fell by and collided with Mr. Baum. In the resultant scramble, I was locked in and only now fight free.

What you have here, in the [book to which this is the Preface], is an attempt made by one of the first people, late in time, to pay attention to a spirited man with a nice old grandma's soul. It is an endeavor to "unburn" the histories of Oz, and shelve the Works where they have rarely, in the history of our country, been shelved: in libraries.

It is not the task of a writer of Prefaces to criticise or super-analyze the work at hand. If Raylyn Moore has done nothing else but begin to stir up some sort of small tempest concerning Oz and the super-evident fact it has stood, unassailed and beautific somewhere beyond Kansas for seventy-odd years, her task will have been commendable.

For Oz has not fallen, has it? Even though legions of bright people with grand good taste, and thousands of librarians have fired cannonades in tandem with hosts of sociologists who fear that the mighty Wizard will pollute their children, Baum, across the years, simply reaches in his pocket and produces, Shaggy Man that he is, the Love Magnet.

And if he is not the Shaggy Man, which he surely is, he is the Pied Piper who takes the adoring children away from their dull and unappreciative parents. Let the older folk survive into starvation with their algebra breakfasts, mathematical luncheons, and computer-data-fact dinners. To the children, Baum cries, "Let them eat cake!" but *means* it, and delivers.

In a story of mine published some twenty-two years ago, *The Exiles*, fine fantasists like Poe and Hawthorne, along with Dickens, and Baum, find themselves shunted off to Mars as the nondreamers, the super-psychological technicians, the book burners of the future, advance through towns and libraries, tossing the last of the great dreams into the furnace.

At the finale of my story, a rocket arrives on Mars, bearing with it the last copies in existence of Poe and Dickens and Baum. The captain of the ship burns these books on a dead Martian sea-bottom, and Oz at long last crashes over into ruins, Tik-Tok runs to rust, the Wizard and all his dusk-time dreams are destroyed, even as Scrooge, Marley, the Three Spirits, the Raven and the Masque of the Red Death fly away into dusks, gone forever.

I do not for a moment believe that day will ever come. The fight between the dreamers and the fact-finders will continue, and we will embody both in equal proportion, or risk all men singing *castrato* soprano for the literary popes.

I have not predicted futures but, as I have often hopefully pointed out, prevented them. How much has my ounce counted for in a world of data dross?

Who can say? I only know that 1984 is not coming after all. For a while there we actually thought it might. Man as mere computer-adjunct data collector realist is losing to man as loving companion to a miraculous universe. By such hopes I must live.

Raylyn Moore, if I read her rightly, has given us a book here of such a size and weight as to knock librarians' heads with, and bang sociologists' elbows with, and knock psychiatrists' hats askew. Whether she intends it or not, in sum here I believe her to say, in all truth:

Shakespeare invented Freud.

Hell, Shakespeare invented *everything!*
And long before the first couch was lain upon and the first psychiatrical confession heard.
Baum is a small and inconsequential flower blooming in the shade of Shakespeare. I suppose I will be reviled for mentioning them in one paragraph. But both lived inside their heads with a mind gone wild with wanting, wishing, hoping, shaping, dreaming. There, if no other place, they touch fingertips.
In a world where books are machine-made for "age groups" and pass through dry-parchment analysts' hands before being pill-fed to kids, Baum deserves this book, because Baum is needed. When the cities die, in their present form at least, and we head out into Eden again, which we must and will, Baum will be waiting for us. And if the road we take is not Yellow Brick why, damn it, we can imagine that it is, even as we imagine our wives beautiful and our husbands wise and our children kind until such day as they echo that dream. . . .

Ozomania Under the Rainbow

· *Alix Kates Shulman* ·

Just over the rainbow from the usual heap of dirty socks, comics, Magic Markers, candy wrappers, old bedsprings, and storage batteries in my thirteen-year-old son's room is a utopian bookcase where order reigns and magic prevails. There the Oz books are kept—all forty-one of them, plus doubles to trade or sell, and several non-Oz books by the Oz originator L. Frank Baum. Besides the precious books themselves, the room contains: homemade life-sized models of the Patchwork Girl of Oz and the Scarecrow, who share the top bunk; a silk hand-sewn Oz flag; a growing collection of Oz journals, Oz maps, and reference works, and

Reprinted from *The Village Voice*, March 3, 1975, pp. 33 and 35. Copyright © 1975 by Alix Kates Shulman. Reprinted by permission of Alix Kates Shulman.

treasured memorabilia from several conventions of the International Wizard of Oz Club and the world of Oz itself.

Stop. I have just been informed that my first sentence contains an error. Despite Judy Garland and MGM, Oz does not lie under the rainbow. If it did, I am told, rainbows could not appear in at least three of Baum's Oz books. I ought to know that one. Oz scholar Noah Seaman has made a study of it and has concluded that Oz must lie somewhere in the South Pacific.

My son is one of approximately 1500 members of the seventeen-year-old International Wizard of Oz Club, many of whom debate such questions with the passion of cultists by mail, by telephone, in the triannual *Baum Bugle* (one of several club periodicals), and if they can somehow swing it, at any of the five regular Oz Club conventions—the Munchkin Convention in the East, the Winkie Convention in the West, the Quadling Convention in the South, the occasional Gillikin Convention in the North, and the Ozmopolitican Convention in the center. Members live as far away as Australia and India, hail from thirteen countries and fifty states (with the best represented, predictably, California), from the first to the eighth decades of life, from the towers of academe, the cubbies of grammar school, behind the footlights of show biz. Fanatics all. Some of the members who may have been attracted to Oz originally by the 1939 MGM musical now share my son's indulgént scorn for the liberties Hollywood took with the text of one of their favorite books. Older members, who may have joined the club originally for reasons of nostalgia, have long since lost such motives in the denser textures and more stringent demands of Ozomania. And now *The Wiz,* the stunning new all-black musical which opened January 5 at the Majestic (and, according to my son, takes fewer liberties with the text, on balance, than did Hollywood), threatens to seduce a new unsuspecting audience down the yellow brick road into the mad land of Ozomania, a place in some ways stranger than Oz itself, and from which they, like many before them, may never return,

Given the inducements and resources available to the new enthusiast, it is not surprising that an Ozophile of any bent—theatrical, literary, artistic, scholarly, acquisitive—once transported would find it difficult to escape. With a beckoning corpus of forty-one published Oz books by six authors (of which 40 percent are out-of-print and almost all ignored by librarians); a substantial non-Oz literature by the self-appointed "Royal Historian" L. Frank Baum; a growing body of criticism; one periodical devoted to Oz scholarshp (*The Baum Bugle*) and original Oz stories, poems, and art (*Oziana*); and a rich theatrical history, including Baum's own Broadway musicals, Hollywood films, and slide shows going back to the beginning of the century, even the secret Ozians, the closet writers with manuscripts tucked away in bottom drawers, the would-be singing Dorothys, or the merely curious may find a membership irresistible. And after the novice has watched, read, appreciated, begun writing, composing, performing, and perhaps collecting (a madness of its own), there are the conventions to experience, with their previously difficult quizzes, their costume contests, musical and dramatic presentations, treasure hunts, workshops (on such esoteric topics as Oz history, Oz geography, restoration of rare books), exhibitions, auctions of books, drawings, and objects, and best of all, community with all those other Ozophiles.

Though I am an outsider, having read (without succumbing) only the 1900 *Wonderful Wizard of Oz*, I confess Ozomania intrigues me. Perhaps every cult exudes its own fascination, but to me there is something particularly appealing about a cult which mixes the generations in such a way that fifty-year-olds revel like children (serving one another the green punch called Ozade, punning incessantly à la Baum, and signing their letters "Ozzily yours") while ten-year-olds turn as scholarly as professors. Most members seem to be middle-aged adults; nevertheless, some of the most respected are the spectacularly learned child bibliophiles, and several of the most honored are distinguished elders like Ruth Plumly Thompson, Baum's major successor and author of some twenty published Oz books of her own, who lives and writes on.[1] There are some other members who literally grew up in the green glow of Oz, turning their fantasies from hobby to calling. Justin Schiller, who founded the club as a lad of thirteen back in 1957, now runs one of New York's better known rare bookstores specializing in children's books, a bibliophile's paradise with a core collection of Oz books. Michael Patrick Hearn, whose definitive *Annotated Wizard of Oz* was published to critical acclaim at the end of 1973, confessed in a recent interview he was nine when he discovered Oz, ten when he joined the club, fifteen when he conceived his book, twenty-one when he completed it, and now at twenty-four, continues to exploit his fantasies as New York editor of the highly regarded children's magazine *Cricket*.[2]

But Ozomania extends will beyond the paid-up rolls of the International Wizard of Oz club; Oz lives offcamera and offstage. Some years back an irreverent porn youth magazine called *Oz* was published and banned in Britain (with the subsequent *Trials of Oz* staged Off-Broadway). The Land of Oz as an amusement park stands on a mountain in

1. Ruth Plumly Thompson died on April 6, 1976 [M.P.H.].
2. Until September 1977 [M.P.H.].

North Carolina, where for a fee you can pretend you are in Kansas, enter a whirling room, and withstand a simulated cyclone.[3] Oz can be seen in the cartoons of Gahan Wilson (himself something of a cult figure to youth); in Erica Jong's poem "The Girl in the Mirror," in part about a character in *Ozma of Oz*, Princess Langwidere (who is not, however, as Jong would have it from the Kingdom of Oz, but rather, as one young scholar of my acquaintance is quick to point out, from the Kingdom of Ev); in Jill Robinson's current popular memoir *Bed/Time/ Story* where Dorothy's Ruby Slippers and Glinda's Magic Kiss (both Hollywood alterations) perform again. Oz might, perhaps even have made it out to space if the government's loony Project Ozma hadn't flopped.

Nor is Ozomania restricted in art and technology. Through the years the Oz corpus has been subjected to a wide range of interpretations, sometimes satirical, sometimes straight, from a Marxist analysis of "The Red Wizard of Oz" that appeared in the 1930s in *The New Masses*, to a Populist interpretation in *American Quarterly* a decade ago, to a Freudian foray in *Psychology Today*, to last year's mythic interpretation in *Unicorn*, to a recent feminist appeal in *Ms.*

Now, while a Marxist or Freudian Oz makes this skeptic smile (as must the inevitable Structuralist version when it comes), I must confess I am tantalized by a feminist Oz. The evidence is impressive. According to *The Annotated Wizard*, Baum was heavily influenced by his mother-in-law Matilda J. Gage, author of the radical *Woman, Church and State* and co-editor with Susan B. Anthony and Elizabeth Cady Stanton of *History of Woman Suffrage*. And indeed, in *The Wizard of Oz*, power, for good or evil, is monopolized by the four witches and Dorothy, females all. Other Oz books, reports Noah Seaman, are even more solidly feminist. In *The Land of Oz*, a General Jinjur organizes an all-girl Army of Revolt to conquer Oz, and though ultimately defeated (through suspiciously unfeminist means), their efforts result in the emergence of a benevolent female ruler, the somewhat androgynous Ozma.

For those who remain doggedly against interpretation, there are scholarly and literary articles on Oz by such eminent literati as Roger Sale, Martin Gardner, Alison Lurie, and Marius Bewley in such serious journals as *The Hudson Review, Chicago Review,* and *The New York Review of Books.* And finally, Oz can boast those indisputable stamps of arrival, Hearn's *Annotated Wizard of Oz,* Jack Snow's 1954 *Who's Who in Oz,* application by the late John Steinbeck to be appointed U.S. Ambassador to the Land of Oz, and a caricature of Baum by David Levine.

---

3. The park has since closed [M.P.H.].

Against all this evidence of legitimacy, and despite the continued popularity of the Oz books among children, the New York Public Library refuses to carry any Oz book but the original *Wizard.* Why? At the urging of my son, who must lend his own collection to reliable friends, and my daughter who though she finds the Oz books "unfeeling" would like to decide for herself whether or not to read them, I called the library to ask. The librarian to whom I spoke offered reasons ranging from priggish (the "poor literary quality" of the series) to disingenuous (we don't want to duplicate the home and school collections) to circular (we find children are content to read only *The Wizard*) to false (we don't carry series), and finally conceded that the policy may soon be "reevaluated."

With or without the library's blessing, the cult of Oz grows. It is as American as Rainbow Sherbet. The latest sign is the Oz Hotline, a "peer counseling crisis intervention center" in Queens, discovered in an underground paper by my husband who has begun to see green like the rest of the family. When asked about the center's connection with Oz, one peer counselor said wistfully, "After all, life is like a yellow brick road."

What does Oz mean? To judge by the critics, everything; according to my son, nothing. Oz doesn't mean. Oz is.

On Rereading the Oz Books

· by Gore Vidal ·

In the preface to *The Wizard of Oz*, L. Frank Baum says that he would like to create *modern* fairy tales by departing from Grimm and Andersen and "all the horrible and blood-curdling incident devised" by such authors "to point a fearsome moral." Baum then makes the disingenuous point that "Modern education includes morality; therefore the modern child seeks only entertainment in its wonder-tales and gladly dispenses with all disagreeable incident." Yet there is a certain amount of explicit as well as implicit moralizing in the Oz books; there are also "disagreeable incidents," and people do, somehow, die even though death and illness are not supposed to exist in Oz.

I have reread the Oz books in the order in which they were written. Some things are as I remember. Others strike me as being entirely new. I was struck by the unevenness of style not only from book to book but, sometimes, from page to page. The jaggedness can be explained by the

Reprinted from *The New York Review of Books*, October 13, 1977, pp. 37–42. Copyright © 1977 by Nyrev, Inc. Reprinted by permission of *The New York Review of Books*.

fact that the man who was writing fourteen Oz books was writing forty-eight other books at the same time. Arguably, *The Wizard of Oz* is the best of the lot. After all, the first book is the one in which Oz was invented. Yet, as a child, I preferred *The Emerald City, Rinkitink,* and *The Lost Princess* to *The Wizard.* Now I find that all of the books tend to flow together in a single narrative, with occasional bad patches.

In *The Wizard of Oz* Dorothy is about six years old. In the later books she seems to be ten or eleven. Baum locates her swiftly and efficiently in the first sentence of the series. "Dorothy lived in the midst of the great Kansas prairies, with Uncle Henry, who was a farmer, and Aunt Em, who was the farmer's wife." The landscape would have confirmed John Ruskin's dark view of American scenery (he died the year that *The Wizard of Oz* was published).

When Dorothy stood in the doorway and looked around, she could see nothing but the great gray prairie on every side. Not a tree nor a house broke the broad sweep of flat country that reached the edge of the sky in all directions.

This is the plain American style at its best. Like most of Baum's central characters Dorothy lacks the regulation father and mother. Some commentators have made, I think, too much of Baum's parentless children. The author's motive seems to me to be not only obvious but sensible. A child separated from loving parents for any length of time is going to be distressed, even in a magic story. But aunts and uncles need not be taken too seriously.

In the first four pages Baum demonstrates the drabness of Dorothy's life; the next two pages are devoted to the cyclone that lifts the house into the air and hurls it to Oz. Newspaper accounts of recent cyclones had obviously impressed Baum. Alone in the house (except for Toto, a Cairn terrier), Dorothy is established as a sensible girl who is not going to worry unduly about events that she cannot control. The house crosses the Deadly Desert and lands on top of the Wicked Witch of the West who promptly dries up and dies. Right off, Baum breaks his own rule that no one ever dies in Oz. I used to spend a good deal of time worrying about the numerous inconsistencies in the sacred texts. From time to time, Baum himself would try to rationalize errors but he was far too quick and careless a writer ever to create the absolutely logical mad worlds that Lewis Carroll or E. Nesbit did.

Dorothy is acclaimed by the Munchkins as a good witch who has managed to free them from the Wicked Witch. They advise her to go to the Emerald City and try to see the famous Wizard; he alone would have the power to grant her dearest wish, which is to go home to

Kansas. Why she wanted to go back was never clear to me. Or, finally, to Baum: eventually, he moves Dorothy (with aunt and uncle) to Oz.

Along the way to the Emerald City, Dorothy meets a live Scarecrow in search of brains, a Tin Woodman in search of a heart, a Cowardly Lion in search of courage. Each new character furthers the plot. Each is essentially a humor. Each, when he speaks, strikes the same simple, satisfying note.

Together they undergo adventures. In sharp contrast to gray flat Kansas, Oz seems to blaze with color. Yet the Emerald City is a bit of a fraud. Everyone is obliged to wear green glasses in order to make the city appear emerald-green.

The Wizard says that he will help them if they destroy yet another wicked witch. They do. Only to find out that the Wizard is a fake who arrived by balloon from the States, where he had been a magician in a circus. Although a fraud, the Wizard is a good psychologist. He gives the Scarecrow bran for brains, the Tin Woodman a red velvet heart, the Cowardly Lion a special courage syrup. Each has now become what he wanted to be (and was all along). The Wizard's response to their delight is glum: " 'How can I help being a humbug,' he said, 'when all these people make me do things that everybody knows can't be done? It was easy to make the Scarecrow and the Lion and the Woodman happy, because they imagined I could do anything. But it will take more than imagination to carry Dorothy back to Kansas, and I'm sure I don't know how it can be done.' " When the Wizard arranges a balloon to take Dorothy and himself back home, the balloon takes off without Dorothy. Finally, she is sent home through the intervention of magic, and the good witch Glinda.

The style of the first book is straightforward, even formal. There are almost no contractions. Dorothy speaks not at all the way a grownup might think a child should speak but like a sensible somewhat literal person. There are occasional Germanisms (did Baum's father speak German?): " 'What is that little animal you are so tender of?' " Throughout all the books there is a fascination with jewelry and elaborate costumes. Baum never got over his love of theater. In this he resembled his favorite author Charles Reade, of whom *The Dictionary of National Biography* tells us: "At his best Reade was an admirable storyteller, full of resource and capacity to excite terror and pity; but his ambition to excel as a dramatist militated against his success as a novelist, and nearly all his work is disfigured by a striving after theatrical effect."

Baum's passion for the theater and, later, the movies not only wasted his time but, worse, it had a noticeably bad effect on his prose style. Because *The Wizard of Oz* was the most successful children's book of the 1900 Christmas season . . . , Baum was immediately inspired to dramatize the story. Much "improved" by other hands, the musical comedy opened in Chicago (June 16, 1902) and was a success. After a year and a half on Broadway, the show toured off and on until 1911. Over the years Baum was to spend a good deal of time trying to make plays and films based on the Oz characters. Except for the first, none was a success.

Since two popular vaudevillians had made quite a splash as the Tin Woodman and the Scarecrow in the musical version of the *Wizard*, Baum decided that a sequel was in order . . . for the stage. But rather than write directly for the theater, he chose to write a second Oz book, without Dorothy or the Wizard. In an Author's Note to *The Marvelous Land of Oz*, Baum somewhat craftily says that he has been getting all sorts of letters from children asking him "to 'write something more' about the Scarecrow and the Tin Woodman." In 1904 the sequel was published, with a dedication to the two vaudevillians. A subsequent musical comedy called *The Woggle-Bug* was then produced; and failed. That, for the time being, was that. But the idiocies of popular theater had begun to infect Baum's prose. *The Wizard of Oz* is chastely written. *The Land of Oz* is not. Baum riots in dull word play. There are endless bad puns, of the sort favored by popular comedians. There is also that true period horror: the baby-talking ingenue, a character who lasted well into our day in the menacing shapes of Fanny (Baby Snooks) Brice and the early Ginger Rogers. Dorothy, who talked plainly and to the point in *The Wizard*, talks (when she reappears in the third book) with a cuteness hard to bear. Fortunately, Baum's show-biz phase wore off and in later volumes Dorothy's speech improves.

Despite stylistic lapses, *The Land of Oz* is one of the most unusual and interesting books of the series. In fact, it is so unusual that after the Shirley Temple television adaptation of the book in 1960,* PTA circles were in a state of crisis. The problem that knitted then and, I am told, knits even today many a maternal brow is Sexual Role. Sexual Role makes the world go round. It is what makes the man go to the office or to the factory where he works hard while the wife fulfills *her* Sexual Role by homemaking and consuming and bringing up boys to be real boys and girls to be real girls, a cycle that must continue unchanged and unquestioned until the last car comes off Detroit's last assembly line and the last all-American sun vanishes behind a terminal dioxin haze.

---

* In 1939, MGM made a film called *The Wizard of Oz* with Judy Garland. A new book, *The Making of The Wizard of Oz* by Aljean Harmetz, describes in altogether too great but fascinating detail the assembling of the movie, which had one and a half producers, ten writers, and four directors. Who then was the "auteur"?

Certainly the denouement of *The Land of Oz* is troubling for those who have heard of Freud. A boy, Tip, is held in thrall by a wicked witch named Mombi. One day she gets hold of an elixir that makes the inanimate live. Tip uses this magical powder to bring to life a homemade figure with a jack-o-lantern head: Jack Pumpkinhead, who turns out to be a comic of the Ed Wynn–Simple Simon school: " 'Now that is a very interesting history,' said Jack, well pleased; 'and I understand it perfectly—all but the explanation.' "

Tip and Jack Pumpkinhead escape from Mombi aboard a brought-to-life sawhorse. They then meet the stars of the show (and a show it is), the Scarecrow and the Tin Woodman. As a central character neither is very effective. In fact, each has a tendency to sententiousness; and there are nowhere near enough jokes. The Scarecrow goes on about his brains; the Tin Woodman about his heart. But then it is the limitation as well as the charm of made-up fairy-tale creatures to embody to the point of absurdity a single quality of humor.

There is one genuinely funny sketch. When the Scarecrow and Jack Pumpkinhead meet, they decide that since each comes from a different country, " 'We must,' " says the Scarecrow, " 'have an interpreter.'

" 'What is an interpreter?' asked Jack.

" 'A person who understands both my language and your own. . . .' " And so on. Well, maybe this is not so funny.

The Scarecrow (who had taken the vanished Wizard's place as ruler of Oz) is overthrown by a "revolting" army of girls (great excuse for a leggy chorus). This long and rather heavy satire on the suffragettes was plainly more suitable for a Broadway show than for a children's story. The girl leader, Jinjur, is an unexpectedly engaging character. She belongs to the Bismarckian *Realpolitik* school. She is accused of treason for having usurped the Scarecrow's throne. " 'The throne belongs to whoever is able to take it,' answered Jinjur as she slowly ate another caramel. 'I have taken it, as you see; so just now I am the Queen, and all who oppose me are guilty of treason. . . .' " This is the old children's game I-am-the-King-of-the-castle, a.k.a. human history.

Among the new characters met in this story are the Woggle-Bug, a highly magnified insect who has escaped from a classroom exhibition and (still magnified) ranges about the countryside. A parody of an American academic, he is addicted to horrendous puns on the grounds that " 'a joke derived from a play upon words is considered among educated people to be eminently proper.' " Anna livia plurabelle.

There is a struggle between Jinjur and the legitimate forces of the Scarecrow. The Scarecrow's faction wins and the girls are sent away to be homemakers and consumers. In passing, the Scarecrow observes, " 'I am convinced that the only people worthy of consideration in this world are the unusual ones. For the common folks are like the leaves of a tree, and live and die unnoticed.' " To which the Tin Woodman replies, " 'Spoken like a philosopher!' " To which the current editor Martin Gardner responds, with true democratic wrath, "This despicable view, indeed defended by many philosophers, had earlier been countered by the Tin Woodman," etc. But the view is not at all despicable. For one thing, it would be the normal view of an odd magical creature who cannot die. For another, Baum was simply echoing those neo-Darwinians who dominated most American thinking for at least a century. It testifies to Baum's sweetness of character that unlike most writers of his day he seldom makes fun of the poor or weak or unfortunate. Also, the Scarecrow's "despicable" remarks can be interpreted as meaning that although unorthodox dreamers are despised by the ordinary, their dreams are apt to prevail in the end and become reality.

Glinda the Good Sorceress is a kindly mother figure to the various children who visit or live in Oz, and it is she who often ties up the loose ends when the story bogs down. In *The Land of Oz* Glinda has not a loose end but something on the order of a hangman's rope to knot. Apparently the rightful ruler of Oz is Princess Ozma. As a baby, Ozma was changed by Mombi into the boy Tip. Now Tip must be restored to his true identity. The PTA went, as it were, into plenary session. What effect would a book like this have on a boy's sense of himself as a future man, breadwinner, and father to more of same? Would he want, awful thought, to be a Girl? Even Baum's Tip is alarmed when told who he is. " 'I!' cried Tip, in amazement. 'Why I'm no Princess Ozma—I'm not a girl!' " Glinda tells him that indeed he was—and really is. Tip is understandably grumpy. Finally, he says to Glinda, " 'I might try it for awhile,—just to see how it seems, you know. But if I don't like being a girl you must promise to change me into a boy again.' " Glinda says that this is not in the cards. Glumly, Tip agrees to the restoration. Tip becomes the beautiful Ozma, who hopes that " 'none of you will care less for me than you did before, I'm just the same Tip, you know; only—only—' "

"Only you're different!" said the Pumpkinhead; and everyone thought it was the wisest speech he had ever made.

Essentially, Baum's human protagonists are neither male nor female but children, a separate category in his view if not in that of our latter-day sexists. Baum's use of sex changes was common to the popular theater of his day, which, in turn, derived from the Elizabethan era when boys played girls whom the plot often required to pretend to be boys. In Baum's *The Enchanted Island of Yew* a fairy (female) becomes a knight (male) in order to have adventures. In *The Emerald City* the hideous Phanfasm leader turns himself into a beautiful woman. When *John Dough and the Cherub* (1906) was published, the sex of the five-year-old cherub was never mentioned in the text; the publishers then launched a national ad campaign: "Is the cherub boy or girl? $500 for the best answers." In those innocent times Tip's metamorphosis as Ozma was nothing more than a classic *coup de théâtre* of the sort that even now requires the boy Peter Pan to be played on stage by a mature woman.

Today of course any sort of sexual metamorphosis causes distress. Although Raylyn Moore in her plot *précis* of *The Enchanted Island of Yew* (in her book *Wonderful Wizard, Marvelous Land*) does make one confusing reference to the protagonist as "he (she)," she omits entirely the Tip/Ozma transformation which is the whole point to *The Land of Oz*, while the plot as given by the publisher Reilly & Lee says only that "the book ends with an amazing surprise, and from that moment on Ozma is princess of all Oz." But, surely, for a pre-pube there is not much difference between a boy and a girl protagonist. After all, the central fact of the pre-pube's existence is not being male or female but being a child, much the hardest of all roles to play. During and after puberty, there is a tendency to want a central character like oneself (my favorite Oz book was R. P. Thompson's *Speedy in Oz*, whose eleven- or twelve-year-old hero could have been, I thought, me). Nevertheless, what matters most even to an adolescent is not the gender of the main character who experiences adventures but the adventures themselves, and the magic, and the jokes, and the pictures.

Dorothy is a perfectly acceptable central character for a boy to read about. She asks the right questions. She is not sappy (as Ozma can sometimes be). She is straight to the point and a bit aggressive. Yet the Dorothy who returns to the series in the third book, *Ozma of Oz* (1907), is somewhat different from the original Dorothy. She is older and her conversation is full of cute contractions that must have doubled up audiences in Sioux City but were pretty hard going for at least one child forty years ago.

To get Dorothy back to Oz there is the by now obligatory natural disaster. The book opens with Dorothy and her uncle on board a ship to Australia. During a storm she is swept overboard. Marius Bewley has noted that this opening chapter "is so close to Crane's ('The Open Boat') in theme, imagery and technique that it is difficult to imagine, on comparing the two in detail, that the similarity is wholly, or even largely accidental."

Dorothy is accompanied by a yellow chicken named Bill. As they are now in magic country, the chicken talks. Since the chicken is a hen, Dorothy renames her Billina. The chicken is fussy and self-absorbed; she is also something of an overachiever: " 'How is my grammar?' asked the yellow hen anxiously." Rather better than Dorothy's, whose dialogue is marred by such Baby Snooksisms as " 'zactly," "auto'biles," " 'lieve," " 'splain."

Dorothy and Billina come ashore in Ev, a magic country on the other side of the Deadly Desert that separates Oz from the real world (what separates such magical kingdoms as Ix and Ev from our realer world is never made plain). In any case, the formula has now been established. Cyclone or storm at sea or earthquake ends not in death for child and animal companion but translation into a magic land. Then, one by one, strange new characters join the travelers. In this story the first addition is Tik-Tok, a clockwork robot (sixteen years later the word "robot" was coined). He has run down. They wind him up. Next they meet Princess Langwidere. She is deeply narcissistic, a trait not much admired by Baum (had he been traumatized by all those actresses and actors he had known on tour?). Instead of changing clothes, hair, makeup, the Princess changes heads from her collection. I found the changing of heads fascinating. And puzzling: since the brains in each head varied, would Langwidere still be herself when she put on a new head or would she become someone else? Thus Baum made logicians of his readers.

The Princess is about to add Dorothy's head to her collection when the marines arrive in the form of Ozma and retinue, who have crossed the Deadly Desert on a magic carpet (cheating, I thought at the time; either a desert is impassable or it is not). Dorothy and Ozma meet, and Dorothy, "as soon as she heard the sweet voice of the girlish ruler of Oz knew that she would learn to love her dearly." That sort of thing I tended to skip.

The principal villain of the Oz canon is now encountered: the Nome King (Baum thought the "g" in front of "nome" too difficult for children . . . how did he think they spelled and pronounced "gnaw"?). Roquat of the Rock lived deep beneath the earth, presiding over his legions of hardworking Nomes (first cousins to George Macdonald's goblins). I was always happy when Baum took us below ground, and showed us fantastic caverns strewn with precious stones where scurrying Nomes did their best to please the bad-tempered Roquat, whose " 'laugh,' " one admirer points out, " 'is worse than another man's frown.' " Ozma and company are transformed into bric-a-brac by Roquat's magic. But Dorothy and Billina outwit Roquat (Nomes fear fresh eggs). Ozma and all the other victims of the Nome King are restored to their former selves, and Dorothy is given an opportunity to ham it up:

"Royal Ozma, and you, Queen of Ev, I welcome you and your people back to the land of the living. Billina has saved you from your troubles, and now we will leave this drea'ful place, and return to Ev as soon as poss'ble."
While the child spoke they could all see that she wore the magic belt, and a great cheer went up from all her friends. . . .

Baum knew that nothing so pleases a child as a situation where, for once, the child is in the driver's seat and able to dominate adults. Dorothy's will to power is a continuing force in the series and as a type she is still with us in such popular works as *Peanuts*, where she continues her steely progress toward total dominion in the guise of the relentless Lucy.

Back in the Emerald City, Ozma shows Dorothy her magic picture in which she can see what is happening anywhere in the world. If Dorothy ever wants to visit Oz, all she has to do is make a certain signal and Ozma will transport her from Kansas to Oz. Although this simplified transportation considerably, Baum must have known even then that half the charm of the Oz stories was the scary trip of an ordinary American child from USA to Oz. As a result, in *Dorothy and the Wizard in Oz* (1908), another natural catastrophe is used to bring Dorothy back to Oz; the long-missing Wizard, too. Something like the San Francisco earthquake happens. Accompanied by a dim boy called Zeb and a dull horse called Jim, Dorothy falls deep into the earth. This catastrophe really got to Dorothy and "for a few moments the little girl lost consciousness. Zeb, being a boy, did not faint, but he was badly frightened. . . ." That is Baum's one effort to give some sort of points to a boy. He promptly forgets about Zeb, and Dorothy is back in the saddle, running things. She is aided by the Wizard, who joins them in his balloon.

Deep beneath the earth are magical countries (inspired by Verne's *Journey to the Center of the Earth*, 1864? Did Verne or Baum inspire Burroughs' *Pellucidar*, 1923?). In a country that contains vegetable people, a positively Golden Bough note is sounded by the ruling Prince: " 'One of the most unpleasant things about our vegetable lives [is] that while we are in our full prime we must give way to another, and be covered up in the ground to sprout and grow and give birth to other people.' " But then according to the various biographies, Baum was interested in Hinduism, and the notion of karma.

After a number of adventures Dorothy gestures to Ozma (she certainly took her time about it, I thought) and they are all transported to the Emerald City where the usual party is given for them, carefully described in a small-town newspaper style of the Social-Notes-from-all-over variety. *The Road to Oz* (1909) is the mixture as before. In Kansas, Dorothy meets the Shaggy Man; he is a tramp of the sort that haunted the American countryside after the Civil War when unemployed veterans and men ruined by the depressions of the 1870s took to the road where they lived and died, no doubt, brutishly. The Shaggy Man asks her for directions. Exasperated by the tramp's slowness to figure out her instructions, she says: " 'You're so stupid. Wait a minute till I run in the house and get my sunbonnet.' " Dorothy is easily "provoked." " 'My, but you're clumsy!' said the little girl." She gives him a "severe look." Then " 'Come on,' she commanded." She then leads him to the wrong, i.e., the magical, road to Oz.

With *The Emerald City of Oz* (1910) Baum is back in form. He has had to face up to the fact that Dorothy's trips from the USA to Oz are getting not only contrived, but pointless. If she likes Oz so much, why doesn't she settle there? But if she does, what will happen to her uncle and aunt? Fortunately, a banker is about to foreclose the mortgage on Uncle Henry's farm. Dorothy will have to go to work, says Aunt Em, stricken. " 'You might do housework for someone, dear, you are so handy; or perhaps you could be a nursemaid to little children.' " Dorothy is having none of this. "Dorothy smiled. 'Wouldn't it be funny,' she said, 'for me to do housework in Kansas, when I'm a Princess in the Land of Oz?' " The old people buy this one with surprisingly little fuss. It is decided that Dorothy will signal Ozma, and depart for the Emerald City.

Although Baum's powers of invention seldom flagged, he had no great skill at plot-making. Solutions to problems are arrived at either through improbable coincidence or by bringing in, literally, some god (usually Glinda) from the machine to set things right. Since the narratives are swift and the conversations sprightly and the invented characters are both homely and amusing (animated paper dolls, jigsaw puzzles, pastry, cutlery, china, etc.), the stories never lack momentum. Yet there was always a certain danger that the narrative would flatten out into a series of predictable turns.

In *The Emerald City*, Baum sets in motion two simultaneous plots. The Nome King Roquat decides to conquer Oz. Counterpoint to his shenanigans are Dorothy's travels through Oz with her uncle and aunt (Ozma has given them asylum). Once again, the child's situation *vis à vis* the adult is reversed.

"Don't be afraid," she said to them. "You are now in the Land of Oz, where you are to live always, and be comfer'ble an' happy. You'll never have to worry over anything again, 'cause there won't be anything to worry about. And you owe it all to the kindness of my friend Princess Ozma."

And never forget it, one hears her mutter to herself.

But while the innocents are abroad in Oz, dark clouds are gathering. Roquat is on the march. I must say that the Nome King has never been more (to me) attractive as a character than in this book. For one thing, the bad temper is almost permanently out of control. It is even beginning to worry the king himself: " 'To be angry once in a while is really good fun, because it makes others so miserable. But to be angry morning, noon and night, as I am, grows monotonous and prevents my gaining any other pleasure in life.' " Rejecting the offer of the usual anodyne, a "glass of melted silver," Roquat decides to put together an alliance of all the wicked magic figures in order to conquer Oz. He looks among his nomes for an ideal general. He finds him: "I hate good people. . . . That is why I am so fond of your Majesty.' " Later the General enlists new allies with the straightforward pitch: " 'Permit me to call your attention to the exquisite joy of making the happy unhappy,' said he at last. 'Consider the pleasure of destroying innocent and harmless people.' " This argument proves irresistible.

The Nomes and their allies make a tunnel beneath the Deadly Desert (but surely its Deadliness must go deeper than they could burrow?). Ozma watches all of them on her magic picture. She is moderately alarmed. " 'But I do not wish to fight,' declared Ozma, firmly." She takes an extremely high and moral American line; one that Woodrow Wilson echoed a few years later when he declared that the United States "is too proud to fight" powerful Germany (as opposed to weak Mexico where Wilson had swallowed his pride just long enough for us to launch an invasion). "Because the Nome King intends to do evil is no excuse for my doing the same.' " Ozma has deep thoughts on the nature of evil; " 'I must not blame King Roquat too severely, for he is a Nome and his nature is not so gentle as my own.' " Luckily, Ozite cunning carries the day.

Baum's nicest conceit in *The Emerald City* is Rigamarole Town. Or, as a local boy puts it,

"if you have traveled very much you will have noticed that every town differs from every other town in one way or another and so by observing the methods of the people and the way they live as well as the style of their dwelling places,"

etc. Dorothy and her party are duly impressed by the boy's endless commentary. He is matched almost immediately by a woman who tells them, apropos nothing:

"It is the easiest thing in the world for a person to say 'yes' or 'no' when a question that is asked for the purpose of gaining information or satisfying the curiosity of the one who has given expression to the inquiry has attracted the attention of an individual who may be competent either from personal experience or the experience of others,"

etc. A member of Dorothy's party remarks that if those people wrote books "it would take a whole library to say the cow jumped over the moon.' " So it would. And so it does. The Shaggy Man decides that there is a lot to be said for the way that people of Oz encourage these people to live together in one town "while Uncle Sam lets [them] roam around wild and free, to torture innocent people.' "

Many enthusiasts of the Oz books (among them Ray Bradbury and Russel B. Nye) point with democratic pride to the fact that there is a total absence, according to Mr. Nye, of any "whisper of class consciousness in Oz (as there is in Alice's Wonderland)." Yet Martin Gardner has already noted one example of Baum's "despicable" elitism. Later (*Emerald City*), Baum appears to back away from the view that some people are better or more special than others. "It seems unfortunate that strong people are usually so disagreeable and overbearing that no one cares for them. In fact, to be different from your fellow creatures is always a misfortune." But I don't think that Baum believed a word of this. If he did, he would have been not L. Frank Baum, creator of the special and magical world of Oz, but Horatio Alger, celebrator of pluck and luck, thrift and drift, money. The dreamy boy with the bad heart at a hated military school was as conscious as any Herman Hesse youth that he was splendidly different from others, and in *The Lost Princess of Oz* Baum reasserts the Scarecrow's position: " 'To be individual, my friends' " (the Cowardly Lion is holding forth), " 'to be different from others, is the only way to become distinguished from the common herd.' "

Inevitably, Baum moved from Chicago to California. Inevitably, he settled in the village of Hollywood in 1909. Inevitably, he made silent films, based on the Oz books. Not so inevitably, he failed for a number of reasons that he could not have foretold. Nevertheless, he put together a half dozen films that (as far as special effects went) were said to be ahead of their time. By 1913 he had returned, somewhat grimly, to writing Oz books, putting Dorothy firmly on ice until the last book of the series.

The final Oz books are among the most interesting. After a gall bladder operation, Baum took to his bed where the last work was done. Yet Baum's imagination seems to have been more than usually inspired despite physical pain and the darkness at hand. *The Lost Princess of Oz*

(1917) is one of the best of the series. The beginning is splendidly straightforward. "There could be no doubt of the fact: Princess Ozma, the lovely girl ruler of the Fairyland of Oz, was lost. She had completely disappeared." Glinda's magical paraphernalia had also vanished. The search for Ozma involves most of the Oz principals, including Dorothy. The villain Ugu (who had kidnapped and and transformed Ozma) is a most satisfactory character. "A curious thing about Ugu the Shoemaker was that he didn't suspect, in the least, that he was wicked. He wanted to be powerful and great and he hoped to make himself master of all the Land of Oz, that he might compel everyone in that fairy country to obey him. His ambition blinded him to the rights of others and he imagined anyone else would act just as he did if anyone else happened to be as clever as himself." That just about says it all.

In *The Tin Woodman* (1918) a boy named Woot is curious to know what happened to the girl that the Tin Woodman had intended to marry when he was flesh and blood. (Enchanted by a witch, he kept hacking off his own limbs; replacements in tin were provided by a magical smith. Eventually, he was all tin, and so no longer a suitable husband for a flesh and blood girl; he moved away.) Woot, the Tin Woodman, and the Scarecrow (the last two are rather like an old married couple, chatting in a desultory way about the past) set out to find the girl. To their astonishment, they meet another tin man. He, too, had courted the girl. He, too, had been enchanted by the witch; had chopped himself to bits; had been reconstituted by the same magical smith. The two tin men wonder what has happened to the girl. They also wonder what happened to their original imperishable pieces.

In due course, the Tin Woodman is confronted by his original head. I have never forgotten how amazed I was not only by Baum's startling invention but by the drawing of the Tin Woodman staring into the cupboard where sits his old head. The Tin Woodman is amazed, too. But the original head is simply bored, and snippy. When asked "What relation *are* we?" ' The head replies, " 'Don't ask me. . . . For my part, I'm not anxious to claim relationship with any common, manufactured article, like you. You may be all right in your class, but your class isn't my class.' " When the Tin Woodman asks the head what it thinks about inside the cupboard, he is told,

"Nothing. . . . A little reflection will convince you that I have had nothing to think about, except the boards on the inside of the cupboard door, and it didn't take me long to think everything about those boards that could be thought of. Then, of course, I quit thinking."

"And are you happy?"

"Happy? What's that?"

There is a further surprise when the Tin Woodman discovers that his old girlfriend has married a creature made up of various human parts assembled from him and from the other man of tin. The result is a most divided and unsatisfactory man, and for the child reader a fascinating problem in the nature of identity.

In Baum's last Oz book, *Glinda of Oz* (posthumously published in 1920), magic is pretty much replaced by complex machinery. There is a doomed island that can sink beneath the waters of a lake at the mention of a secret word, but though the word is magic, the details of how the island rises and sinks are straight out of *Popular Mechanics.*

Ozma and Dorothy are trapped beneath the water of the lake by yet another narcissistic princess, Coo-ee-oh. By the time Glinda comes to the rescue, Coo-ee-oh has been turned into a proud and vapid swan. This book is very much a last round-up. . . . Certainly there are some uncharacteristic sermons in favor of the Protestant work ethic: "Dorothy wished in her kindly, innocent heart, that all men and women could be fairies with silver wands, and satisfy all their needs without so much work and worry. . . ." Ozma fields that one as briskly as the Librarian of Detroit could want:

"No, no, Dorothy, that wouldn't do at all. Instead of happiness your plan would bring weariness. . . . There would be no eager striving to obtain the difficult. . . . There would be nothing to do, you see, and no interest in life and in our fellow creatures."

But Dorothy is not so easily convinced. She notes that Ozma is a magical creature, and *she* is happy. But only, says Ozma, with grinding sweetness, " 'because I can use my fairy powers to make others happy.' " Then Ozma makes the sensible point that although she has magical powers, others like Glinda have even greater powers than she and so " 'there still are things in both nature and in wit for me to marvel at.' "

In Dorothy's last appearance as heroine, she saves the day. She guesses, correctly, that the magic word is the wicked Coo-ee-oh's name. Incidentally, as far as I know, not a single Oz commentator has noted that Coo-ee-oh is the traditional cry of the hog-caller. The book ends with a stern admonishment, " 'it is always wise to do one's duty, however unpleasant that duty may seem to be.' "

Although it is unlikely that Baum would have found Ruskin's aesthetics of much interest, he might well have liked his political writings, particularly *Munera Pulveris* and *Fors.* Ruskin's protégé William Morris would have approved of Oz, where

Everyone worked half the time and played half the time, and the people enjoyed the work as much as they did the play. . . . There were no cruel overseers set to watch them, and no one to rebuke them and find fault with them. So each one was proud to do all he could for his friends and neighbors, and was glad when they would accept the things he produced.

Anticipating the wrath of the Librarian of Detroit, who in 1957 found the Oz books to have a "cowardly approach to life," Baum adds, slyly, "I do not suppose such an arrangement would be practical with us. . . ." Yet Baum has done no more than to revive in his own terms the original Arcadian dream of America. Or, as Marius Bewley noted, "the tension between technology and pastoralism is one of the things that the Oz books are about, whether Baum was aware of it or not." I think that Baum was very much aware of this tension. In Oz he presents the pastoral dream of Jefferson (the slaves have been replaced by magic and goodwill); and into this Eden he introduces forbidden knowledge in the form of black magic (the machine) which good magic (the values of the pastoral society) must overwhelm.

It is Bewley's view that because "the Ozites are much aware of the scientific nature of magic," Ozma wisely limited the practice of magic. As a result, controlled magic enhances the society just as controlled industrialization could enhance (and perhaps even salvage) a society like ours. Unfortunately, the Nome King has governed the United States for more than a century; and he shows no sign of wanting to abdicate. Meanwhile, the life of the many is definitely nome-ish and the environment has been, perhaps, irreparably damaged. To the extent that Baum makes his readers aware that our country's "practical" arrangements are inferior to those of Oz, he is a truly subversive writer and it is no wonder that the Librarian of Detroit finds him cowardly and negative, because, of course, he is brave and affirmative. But then the United States has always been a Rigamarole land where adjectives tend to mean their opposite, when they mean at all.

Despite the Librarian of Detroit's efforts to suppress magical alternative worlds, the Oz books continue to exert their spell. "You do not educate a man by telling him what he knew not," wrote John Ruskin, "but by making him what he was not." In Ruskin's high sense, Baum was a true educator, and those who read his Oz books are often made what they were not—imaginative, tolerant, alert to wonders, life.

L. Frank Baum and
the "Modernized Fairy Tale"

· by Michael Patrick Hearn ·

As has often been noted fairy tales rarely deal with fairies, what J. R. R. Tolkien described as that "long line of fluttering sprites with antennae that I so disliked as a child and which my children in their turn detested."[1] For three hundred years this literary form inadequately labeled "fairy tale" has worn as many disguises as its enchanted princes and princesses. One of these transformations is the "modernized fairy tale" as defined by L. Frank Baum in *The Wonderful Wizard of Oz.*

Although not a scholar, Baum was well read in the traditions he wished to alter. Being the father of four sons, he was familiar with most of the nursery classics (he prefaced his first children's book *Mother Goose in Prose* with an erudite discussion of the Mother Goose legend); he knew well the work of Perrault, Grimm, and Andersen, and the blue, red, and other-colored fairy-tale collections of Andrew Lang. Among his predecessors, Baum admired Frank R. Stockton and Howard Pyle for their distinctive contribution to the American fantasy tradition; and among his contemporaries' works, he enjoyed Frances Hodgson Burnett's *Racketty Packetty House* and the Edwardian novels of E. Nesbit (an author whose fantasies were perhaps most in harmony with Baum's tales), as well as the stories of the now-neglected Tudor Jenks and Albert Stearns. In 1900, in his introduction to *The Wonderful Wizard of Oz*, Baum offered an audacious approach to juvenile literature. Concluding that the stories of Grimm and Andersen were now of only historical importance, he proposed "a series of newer 'wonder tales' in which the stereotyped genie, dwarf, and fairy are eliminated, together with all the horrible and blood-curdling incident devised by their authors to point a fearsome moral to each tale." *The Wonderful Wizard of Oz* was designed solely to entertain the young as "a modernized fairy tale, in which the wonderment and joy are retained and the heartaches and nightmares are left out."

Technically, *The Wonderful Wizard of Oz* is a descendant not of the *conte de fées*, but rather of the *voyage imaginaire*, a genre that flourished in the eighteenth century—the most notable examples are *Robinson Crusoe* and *Gulliver's Travels.* Tolkien distinguished between such

1. J. R. R. Tolkien, "On Fairy-Stories," *Tree and Leaf* (Boston, 1965), p. 6.

Reprinted from *Children's Literature in Education*, Spring 1979, pp. 57–66. Copyright © 1979 by Michael Patrick Hearn.

"traveler's tales" and true fairy stories in that such places as Lilliput, Atlantis, and the Land of Oz contain only those "marvels to be seen in this world in some other region in our own time and space: distance only conceals them."² These books do not deal with the realm of *Faërie*, the spiritual world which occasionally communes with that of mortal men. The fairies of Oz are not within this, the Celtic tradition: Baum's immortals do not possess the power to pass at will from their world to the profane.

To understand Baum's conception of the Land of Oz, one must consider his cosmography. Baum briefly dabbled in Theosophy, that nineteenth-century attempt to define theology according to modern physical science. The Theosophists studied Paracelsus, who explained the Aristotelian material world of earth, air, fire, and water as being guarded by spirits. Baum argued, "Every bit of wood, every drop of liquid, every grain of sand or portion of rock has its myriads of inhabitants. . . . These invisible and vapory beings are known as Elementals and play an important part in the lives of humanity. They are soulless, but immortal."³ From the Lovely Lady of Light (in *Tik-Tok of Oz*) to the Nome King in his Underground Dominions (in *Ozma of Oz*), Baum offered in his Oz books glimpses of each Paracelsian order of immortal. Unlike the Darwinians, the Theosophists saw nothing contradictory between theology and the Newtonian system of the universe; both were interpretations of the same natural forces, one spiritual, the other physical. Both disciplines, in that sense, are sciences.

Unlike Tolkien, Baum did not fear "the vulgar devices of the laborious, scientific magician."⁴ Indeed, the greatest magician in Baum's kingdom, the Wizard of Oz, carries his black bag of magic tools just like a general practitioner on a house call. When the Shaggy Man (in *The Patchwork Girl of Oz*) accurately describes Ozland as a place "where magic is a science," he reflects Baum's lifelong interest in mechanical gadgetry. "Some of my youthful readers are developing wonderful imaginations," he wrote in his preface to *The Lost Princess of Oz.* "This pleases me. Imagination has given us the steam engine, the telephone, the talking-machine and the automobile, for these things had to be dreamed of before they became realities. So I believe that dreams are . . . likely to lead to the betterment of the world." On the question of technical progress, however, the author of the Oz books was ambivalent. Oz remained rural, for Baum apparently agreed with John Ruskin

2. Ibid., p. 12.
3. In an article on clairvoyants, *Aberdeen* (South Dakota) *Saturday Pioneer,* April 5, 1890.
4. Tolkien, "On Fairy-Stories," p. 10.

that "all the best fairy tales have owed their birth, and the greater part of their power, to narrowness of social circumstances; they belong properly to districts in which walled cities are surrounded by bright and unblemished country."[5] The machines in Baum's garden are merely diversions, automatons to amuse their inventor.

Oz magic is limited. Not just anything can happen on the other side of the Deadly Desert. Just as the Natural World has its rules, so too must the Secondary World. "Its creator, like the inventor of a game, is at liberty to decide what the laws shall be," W. H. Auden has written, "but, once he has decided, his story must obey them."[6] At Ozma's ascent to the throne (in *The Marvelous Land of Oz*), the concept of Oz differs from Baum's original inspiration. Certain new rules (such as the impossibility of killing anyone, the absence of aging and death, and the abolishment of currency) are introduced, and, in the sequels, once he has defined his universe, Baum rarely disobeys its laws.

Just as his fairyland has its restrictions, so Baum also limited the form in which to express his ideas. He was convinced that what children wanted in their storybooks was "action," "something doing every minute," "exciting adventures, unexpected difficulties to overcome, and marvellous escapades."[7] E. M. Forster has argued that a story may have any fault but one: "that of making the audience not want to know what happens next."[8] And Baum generally avoided this difficulty in the Oz books. One suspects that when Baum thought he was losing his reader, he threw in something completely unexpected, just as Dickens did when he feared he was out of step with his public. Often there are strange twists and turns in Baum's plots, which cannot be justified by traditional theories of plot. His stories rarely contain the conventional balance between intent and expression, and, at times, he does not seem to have fully worked out his ideas. "My characters just won't do what I want them to!"[9] he was known to complain. Ironically, it may be the delight of the unexpected resulting from just such seemingly crossed purposes which has kept his readers' interest for over seventy-five years.

Baum's creations are generally what Forster calls "flat characters," people "constructed round a single idea or quality."[10] The Scarecrow is

5. John Ruskin, "Fairy Stories" (1886), in *The Complete Works of John Ruskin*, vol. 19 (London, 1905), p. 237.

6. W. H. Auden, "Afterword," *The Golden Key* by George Macdonald (New York, 1967), p. 83.

7. L. Frank Baum, "Modern Fairy Tales," *The Advance*, August 19, 1909.

8. E. M. Forster, *Aspects of the Novel* (New York, 1927), p. 27.

9. Quoted by Harry Neal Baum, "How My Father Wrote the Oz Books," *American Book Collector*, Special Number (December 1962), p. 17.

10. Forster, *Aspects of the Novel*, p. 67.

wise, the Tin Woodman kind, the Cowardly Lion cowardly. What George Orwell noted about Dickens' personages is also true of Baum's—that they "have no mental life. They say perfectly the thing they have to say, but they cannot be conceived as talking about anything else. They never learn, never speculate."[11] Perhaps not; but the reader does learn, at least by a character's example. For instance, in *The Emerald City of Oz*, Ozma has no other choice than to refuse to defend her nation against the Nome King and his invaders. The frustrating tension of the story lies in the conflict between personalities: the pacifist Ozma and the tyrannical Roquat. Neither may go against his nature. Similarly, in *The Patchwork Girl of Oz*, after wandering throughout the often dangerous Land of Oz, Ojo the Unlucky finds the left wing of a yellow butterfly, the final ingredient needed for a magic potion to save his uncle; but he is denied it by the tender-hearted Tin Woodman who will not allow even a butterfly to suffer in his kingdom. His decision is predictable, and yet it still comes as a shock after following all the adventures the boy has already survived. In a conventional scheme, the book would have had to conclude once the yellow butterfly had been discovered; whatever happened next would be only anticlimactic. But Baum was not ready to settle his narrative, and he handles the conflict so convincingly that indeed the reader does want to know what will happen next.

In other instances, Baum shares with other authors the difficulty of sustaining the reader throughout a multivolumed work. For an illustrious comparison, in *The Divine Comedy*, Paradise proves disappointing after the high adventure of Inferno. Structurally, Dante must take his hero throughout all levels of the spiritual world, but dramatically even the great Florentine poet could not sustain narrative tension. Not all readers have bothered to make the climb through Paradise once they have struggled through Purgatory. Perhaps the best example of Baum's wrestling with this Dantean dilemma is *Dorothy and the Wizard in Oz*. The marvelous adventures underground (sometimes as gripping as those through Dante's Hell) through the Vegetable Kingdom, through the Valley of Voe with its terrible Invisible Bears, through the lands of the fierce Wooden Gargoyles and the hungry Dragonettes, are all put out of sight and out of mind once the travelers reach the Emerald City; the tedious trial of Eureka the kitten is hardly a suitable conclusion to the exciting yarn that went before it.

As the series continued, and the Land of Oz grew closer to Baum's ideals of political perfection, the author had increasing difficulty writ-

11. George Orwell, "Charles Dickens," *Critical Essays* (London, 1946), p. 52.

ing about his fairyland. In *The Emerald City of Oz*, the sixth Oz book, Baum created a Utopian social structure for the Land of Oz; in this kingdom, the people worked half time and played the other half, and they had all that they desired and were content. But one cannot have a story without tension. In this book, Baum bothered to describe the politics of Oz in detail to contrast Ozma's benevolent rule with that of the cruel Nome King; perhaps he also tried to perfect his concept of Oz to eliminate the possibility of further adventures in his enchanted world. Significantly, he attempted to end the series in this book by isolating his fairyland from the rest of the world behind a Barrier of Invisibility.

Even before his clumsy attempt to end the Oz series, Baum escaped from the Land of Oz more often than is generally acknowledged. In his introductions, he complained that he had other tales to tell than those about the Land of Oz, but the children would have nothing else from him. Many of the stories, however, are only thinly disguised as Oz books. *Ozma of Oz*, one of his finest tales, takes place almost entirely in a land on the other side of the Deadly Desert. The travels along *The Road to Oz* are far more interesting than those encountered after the desert has been crossed. Once Baum revived contact with the Emerald City by wireless in *The Patchwork Girl of Oz*, the Royal Historian had to deal once more with what had become a static culture. Now he had to look again beyond Oz for new adventures, to the Rose Kingdom and Pessim's Island, to Pingaree and the Nome Kingdom. Baum was eventually forced to expand the borders of the original kingdom to include secondary cultures hidden from Ozma's just reign. "This fairyland is so big," Baum explained in *The Magic of Oz*, "that all of it is not yet known to its girl Ruler, and it is said in some far parts of the country, in forests and mountain fastnesses, in hidden valleys and thick jungles, are people and beasts that know as little about Ozma as she knows of them." Baum's widening of his original conception of the Land of Oz enabled his numerous successors to continue the popular Oz series for another twenty-six titles.

While broadening his secondary world, Baum was not always successful in eliminating all disagreeable incidents from the Oz stories. Of all Baum's critics, James Thurber was particularly thin-skinned about these books: "I know that I went through excruciatingly lovely nightmares and heartaches when the Scarecrow lost his straw, when the Tin Woodman was taken apart, and when the Saw-Horse broke his wooden leg (it hurt for me, even if it didn't for Mr. Baum)."[12] But even in the

12. James Thurber, "The Wizard of Chittenango," *The New Republic*, December 12, 1934, p. 141.

most brutal of the series, *The Wonderful Wizard of Oz*, Baum's villainly rarely possesses the terrors so characteristic of European folklore. Baum's Wicked Witch does not have fences of human bones and lanterns of men's skulls as does the cannibalistic Russian witch Baba Yaga; the only punishment Dorothy is threatened with is not to dance in a pair of hot iron shoes or to be strangled by an enchanted girdle, but rather merely to do the house cleaning at the castle. Of course, Baum recognized that drama derives from menace, and there are many dangers (many of them terrifying) to be overcome in the Oz books. What distinguishes his stories from those of most of his predecessors is that he never introduced such unpleasant details as mere didactic devices. While he did not create these tales to embody some fearsome moral, Baum's work is always moral. Baum admitted to not knowing of any memorable fairy tale "wherein the good did not conquer the evil and virtue finally reign supreme."[13] In the Oz books, Good always triumphs over Evil.

Baum objected to including in children's books not only "murders or cruelties" and "terrifying characters" but also "mawkish sentimentality, love and marriage."[14] Ruskin, too, found the concept of love as displayed in contemporary fairy tales "too often restrained and darkened into the hieroglyph of an evil mystery, troubling the sweet peace of youth with premature gleams of uncomprehended passion, and flitting shadows of unrecognized sin."[15] Although not so pious as the British critic, Baum also believed that love, "as depicted in literature, is a threadbare and unsatisfactory topic which children can comprehend neither in its esoteric nor exoteric meaning. Therefore it has no place in their storybooks."[16] Baum also hesitated on the subject of sexual reproduction. Because in Oz there is no death and no one, not even a baby in his crib, grows any older, one must conclude that birth too was an impossibility after the country was fully enchanted. Billina the Yellow Hen is an excellent example of the superstition of spontaneous regeneration; although she is said to be the only chicken in the Land of Oz, she is the mother of a brood of chicks. The implication that each egg laid by a hen is fertilized with or without a rooster is an odd assumption to be made by this former chicken breeder who was once secretary of the New York state poultry association.

Romance appears on occasion in the Oz books, especially in the later titles. Except for some fleeting references to the Tin Woodman's love

13. Baum, "Modern Fairy Tales."
14. Ibid.
15. Ruskin, "Fairy Stories," p. 234.
16. Baum, quoted in an interview, St. Louis *Republic*, May 30, 1903.

for the Munchkin girl and that of the sorceress Gayelette for Quelala in *The Wonderful Wizard of Oz*, the early stories are free of any "love interest"; but Baum compromised his ideals in *Tik-Tok of Oz* by matching the Rose Princess with Private Files, and in *The Scarecrow of Oz* by recording the frustrated courtship of Pon the Gardener's Boy and Princess Gloria of Jinxland. As both books were in part derived from dramatizations,[17] the introduction of romance into these children's stories is understandable, but perhaps because of it, these titles did not sell as well as the earlier ones in the series. When his publishers suspected that this new element demonstrated "a slight tendency in your later books to get away from the youthful viewpoint,"[18] Baum countered, "In *The Scarecrow*, I introduced a slightly novel theme, for me, in the love and tribulations of Pon . . . and Princess Gloria. It smacked a bit of the Andersen fairy tales and I watched its effect upon my readers. They accepted it gleefully, with all the rest, it being well within their comprehension."[19] Baum was apparently convinced (even if his publishers were not) that his readers were ready to accept, in *The Tin Woodman of Oz*, Nick Chopper's quest for his former sweetheart. How well Baum dealt with romance is questionable; the love of Private Files and Princess Ozga is supplementary to the plot of *Tik-Tok of Oz* and thus does not distract the child's attention from the search for the Shaggy Man's brother, but the freezing of Gloria's heart is a subtle comment on the fickleness of human desire that only the mature reader is likely to appreciate.

Such matters rarely troubled Baum, for the trials of these princes and princess were of only secondary concern to their creator. It is Dorothy, a contemporary child, who is his central protagonist. His Kansas girl was in part inspired by Lewis Carroll's heroine, and Baum argued that it was "fair to state that children loved Alice better than any prince or princess that Andersen ever created. The secret of Alice's success lay in the fact that she was a real child, and any normal child could sympathize with her all through her adventures."[20] One of Baum's strengths as a writer of fairy tales is that his child heroine is so easily identifiable by any young reader.

The concept of the "modernized fairy tale" determined Baum's style as much as his form. Andrew Lang had noticed, as did Baum, the nine-

17. *Tik-Tok of Oz* was largely based on Baum's 1913 musical comedy, *The Tik-Tok Man of Oz*; the latter part of *The Scarecrow of Oz* incorporated material from *His Majesty, the Scarecrow of Oz*, a silent film released in 1915 as *The New Wizard of Oz*. See Fred M. Meyer's "Dramatic Influence on Oz," *The Baum Bugle*, August 1962, pp. 5–8.

18. In a letter from Frank K. Reilly to L. Frank Baum, January 12, 1916.

19. In a letter from Baum to Reilly, January 17, 1916.

20. Baum, "Modern Fairy Tales."

teenth-century tendency to fill original fairy tales with "huge cantacles of description and word-painting, which are just as tedious to a child as to a grown-up reader."[21] Both Baum and Lang preferred the simple, direct style of the Brothers Grimm to that of their more verbose contemporaries. "The child skips descriptive passages because it cannot understand or appreciate them," Baum explained. He knew they avoided such passages, because he had done the same as a boy. "Such writers as Andersen, with all their kindly sympathy for the little ones, forget that their own keen appreciation of the beauties of nature is not shared by their youthful and inexperienced readers." Although Baum did not clutter his prose with gratuitous detail and his style may be praised for its clarity and energy, a good editor would have pruned Baum's redundancies and discouraged the overuse of the word "and." Baum was not a self-conscious stylist; his principal concern in his writing was that he be understood by his intended audience.

L. Frank Baum was surely among the most experimental and purposeful of American writers for children. In the pursuit of novelty in his stories, he continually tried out new methods of composition and expression, and, ever conscious of their young needs and capabilities, he carefully watched the effects of his literary experiments on his child readers. Despite the superficial contradictions between some of his theories and their practice in his work, Baum through his "modernized fairy tale" made a significant contribution to twentieth-century juvenile literature.

21. Andrew Lang, "Modern Fairy Tales," *Illustrated London News,* December 3, 1892, p. 714.

Oz

· *by Brian Attebery* ·

In 1900, when L. Frank Baum, with two successful children's books already in print, approached his publisher with a new project, the publisher turned him down. "He advised the author it was the consensus of the book trade that children were satisfied with the fairy tales already on the market, and that their parents would not buy anything as uncon-

Reprinted from *The Fantasy Tradition in American Literature.* Bloomington: Indiana University Press, 1980, pp. 83–108. Copyright © 1980 by Brian Attebery. Reprinted by permission of Indiana University Press.

ventional as an American fairy tale."[1] According to his biographers, Baum and his illustrator, W. W. Denslow, finally had to put up their own money for printing and binding.[2] We have seen . . . how many fairy tales were on the market, and how few of the good ones were significantly American. But where the publisher might have looked at the facts and said to himself that American fairy tales do not work, and that there were enough of the other kind, Baum made the opposite conclusion. If there were a great many fairy tales already, that meant they were well liked, and if there were no new, native fairy tales, then it was high time one was written.

Baum was right. Even though it was considered, as Mrs. Baum later recollected, "too different, too radical—out of the general line,"[3] his American fairy tale became one of the best-known and best-loved children's books of all time and marked a turning point in the development of American fantasy. For the first time, as Edward Wagenknecht points out, an American writer "can honestly be said to have created a world. . . ."[4]

It is the nature of that created world that enables us to say, with emphasis, that *The Wizard of Oz* is an American fairy tale. It does not take place in Kansas, any more than *A Connecticut Yankee in King Arthur's Court* takes place in Connecticut. It only starts there. But there is something about Oz itself that makes it more American than Mark Twain's Camelot or Christopher Cranch's Huggermugger Island. Somehow L. Frank Baum put together a fairyland, like none before it, that we recognize as our own, a fairyland so stamped with the national culture that the English, those connoisseurs of fairylands, often find it more bewildering than wonderful.[5] But Oz struck such a chord in American readers that they went on to demand a dozen sequels by the author, a number of musical comedy adaptations, three filmed versions (one of which is now a national icon), and countless continuations by lesser writers. . . .

1. Frank Joslyn Baum and Russell P. MacFall, *To Please a Child* (Chicago: Reilly & Lee Co., 1961), pp. 112–113.

2. Ibid., p. 113. Michael Patrick Hearn, in his introduction to *The Annotated Wizard of Oz* (New York: Clarkson N. Potter, Inc., 1973), p. 28, dismisses the story, saying that publisher George M. Hill accepted the book with no reservations except about the time of release. If so, Hill showed more acuity than one would expect: the book was an undoubted novelty and therefore a gamble.

3. Maud Gage Baum, in a letter quoted by Martin Gardner in "The Royal Historian of Oz," *The Wizard of Oz and Who He Was,* by Gardner and Russel B. Nye (East Lansing, Mich.: Michigan State University Press, 1957), p. 25.

4. Edward Wagenknecht, " 'Utopia Americana' A Generation Afterwards," *American Book Collector* 13 (December 1962):13.

5. Raylyn Moore, in her monograph, *Wonderful Wizard, Marvelous Land* (Bowling Green, Oh.: Bowling Green University Popular Press, 1974), p. 29, cites a British reviewer in recent years who felt compelled to explain to her readers the plot of *The Wizard*—and got it wrong.

It remains to be shown how Baum, unlike his predecessors, created a fairyland with such solid outlines that it remains recognizable in reproduction after reproduction, like a drawing still clear after a thousand tracings. Where did it come from? To begin with, it is defined through contrast with a place we know well, at least after Baum's opening description. Oz is, as Dorothy says to Toto in the film version, certainly not Kansas. Kansas is:

nothing but the great gray prairie on every side. Not a tree nor a house broke the broad sweep of flat country that reached the edge of the sky in all directions. The sun had baked the plowed land into a gray mass, with little cracks running through it. Even the grass was not green, for the sun had burned the tops of the long blades until they were the same gray color to be seen everywhere.[6]

This is just the opposite of the atmospheric magic that introduces "Rip Van Winkle." It is a way of describing landscape, in terms borrowed from Baum's naturalistic contemporaries, that cries out for relief. Baum is doing what a painter does when he paints a large, flat, colorless area on canvas: he is creating negative space which acts to make any positive design all the more vivid. Kansas is gray, so we begin to think about color. It is flat, so we long for contour. It is vast, so we wish for something on a human scale. It is featureless, so we imagine the absent trees and houses. It is harsh, so we think of fertility. Before the paragraph is done, we have been given, by contraries, a picture of Oz.

When Dorothy arrives in Oz, all of our expectations are met. Baum's description emphasizes the exact contrast:

The cyclone had set the house down, very gently—for a cyclone—in the midst of a country of marvelous beauty. There were lovely patches of green sward all around, the stately trees bearing rich and luscious fruits. Banks of gorgeous flowers were on every hand, and birds with rare and brilliant plumage sang and fluttered in the trees and bushes. A little way off was a small brook, rushing and sparkling along between green banks, and murmuring in a voice very grateful to a little girl who lived so long on the dry, gray prairies [p. 100].

As the story goes on, the opposition of Kansas and Oz continues in subtler ways. Kansas is a dead land, where even the grass is scorched and gray. Oz is a place of such fertility that a scarecrow can come alive spontaneously. Kansas is a place of isolation where people do not talk

6. All quotations from *The Wizard of Oz* are taken from the *Annotated Wizard of Oz*, ed. Michael Patrick Hearn. Hearn's text is taken from the original George M. Hill edition of 1900, actually titled *The Wonderful Wizard of Oz*. His introduction and annotations summarize most of the critical and biographical work done on Baum to date, and the reproductions of text and illustrations are of uniformly high quality.

to one another. In Oz, Dorothy is able to talk not only with people, but with all of the animals as well. In a later book, *The Road to Oz*, the first clue that Dorothy and her companions have left Kansas and entered fairyland is a city of speaking foxes:

"What a queer notion!" cried the Fox-King, beginning to laugh. "Whatever made you think this is Kansas?"

"I left Uncle Henry's farm only about two hours ago; that's the reason," she said, rather perplexed.

"But, tell me, my dear, did you ever see so wonderful a city as Foxville in Kansas?" he questioned.[7]

In addition to all this life and color and wonder, Oz is fabulously wealthy. Its farms are prosperous, its capital city littered with precious stones. No one must dress in rags, go hungry, or work harder than is good for him. Later, Baum began to develop a systematic utopian scheme for administering Oz, but the riches are there from the beginning. In *The Emerald City of Oz*, when Dorothy finally leaves Kansas for good, it is because the gap has grown too great between her poverty there and her rank in Oz, where she is now a princess. Oz is not plagued with droughts and crop failures, nor with bankers and mortgages, as Kansas most assuredly was. In Oz, a man who worked as hard as Uncle Henry could not help but succeed.

But Oz is not defined only by its unlikeness to Kansas. There are also certain striking similarities between the two. Both are landlocked, bordered, not by perilous seas, but by impassable desert. Oz expresses simultaneously the two symbolic landscapes that Henry Nash Smith says form American's image of the western frontier: it is the Garden of the World set in the midst of the Great American Desert.[8]

Oz is filled, too, with homely, familiar, Kansas-type things. The flora and fauna in the first book include cornfields, peach trees, crows, beetles, wildcats, storks, and field mice. Sprinkled among the familiar creatures are a few exotics, like the Cowardly Lion, and inventions, like the fierce, heraldic Kalidahs. But Baum rarely interrupts the story to introduce some strange, unheard-of plant or animal when he can slip a common one in without fuss. What wonders there are stand out because the matrix is so down-to-earth. He seems to have been guided not at all by conventional notions of which creatures belong in a fairy tale: there is not a single nightingale, for instance, in any of the Oz stories,

---

7. L. Frank Baum, *The Road to Oz* (1909; reprint ed., Chicago: Rand McNally & Co., n.d.), p. 43.

8. Henry Nash Smith, *Virgin Land: The American West as Symbol and Myth* (Cambridge, Mass.: Harvard University Press, 1950), pp. 174–183.

but an important part is played by a farmyard hen named Bill (Dorothy changes this to Billina).

Inanimate objects, too, are familiar. Michael Patrick Hearn, in his annotations to *The Wizard of Oz*, points to the magic slate used by the Good Witch of the North as an unexpectedly homely touch, along with the clothes basket that the Wizard attaches to his balloon, the Tin Woodman's funnel hat and oil can, and the Scarecrow himself.[9] All of these things except the basket are connected with magic. Chalk marks appear miraculously on the slate, the funnel and oil can are signs of the Woodman's strange transformation from flesh to tin, and the Scarecrow is an example of spontaneous animation. Other household items take on magical associations in this and later books. The Wicked Witch of the West carries, not the traditional broomstick, but an umbrella, appropriate, as Hearn points out, to her fear of water (p. 231). In later volumes a sawhorse, a patchwork quilt, and a phonograph come to life. Elements of daily life not only appear, but are intimately connected with the heart of the magic itself. The only American antecedents to this technique—or, more than technique, this philosophy of fantastic composition—are the talking chairs of Eggleston's *Queer Stories* and the contents of Davy's pockets in *Davy and the Goblin*, both undercut by the disjointed, affectless quality of dream narration, and Hawthorne's remarkable "Feathertop," which will be discussed later in connection with Baum's invention of characters.

Oz is also Kansas in that it is the agrarian promised land. It is essentially rural and democratic, though it has a capital city and a queen. Its many farmers and woodsmen act and speak with the assurance of yeomen, rather than with the cautious humility of peasants; servants are few and independent; the army has been reduced to a comical and impotent handful of officers; and titles, like Dorothy's, seem to be awarded by popular acclaim. It is too much to say, as Henry Littlefield does, that *The Wizard* is a "Parable on Populism," but it does share many of the Populist concerns and biases.[10] Taken loosely, with a grain of salt, Littlefield's readings help indicate much about the relationship between Kansas and Oz: the silver shoes are a little like William Jennings Bryan's silver ticket to prosperity, the Scarecrow is, in a sense, the troubled farmer, the Tin Woodman can stand for the industrial laborer, the Cowardly Lion is a witty analog of Bryan himself, the Wizard could be any ineffectual president from Grant to McKinley, and the band of petitioners are another Coxey's Army descending on Washington (Littlefield, throughout). I might even propose one more analogy.

9. Hearn, *The Annotated Wizard*, p. 106.
10. Henry Littlefield, "The Wizard of Oz: Parable on Populism," *American Quarterly* 16 (Spring 1964): 47–58.

Dorothy, bold, resourceful, leading the men around her toward success, is a juvenile Mary Lease, the Kansas firebrand who told her neighbors to raise less corn and more hell, or an Annie Diggs, the Populist temperance reformer. Baum and the Populists promoted an active role for women in the rural utopia. Incidentally, the real surname of the Wizard of Oz is Diggs.

Baum created Oz, then, with the aid of a paradox. It is Kansas—or rather, let us say, since most of the elements we are dealing with are applicable to a broader area than Dorothy's Kansas, it is the United States—and it is also everything that conditions in the United States make us wish for. Oz is America made more fertile, more equitable, more companionable, and, because it is magic, more wonderful. What Dorothy finds beyond the Deadly Desert is another America with its potential fulfilled: its beasts speaking, its deserts blooming, and its people living in harmony.

If Oz is America, then Dorothy is its Christopher Columbus. *The Wizard of Oz* is primarily a story of exploration, and one of its principal strengths is the feeling of "wild sunrise" that Keats ascribed to Cortez and his men. Dorothy is the discoverer who opens up the newest new world; later she and other children—the Cabots, Drakes, and Hudsons of this fairyland—chart the unknown regions remaining in Oz and the lands around it. All of the stories are based on movement. They whisk one away from known lands with a dizzying swoop, proceed over land, water, and air toward a brief action, then take off again for home. In *The Road to Oz*, indeed, there can be said to be no plot at all except the journey of Dorothy, Button Bright, Polychrome, and the Shaggy Man to Oz. The journey motif owes something to traditional fairy-tale structure, as we will see, but it owes as much or more to an American tradition of restlessness and curiosity. Happily, the discovery of Oz undoes some of the evils that accompanied the discovery of America. The natives accept the invaders, who, in turn, leave them in possession of their lands. Profit and progress are firmly excluded, and Oz remains the sleepy paradise it began.

Selma Lanes points out in her essay on "America as Fairy Tale" that the discovery of Oz coincided with a change in America's image of itself. Not until we realized that we were not living in a fairyland of peace and plenty could we begin to draw upon the power of that archetype in our fictions. "Having long had a thin tradition of American fairy tales precisely because of a deeply held faith in the fairy-tale aspects of the American dream, we have in our time lost that faith and are creating new and more convincing American fairy tales and fantasies."[11]

11. Selma Lanes, *Down the Rabbit Hole* (1971; reprint ed., New York: Atheneum, 1976), p. 111.

Oz is at the turning point. It could only have been invented by someone who, like Baum, personally felt the gap between American ideals
and American life. In this regard it is interesting to compare the Oz
books, as Fred Erisman does, with another of Baum's series, the "Aunt
Jane's Nieces" stories. The same values are upheld in both: generosity,
simplicity, individuality, and industry; but, whereas in Oz the virtues
define society, in the fictional "real world" they struggle for minor
victories within a system responsive only to power and prestige. Aunt
Jane's nieces rely on wealthy benefactors and on a shady detective
named Quintus Fogerty to help them clean up patches of corruption,
but Dorothy, in Oz, can destroy a witch with a bucket of water.[12]

The successful creation and immediate acceptance of Oz indicates
that Americans by 1900 had finally begun to feel the need of an ideal
world apart from America itself, as it was believed to be or as it was
expected to become. Many critics associate Oz with the host of utopian
writings that appeared in the final years of the nineteenth century, and
indeed it is a product of the same hunger for a more equitable world
that produced Edward Bellamy's *Looking Backward*. However, Bellamy's book, published in 1888, is a prospectus, set in a Boston-that-is-
to-come, for America's future development. It extrapolates; it proposes;
it relies on a science fiction rationale to lend plausibility to its ideas.
After it appeared, Bellamy-ite societies sprang up all over the world,
dedicated to bringing the course of history into line with Bellamy's
speculations. But twelve years later there were no Baumite societies.
No one proposed to govern Boston after the manner of the Emerald
City. Far from having scientific verisimilitude, Oz is punctuated with
marvels, each of which widens the gap between the lived world and the
imagined. Both Bellamy and Baum capture the energy of the Progressive
impulse, but while *Looking Backward* represents it at its most optimis-
tic, outward-reaching point, *The Wizard of Oz* reveals a shift toward
introspection and the redefinition of values.

That is not to say that Americans, including Baum, immediately and
totally transferred their allegiance from this world to various Others.
The perfections of Oz would not be so poignant if they did not so
strongly suggest qualities of American life at its rare best. In this respect, I would say that the primary source of secondary belief taken
advantage of by Baum is the powerful but receding faith in the American Dream, rather than any corpus of supernatural legend. That faith
has not yet left us entirely (it is kept alive partly by having been realized imaginatively in Oz) so that if Kansas, for example, is proven to be

12. Fred Erisman, "L. Frank Baum and the Progressive Dilemma," *American Quarterly*
20 (Fall 1968): 616–623.

a part of the fallen world, there is still a glimpse of earthly paradise farther on, in California or Alaska or on the moon. As a matter of fact, Oz shares many of its characteristics with the popular image of California: fertility, mineral wealth, kindly climate, and a profusion of colorful eccentrics. It is no accident that Baum moved to California when his writings earned him enough money. If Oz were open to immigration, the Emerald City would soon be as big as Los Angeles.

That, then, is Oz, a photograph of America with its blemishes filtered out, hand-tinted with the colors of the imagination. Topographically, the four quadrants of Oz seem to represent Baum's own personal geography. The East is Baum's New York childhood, a gentle land of forest and farm, with its residents scaled down just enough to make a child comfortable. One has the impression that the land of the Munchkins is a little older, more settled, than the other regions, and there are traces there of an "old-world" heritage, analogous to the costumes and customs retained by, say, Pennsylvania Germans. Baum's own family was German, and his father made at least one trip back to the old country. Could it be that the Munchkins, though the name is rich in other associations, derive ultimately from the child statue that overlooks the capital of Bavaria from its town hall? It is known as the Munich Child—*Münch Kind*. Bavaria's "official" color, like that of the Munchkins, is blue.

If the Munchkins live in the settled East, the Winkies are western frontiersmen. The western quarter of Oz is roughly equivalent to South Dakota, the westernmost point of Baum's early wanderings. The Winkie country is wild: "As they advanced the ground became rougher and hillier, for there were no farms nor houses in this country of the West, and the ground was untilled" (p. 220). It has hoards of marauding beasts—wolves, crows, and locust-like black bees—and a tribe of savages (in the form of winged monkeys) who attack Dorothy's band of pioneers. In heading west, the travelers leave the protective forest and enter a harsh prairie: "In the afternoon the sun shone hot in their faces, for there were no trees to offer them shade; so that before night Dorothy and Toto and the Lion were tired, and lay down upon the grass and fell asleep, with the Woodman and the Scarecrow keeping watch" (p. 221).

Baum was not a farmer, but as one-time editor of a small-town newspaper in Aberdeen, South Dakota, he was intimately concerned with the farmer's plight. As agriculture suffered in the late years of the nineteenth-century from drought, high expenses, and low prices, so did his paper suffer and eventually fold. Dorothy's Kansas is evidence that he was sensitive to the problems of his rural neighbors; it is a one-sided picture of the hardships of life on the prairies. The land of the Winkies is again a reflection of pioneer life, but with an element of optimism transforming gray waste into golden plenty. Though the West of Oz seems stern and forbidding, with a malevolent nature spirit—the Witch—in command, once the witch is vanquished we see it in a new light. The Winkies, out from under the thumb of cruel necessity, prove to be friendly and helpful. They are sturdy farmers and craftsmen, and they help Dorothy rescue and repair her friends in something of the spirit of a neighborhood barn raising. The chosen color of the Winkies is the yellow of ripe grain.

North and South are less clearly defined. Dorothy does not visit the northern land of the Gillikins in the first volume, and by the time Baum began to explore it, Oz had become well established in its own right and did not reflect American geography so closely. We do know that its color is purple and that it is a mountainous, timbered, largely unsettled region. It vaguely suggests northern Michigan, were Baum spent vacations, or Minnesota, or the great untracked expanse of Canada. The South is primarily a region of isolated communities of eccentrics, like the people made all of china in the first book. There is no clear connection between the land of the Quadlings and the American South, with which Baum was not familiar. Its queen, Glinda, is revered as a near-goddess, suggesting the southern worship of genteel womanhood, but then Oz itself becomes a matriarchy when Ozma comes to power. South, for Baum, more probably meant the hills of southern Illinois, Indiana, and Missouri, where he traveled selling china (the origin of the china country?) after the failure of his newspaper. The hostile Hammer-Heads who attempt to block Dorothy's southward journey are not unlike conventional hillbillies, save for their unusual physical characteristics—they are armless and have heads like battering rams on elastic necks.

The sections of Oz are unquestionably influenced by American sectionalism, though their characteristics reflect Baum's own experience rather than traditional political or economic divisions. The Munchkins do not engage in New England–style manufacturing nor the Quadlings in sharecropping: neither would be in keeping with an idealized fairyland. Nevertheless, the analog is clear. But what of the center, the radiant Emerald City? What, to Baum, was the capital and heart of the country? The answer must be Chicago, the scene of his first successes, the home to which he returned after his sales trips, the site of a growing artistic community of which Baum felt himself an integral part. His Chicago was not the jungle of Upton Sinclair's shocking exposés, nor the brawling hog-butcher of Carl Sandburg's apostrophes. It was the shining, hopeful White City, built on the shores of Lake Michigan for the great Columbian Exposition. The beaux arts brilliance of the White City inspired another writer to dream of utopia: to Henry Demarest Lloyd it was the seed of a new society, as described in his sketch "No Mean City."[13] The buildings of the White City soon came down, and the city of fairy-tale splendor passed into fairy tale, altered in color but not in meaning.

We have seen something of how Baum utilized American material to create his Other World. Other writers, like Bellamy or Lloyd, did much the same thing: they too played on national hopes and disappointments in creating fictional landscapes. But Oz is not a utopia, though it has many utopian elements. It is something more lasting, a fairyland. The difference is that Oz, like any fantasy world, allows for—rather, de-mands—the existence of the impossible. How does Baum integrate the impossible into a setting derived from pragmatic American experience? The best way to point out his techniques is to look at our earmarks of fantasy: narrative structure, hero, nonhuman characters, and a coherent system of magic and significance. The fact that Baum's work, American as it is, lends itself to analysis along these lines, which were drawn originally from the British fantasy tradition, is a sign of his unprece-dented entry into the mainstream of fantasy after our hundred or so years of apprenticeship.

The land of Oz is a constant throughout the series, and so may be described as if all fourteen volumes were one evolving work. But there is no overall story structure to the set; each book must be considered individually. The most important story, and the most highly structured, is that of *The Wizard of Oz*. ... [T]he basic pattern for most successful fantasy is derived from the traditional fairy tale, being that pattern of journey, conflict, return, and reward outlined by Vladimir Propp in his *Morphology of the Folktale*.

Baum was probably unaware of most of the scholarly work being done in this time by folklorists, and in any case he lived before the important analyses of the folktale, like Propp's, had been made. If his story corresponds in any significant measure to the traditional struc-ture, it indicates not a studied imitation but an intuitive grasp of the fundamental dynamics of the folktale. And *The Wizard* does, indeed, follow the traditional pattern, with the additional multiplication of ele-ments and overlaying of action we expect of a written work, though a good oral storyteller can do the same things.

The rapid opening of *The Wizard* corresponds to Propp's first set of

13. Cited in Daniel Aaron, *Men of Good Hope: A Story of American Progressives* (New York: Oxford University Press, 1961), pp. 135–136.

"functions." . . . First of all, there is an original, presumably idyllic, situation. In this case, the original state occurs some time before the book begins, when Dorothy was living with her parents somewhere other than Kansas. Next is what Propp called "absentation," when one or both parents leave the formerly happy home. Dorothy's parents die, leaving her in the care of Uncle Henry and Aunt Em. On a symbolic level, Uncle Henry and Aunt Em are Dorothy's parents, but she is unable, at this point, to accept them as such: hence the importance of her final reunion with them. Next in the fairy-tale morphology we have a command or interdiction of some sort, and an act of disobedience. Aunt Em calls out to Dorothy to get into the cellar, but Dorothy runs after her dog instead. At this point in a fairy tale the element of magic enters into what usually begins as an ordinary domestic scene. The villain may come snooping around or leave a trap for the hero, or as in this case, the hero may fall by accident under the influence of a magical agent, like the cyclone which carries Dorothy to Oz.

Now the fairy-tale action proper begins. Either there is an act of villainy, or else a need or lack is discovered. The hero is informed of it and dispatched to go fill the need. The first thing he usually encounters is a figure Propp calls the "donor," who tests the hero in some way, awards him a magical agent to aid in the quest, and points the way. For Dorothy, these two segments, the dispatch and the meeting with the donor, are compressed into one. The first person she meets in Oz is the Good Witch of the North. The Witch informs her of her lack—she is no longer in Kansas and there is no way to get back—and also presents her with the magical silver shoes and a protective kiss on the forehead. Then she shows her the yellow brick road and sends her off on the next stage of her adventure.

The journey to the Emerald City figures in Propp's morphology as a single function, the delivery to the appointed place of action. But Baum expands this element into a symmetrical set of complications. First, Dorothy meets her three companions: the Scarecrow, the Tin Woodman, and the Cowardly Lion. These are the hero's customary helpers, animated forms of the magical agent. They are also, in this instance, heroes themselves of parallel subplots. Each has a lack of his own— brains, heart, and courage—and to each Dorothy acts as the dispatcher, sending them off to the Emerald City. After the three companions appear we got three obstacles: wild beasts, a river, and a field of deadly poppies, before reaching the goal.

At this point in the fairy-tale morphology we should meet the villain, usually an ogre or evil wizard. Dorothy finds a wizard, but instead of taking the villain's part, the Wizard of Oz assumes the role of a second dispatcher. He informs the travelers of a new need: they must kill the Witch of the West. The subsequent trip to the land of the Winkies is an embedded adventure within the main one. The secondary adventure proceeds apace, with a struggle, a victory, and a return. The Witch is dead, the quest accomplished, and the Wizard should now revert to his original role. He is defeated, his conditions met; now he is responsible for solving the problems of the heroes. With the auxiliary heroes he can do so. They get what they lack. But Dorothy discovers that she is no closer to home than before. With her, the Wizard was falsely assuming the positions of donor and villain. He has nothing to give her, nor does it solve her lack to defeat him. So we get something not unknown in fairy tales: the hero sets out once again in search of the still elusive goal.

With a fine balancing of beginning and end, Dorothy meets at last the one who can help her, and it is Glinda, the Good Witch of the South, essentially a double of the Witch of the North who launched her on her quest. Now the resolution comes, but in a divided form. Most fairy tales end with a wedding or an accession to the throne, or both. No one is paired off at the end of *The Wizard*, but the three companions all assume thrones. The Scarecrow goes back to rule the Emerald City, the Woodman becomes Emperor of the Winkies, and the Lion becomes king of the forest. For Dorothy, the resolution is one which does not appear in Propp's morphology, unless we stretch the meaning of such a term as Function K^{10}, "release from captivity," but we know it from such tales as "Hansel and Gretel." It is a return to the family, now seen not as cruel step-parents but as loving parents, though still in the guise of aunt and uncle.

Baum not only intuitively understood fairy-tale structure, but he was also able to adjust it at will to fit his needs. The sharp break between the opening segment and the ensuing action, for example, he made serve as a crossing of the threshold into another world. By doubling and tripling certain elements he was able to take advantage of his major strengths as a writer, the portrayal of movement and the quick and comical delineation of character. The embedded plot is neatly introduced by having one character, the Wizard, take on two functional roles. The Wizard is also placed in a central position in the book, structurally and geographically, with the result that at the heart of fairyland we find Omaha-born Oz Diggs, a reminder of the opening scene of the book and a forecast of its end. Baum's skill in handling the fairy-tale story line—in making it his own—surpasses, I believe, that of any of the imitators of European style fairy tales, . . . just as his grasp of American character and landscape surpasses that of all his predecessors in the native, fairies-in-America line.

Baum's first stories were actually much like those of Howard Pyle or the lesser retellers from European tradition. They were transformations into *Märchen* form of familiar Mother Goose motifs, short and clever but in no way innovative.[14] At the time he was preparing *The Wizard* for publication he was also readying *A New Wonderland*, a set of stories in the familiar comic fairy court vein of Thackeray's *The Rose and the Ring* or Andrew Lang's original tales.[15] Between Oz books he also continued to write more or less traditional fairy stories, the finest of which is *Queen Zixi of Ix*.[16] These books show that Baum was familiar with the kind of competent fairy-tale writing that magazines like *St. Nicholas* made popular. Indeed, Zixi herself appeared in *St. Nicholas*, from November 1904 to October 1905. If Baum had written more for *St. Nicholas* and similar prestigious journals, and if he had limited himself to their standard fare, his achievement would have been less striking, but his reputation would probably not have suffered such an eclipse among critics of children's literature.

Baum made a clear distinction between his conventional stories and those he called modernized fairy stories, like *The Wizard*, but, as he indicates in his introduction to that book, both kinds shared the same prototypes:

Folk lore, legends, myths and fairy tales have followed childhood through the ages, for every healthy youngster has a wholesome and instinctive love for stories fantastic, marvelous, and manifestly unreal. The winged fairies of Grimm and Andersen have brought more happiness to childish hearts than all other human creations [p. 85].

Baum is clearly thinking of "folk lore" here as something belonging to other cultures and other times. He gives it credit for originating the fairy tale, but seeks something more in tune with present-day life: "for the time has come for a series of newer 'wonder tales' in which the stereotyped genie, dwarf and fairy are eliminated, together with all the horrible and blood-curdling incident devised by their authors to point a fearsome moral to each tale" (p. 85). If he had known more of authentic oral tradition, he would have known that most tales are free of both winged fairies and morals. By reacting against the sentimental writers

14. L. Frank Baum, *Mother Goose in Prose* (1897; reprint ed., Indianapolis, Ind.: The Bobbs-Merrill Company, 1905).
15. L. Frank Baum, *A New Wonderland* (New York: R. H. Russell, 1900), was revised and retitled *The Surprising Adventures of the Magical Monarch of Mo and His People* in 1903 (Indianapolis: The Bobbs-Merrill Company; reprint ed., New York: Dover Publications, Inc., 1968).
16. L. Frank Baum, *Queen Zixi of Ix; or the Story of the Magic Cloak* (New York: Century Co., 1905).

that he knew (more likely the Virginia Bakers and Lily Wesselhoefts of this country than the Grimm collection or Andersen), he was reaching past them to sources he had never actually seen or heard.

As Baum continued to write "modernized" tales, he grew bolder in his treatment of the fairy-tale structure. *The Land of Oz* has an unconventional ending: the boy hero is revealed at last to be, not a king in disguise, but a queen, transformed by witchcraft into male form. In *Ozma of Oz* and several of the later Oz books, Dorothy becomes a sort of heroine errant, performing quests not for her own sake but for other, lesser characters; the hero role is broken up, that is, into an active but unconcerned protagonist and one or more passive but needy companions. *The Scarecrow of Oz* contains a fairy tale in burlesque, the "hero" of which is the most ineffectual character in the story. Some of the books, like *Dorothy and the Wizard in Oz* and *The Road to Oz*, suppress all phases of the fairy-tale morphology except the quest–journey, but they still follow the proper sequence for that segment of the full structure. In others, like *The Emerald City of Oz, Tik-Tok of Oz,* and *Glinda of Oz*, a rival story line of conquest and siege all but overpowers the individualistic fairy-tale development, perhaps reflecting America's growing awareness of international strife up to and during World War I. But the underlying pattern remains constant and occasionally, as in *Rinkitink of Oz*, reappears in classic form.

Though Baum's familiarity with fairy-tale style and structure does not mean that he was in touch with the Jack tales and other American versions of *Märchen*, still he was able to do what oral storytellers often do, adapt a borrowed pattern to local conditions, local habits of thought. There are genuine bits of oral tradition in his stories, mostly on the level of language: prose rhythms, metaphors, and jokes. A structure is a very neutral thing, so that no matter where Baum learned the pattern for a fairy tale, his fantasies came out unmistakably American because of their sound, their sense of place, and, to move into the next area of concern, their characters.

The third point noted about the English fantasies . . . is that their protagonists, like the heroes of fairy tale, are generally the representatives of common, unexceptional humanity in worlds of miracle. They are lenses through which the reader can view the unfamiliar without having to lose his orientation in the familiar. If they accomplish prodigious feats it is only with agonizing effort—or luck. They are high-spirited, but must frequently be helped by the grander figures around them. Their greatest strengths are an active curiosity that gets them into awkward situations, and a measure of common sense that gets them out again.

The one unforgettable protagonist of Baum's books is Dorothy. Dorothy is all of the above things: ordinary, human, lucky, plucky, surrounded by protectors, curious, and sensible. She suggests Gretel (another witch killer), Cinderella , and Jack—all the intrepid *Märchen* heroes. But Dorothy and her lesser avatars, Tip, Prince Inga, Betsy Bobbin, and Trot, are more complex than characters in traditional tales. Other sides of Dorothy's character point to sources and analogs in other modes of literature.

An important literary source for *The Wizard*, and probably the primary inspiration for Dorothy herself, is Lewis Carroll's *Alice in Wonderland*. When Baum set about to construct a modernized fairy tale, *Alice* was one of the few examples available to him, although it may be called a fairy tale only in the very broadest sense, being much less closely aligned with oral tradition in detail or overall conception than *The Wizard*. Nevertheless, Baum considered Alice's adventure, "rambling and incoherent as it is," to be "one of the best and perhaps the most famous of modern fairy tales."[17] Rambling and incoherent in comparison with folk or literary *Märchen* it is, because it is nonsense: a wild mutation away from the parent form, with its own logic and order; but for Baum, who was considering it as a source book, the important thing about *Alice* is not its discovery of the absurd but its development of the fairy-tale hero into a distinctive, perceiving individual. In an essay on "Modern Fairy Tales," Baum, after decrying Carroll's "whimsical" treatment of fantastic themes, says that, nonetheless:

> . . . it is but fair to state that the children loved Alice better than any prince or princess that Andersen ever created. The secret of Alice's success lay in the fact that she was a real child, and any normal child could sympathize with her all through her adventures. The story may often bewilder the little one—for it is bound to bewilder us, having neither plot nor motive in its relation—but Alice is doing something every moment, and doing something strange and marvelous, too, so the child follows her with rapturous delight.[18]

In contrast with Charles Carryll, whose *Davy and the Goblins* copies all of Carroll's techniques except that of giving life to his characters (and thence to his story), Baum threw away offhand everything but the spirit of *Alice in Wonderland*, and in doing so produced a far worthier successor. Dorothy and Alice are two of the most likeable heroines in literature, two witty and contemporary character sketches of the sort one finds in the best domestic comedies. Carroll discovered that such a

17. L. Frank Baum, "Modern Fairy Tales," *The Advance* (19 August 1909), quoted in Hearn, *The Annotated Wizard*, p. 91.
18. Ibid.

character could be removed from the social world into the world of dream, and Baum took things one step further (in terms of violations of reality) into a world of waking marvels.

Though Alice and Dorothy are both portraits of believable, modern-day children, there are important differences between them. Dorothy, unlike Alice, never wonders who she is, where she is going, or why the world has suddenly turned upside down. "My name is Dorothy," she says to the Scarecrow after only one day in the land of Oz, "and I am going to the Emerald City, to ask the great Oz to send me back to Kansas" (p. 118). Even while whirling through the air in the middle of a tornado, she keeps her self-possession:

At first she had wondered if she would be dashed to pieces when the house fell again; but as the hours passed and nothing terrible happened, she stopped worrying and resolved to wait calmly and see what the future would bring. At last she crawled over the swaying floor to her bed, and lay down upon it; and Toto followed and lay down beside her [pp. 95–96].

Alice is English; Dorothy is aggressively, triumphantly American. As the primary link between the naturalistically portrayed Kansas of the beginning and the transmogrified America that is Oz, she must be able to make explicit the comparisons between the two, and to do so she must be accepted by the reader as a valid representative of all things American. Therefore, Dorothy is not merely a fairy-tale heroine, or a believable child, she is also heir to an American conception of character, especially of its own character. And what is the essential American character? Often it is the explorer, the wanderer, who penetrates ever wilder regions of the world or the mind and comes back relatively unscathed.

Rip Van Winkle, in the first successful American romance, is such a wandering hero. He too, like Dorothy, explores for a time the perilous regions of fantasy, facing the strangest events with mild surprise. Rip ages during his adventure, but he can hardly be said to be otherwise changed by it, except perhaps to be more appreciative of his lost and regained home. Rip is childlike, in comparison to those around him; he represents a vanishing peasant simplicity, organically related to that of a fairy-tale hero, that lets him accept without question whatever may happen.

Edgar Allan Poe's explorers are of a different cast. Like Rip, like Dorothy, they are plunged into a universe of marvels, but their reaction is more likely to be an exultant horror than calm curiosity. A Poe hero represents the American mind in conflict with itself. Enamored, on the one hand, of system and logic, he is drawn, on the other, to the wild unpredictability of the universe. When adventure comes to him, his two desires clash. He may become totally irrational, possessed by sensation, like Roderick Usher. Or he might take refuge in blind reason, an artificial order that has no bearing on the outside world, like Usher's friend, or like the oh-so-reasonable narrator of "The Tell-Tale Heart." In both cases, the madness buried at the beginning surfaces by the end. Twain's Connecticut Yankee portrays a similar conflict between reason and miracle.

By using a child version of the explorer, Baum is able to sidestep such an intellectual dilemma. Dorothy and Arthur Gordon Pym mark the boundaries of this American type, the explorer or stranger in a strange land. Somewhere between the two we find Melville's not very mature Taji, in the water world of *Mardi*, his Ishmael, who seems to poise exactly between the dark and light views of his world, and the mature child Huckleberry Finn, under whose seeming acceptance there is a great deal of Poesque despair. What all of these characters share is their ability to discover new worlds, to move through them and learn from them, and then to emerge from them paradoxically the same as when they started. Even Pym escapes long enough to tell the tale. Some of them are Gothic heroes, some picaros, some heroes of *Märchen*, but whatever the narrative mode, the commanding motivation remains the same. It is to see what is around the next corner or over the next range, and that is true whether the hero looks ahead with fear or with delight.

Since Dorothy is female and a westerner, she suggests one other category of character, another peculiarly American one: the pioneer woman. There are two classes of pioneer women in the popular imagination. One is faded and bleak and particularly appealing to local color writers with a naturalistic vision. That is Aunt Em. The other is lively and attractive, drawing her strength from the earth she lives so close to. That is, of course, Dorothy, who is to some degree a forerunner of the Nebraska heroine in Willa Cather's *My Ántonia*.[19] Throughout *The Wizard*, Dorothy gives her comrades guidance and encouragement, like a little mother; and if men of tin or straw could eat, or if lions were vegetarians, she would undoubtedly nurture them as well. She does an admirable job of keeping herself and Toto provided for on an arduous journey. Nurture, comfort, and guidance: these, in mythology, are the functions of the Earth Mother. If Dorothy were allowed to mature, we might imagine her something like the grown-up Ántonia, full-figured, sun-burned to earth colors, radiating order, contentment, and fertility.

19. The road to Ántonia's house is lined with sunflowers and described as "a gold ribbon across the prairie"—another yellow brick road? Willa Cather, *My Ántonia* (Boston and New York: Houghton Mifflin Company, 1946), p. 19.

She does not grow up, however. An adult heroine would, as I say, bring back all those troublesome questions of belief and reason that drove Poe's heroes mad. So Baum imposed on Oz an end to aging, and Dorothy, rather than maturing, began to fall into a rather gushing girlishness. That is one of the primary weaknesses of the later books, so important is Dorothy's earthiness to the fantasy.

How are all these conceptions of Dorothy related? The first, the fairy-tale hero, is a basic guideline, like the Proppian story outline. It merely says that the hero must be perceivably one of us, and not a partaker of the strangeness of the Other World. The qualities of a good fairy-tale hero keep the story moving, because he is bold and curious, and make the outcome meaningful, because he is universal. But a writer who wishes to expand the role of hero to the status of rounded character, and the brief tale into full-length fantasy, must fill in the outlines from other sources.

If the fairy tale gave Baum an outline for his main character, one might say that Lewis Carroll taught him how to draw in features and make them appear three-dimensional. Carroll's Alice comes to life because she has a family, a history, habits, opinions, and a unique point of view. These are things that are difficult to generate unless the author is familiar with the character's milieu, or unless he knows more about his fictional society than he could ever fit into a book. It is possible to so immerse oneself in a fantasy world (I am speaking of art, not psychopathology) that a member of that world can become a fully developed personality and our representative in the world, like certain of J. R. R. Tolkien's hobbits, but it is easier to draw a character more directly from life.

With an outline and a set of features, Dorothy still needed color. It is not enough to say, "I will create a character who seems to be a living, breathing American child." One must have some notion of what it means to be such a creature. Part of what it meant to Baum is to be healthy, confident, exploratory, and full of pioneer spirit, to the point of invoking the quasi-mythic conception of frontier womanhood. This side of Dorothy's character reveals Baum's regional-minded optimism: what wonderful children we are raising in the West, he is saying; they are the hope of the country. Dorothy from Kansas, Betsy Bobbin from Oklahoma, and Trot from California all move through his stories gently wreaking order and distributing love. Baum was fond of all children, but he had no such faith in those from eastern cities. Button-Bright from Philadelphia is a charming boy, but completely helpless. In the matter of character, as in setting, Baum is all the more an American writer for being a regional one as well.

What about the characters around Dorothy? Just as she is the essential tie with the familiar, they are the wonder-working helpers and adversaries who must carry us into the marvelous. How does Baum stand up on our fourth element of fantasy, the assortment of nonhuman characters? Excellently, for the most part. From the Good Witch at the beginning of *The Wizard* to the fascinating Yookoohoo in *Glinda of Oz*, his last book, Baum produced with seeming ease a host of vivid, unquestionably magical beings: he brought a scarecrow to life, made an engaging eccentric out of an insect, revealed a common tramp to be a wonder worker, and made witches seem like his own invention.

The secondary characters in Baum's Oz fall into four overlapping groups: there are Class A figures, bold, humorous, unforgettable characters who nearly assume hero status; Class B, not so grand as Class A, but still strong; Class C, a group of spear carriers, thrown in to keep the story rolling, which they do competently enough; and, unfortunately, Class D, weak or whimsical groups that never come to life at all.

In Class A I would put the Big Three: the Scarecrow and the Tin Woodman from *The Wizard* and Jack Pumpkinhead from *The Land of Oz*. These three characters establish Baum as the Dickens of fantasy. Like Pickwick and his friends, they are a perfect blend of the grotesque and the lovable. They demonstrate Baum's remarkable ability to assume the viewpoint of even the oddest creature.

What kind of personality does a living scarecrow have? Baum, without hestitating, answers that this particular Scarecrow, at least, is a close and careful observer (through those lovely, blue, mismatched, painted eyes), a wit (though his jokes are often, appropriately enough, corny), a humble fellow (having started out in life as a sort of farm laborer), but with some understandable vanity about his wizard-made brains. From having spent his early life stuck on a pole, he is something of a philosopher, of the pragmatic school:

"I am never hungry," he said; "and it is a lucky thing I am not. For my mouth is only painted, and if I should cut a hole in it so I could eat, the straw I am stuffed with would come out, and that would spoil the shape of my head" [p. 124].

His mood is always sunny, which may be due to the fact that his mouth is painted in a perpetual smile. It is not much use asking whether he is always smiling on the inside, since his insides are only straw. He is a case of clothes making the man, and doing a pretty good job of it. Unlike Dorothy, who is never described in much detail since we are more interested in her impressions than in her appearance, the Scarecrow, being all outside, as it were, is described quite exactly, and with frequent subsequent references to his peculiar looks:

Dorothy leaned her chin upon her hand and gazed thoughtfully at the Scarecrow. Its head was a small sack stuffed with straw, with eyes, nose, and mouth painted on it to represent a face. An old, pointed blue hat, that had belonged to some Munchkin, was perched on this head, and the rest of the figure was a blue suit of clothes, worn and faded, which had also been stuffed with straw. On the feet were some old boots with blue tops, such as every man wore in this country, and the figure was raised above the stalks of corn by means of the pole stuck up its back [p. 116].

The Scarecrow's first act is a friendly wink at Dorothy, and he continues to demonstrate his feelings with broad gestures as well as with a distinctive style of speaking. Baum has a way of portraying character through costume and through repeated bits of action, like the Scarecrow's many tumbles, that is probably a holdover from his youth, when he wrote and acted in popular plays. The Scarecrow and the Tin Woodman are very much like a pair of comic players, a team of vaudevillians, and it is no wonder that old vaudevillians Montgomery and Stone on Broadway and Ray Bolger and Jack Haley in the movie struck such a response in the roles.

At his most human, the Scarecrow resembles a kindly farmer. The Tin Woodman resembles, to no one's surprise, a woodsman: a hunter or trapper or logger operating just beyond the cleared land. And that is what he once was, until, through a gradual replacement of body parts, he became a man of metal, with his memory and identity intact, but no longer human.

In many ways, the Tin Woodman complements the Scarecrow. The Scarecrow is contemplative, the Woodman a man of action. The Scarecrow comes from settled land, the Woodman from the virgin forest. The Scarecrow was once inanimate matter that became a man; the Tin Woodman a man that has grown to resemble an inanimate object. The Scarecrow aspires to human intelligence, while the Tin Woodman longs for human sympathies. On that last point hangs their entry into the plot, and throughout the story questions of intellect center on the Scarecrow and questions of sentiment on the Woodman.

Many critics have pointed to the Tin Woodman as the first entry of the machine into the field of fantasy, but the Tin Woodman is not a machine, nor is he ever connected with things mechanical. Baum does bring in a mechanical man, Tik-Tok, in the third Oz book, and he is a very different character from the Woodman. The Tin Woodman's distinctive characteristic is the tender human spirit within his hard and shiny body; it makes him a rather poignant character, and, since he accepts his fate without self-pity, an admirable one, a symbol of resistance to dehumanization.

Jack Pumpkinhead is not so witty as the Scarecrow, nor as staunch as the Tin Woodman, but he is their equal in strangeness. Jack is a man made of wood, with a Jack O'Lantern for a head, dressed in some un-known gentleman's cast-off clothes. He is meant only for a joke, but his comical appearance strikes the fancy of an old witch, and so she brings him to life. If that sounds familiar, it ought to, because Jack is Haw-thorne's "Feathertop," given another chance at existence. Feathertop was too good a creation to disappear after just one story. Baum proves that his comical potential was barely tapped in Hawthorne's tale.

I know of no evidence that Baum read Hawthorne. He was not gener-ally much of a reader, but he had a taste for anything partaking of the marvelous, and . . . there were few American writers besides Hawthorne who were able to make effective use of fantasy. The resemblance be-tween the two scenes of animation is quite striking: in place of Mother Rigby's hell-fired pipe we have the Powder of Life in Mombi's pepper box, and, Mombi did not make the mannequin himself as Mother Rigby did, but other details—the pumpkinhead's calm acceptance of life and the witch's shifts from fury to glee—are identical. Baum's account even suggests something of Hawthorne's amused style:

Jack Pumpkinhead stepped back a pace, at this, and said in a reproachful voice:
    "Don't yell like that! Do you think I'm deaf?"
    Old Mombi danced around him, frantic with delight.
    "He lives!" she screamed: "he lives! he lives!"
    Then she threw her stick into the air and caught it as it came down; and she hugged herself with both arms, and tried to do a step of jig; and all the time she repeated, rapturously:
    "He lives!—he lives!—he lives!"[20]

Marius Bewley suggests that Jack Pumpkinhead is not the only thing in Oz to show Hawthorne's influence.[21] Many of Baum's magical events sound like possible entries in Hawthorne's notebooks: a girl's heart is frozen so she cannot love; a man meets his own cast-off head and cannot decide which of the two is the real individual; a straw man wants a brain and finds that one made of pins and needles serves him perfectly; a mechanical man moves, speaks, and thinks—but does he live? What is the difference between these conceits and those of Hawthorne such as "The Bosom Serpent"; "Ethan Brand," whose sin has turned his heart to marble; "The Birthmark" that is all that stands

20. L. Frank Baum, *The Land of Oz* (1904; reprint ed., Chicago: Rand McNally & Co., n.d.), p. 14.
21. Marius Bewley, "The Land of Oz: America's Great Good Place," *The New York Review of Books* (3 December 1964), reprinted in his *Masks and Mirrors* (New York: Athe-neum, 1970), pp. 259–260.

between a woman and perfection—and death; or the mechanical yet seemingly living butterfly created by "The Artist of the Beautiful"? The difference is partly one of tone—Baum is in every case more light-hearted, less concerned with dark implications and motivations—and partly one of framework. Hawthorne wrote allegorical romance, Baum fantasy. And the difference between those two modes is in the placing of secondary belief: the one continually points beyond itself to the moral or metaphysical truths under examination, while the other pretends to signify only itself, to be no more than a recounting of "actual" events, although those events may lead to the same philosophical questions that the allegory explicitly raises.

I will say more about meanings in Baum shortly, for that is the final point of my analytical description of fantasy, but for now I will say only that Hawthorne's techniques of speculation seem to form the basis for Baum's creation of magical characters. The most important characters, like the three discussed above, always combine more than one allegorical message. They are more on the order of Chillingworth, who is at one time wronged husband, man of the wilderness, devil, and Faustian antihero of *The Scarlet Letter*, than like the one-dimensional characters of the sketches. Jack Pumpkinhead, for instance, goes beyond Feathertop's single issue: our willingness to be fooled by a handsome facade. He also plays the child to Tip, his maker, raising questions of parental responsibility and love for the imperfect child. At times he is a wise fool, a Touchstone, revealing the inconsistencies of those around him. He is, like the Scarecrow, a symbol that a man should be judged by his acts rather than his origins. And he becomes an embodiment of the paradox of mortal body and immortal soul when his pumpkin head—surely the major part of him—spoils and is buried, leaving Jack as good as new with a replacement.

Other characters play more limited roles and have less complex meanings. The group of individuals I called Class B generally have one notable attribute apiece, but each can, if given the opportunity, break into three-dimensionality. Among this class are the witches, good and evil; various animals, especially the Cowardly Lion and Billina, the forthright yellow hen; the other Americans who make their way to Oz, all of them children or eccentrics like the humbug Wizard or the Shaggy Man; solitary magicians, neither good nor evil, like Red Reera the Yookoohoo or the Lonesome Duck; the archvillains of Oz, the Nomes; and characters like the Patchwork Girl and the Frogman who might have been Class A except that they do not appear until the later, lesser books and thus are not granted the development given to the Scarecrow or Tin Woodman. The Nomes are an interesting race, strongly reminiscent of the gnomes in Christopher Cranch's *The Last of the Huggermuggers.* They are never portrayed as entirely evil creatures; indeed, the Nome King bears a curious resemblance to Santa Claus, and he can be charming on occasion. But the Nomes are earth spirits, guardians of underground treasures, and their wealth often leads them into greed. They value jewels too much and other living creatures too little. Baum shows a nice insight into his own symbols when he makes the Nomes fear, more than any other thing, the egg, symbol of new life.

Class C characters never go beyond their single significance. They include most of the adult Ozites, who may be subdivided into Helpful and Unhelpful Strangers. Also in this group are Uncle Henry and Aunt Em after they get to Oz, where they degenerate into low humor: country folk touring a foreign country. In Class C, too, I would put some of the tribes of grotesque beings that impede the progress of Dorothy and her friends. Among these are the Hammer-Heads, Wheelers, Mangaboos, Gargoyles, Scoodlers, and Growlywogs. When Baum is interested in a group like the Wheelers, they can be bright spots in the narrative, like items in a well-written travelog or bestiary. When he is not, they sink into Class D.

Class D creatures are those one would rather were left out of the story. They are boring at best, and sometimes make one acutely uncomfortable. Among them are the living utensils of Utensia and the edible people of Bunbury, both from *The Emerald City of Oz.* They are in the unmemorable kitchen-fantasy tradition of *Prince Carrotte.* There are other ill-conceived individuals, like the animated phonograph in *The Patchwork Girl of Oz* and Kiki Aru, the tiresome Munchkin boy who makes trouble in *The Magic of Oz.* There are also times when a Class B, C, or even A character can behave in a Class D manner. Both the Scarecrow and the Patchwork Girl, for instance, develop a terrible case of doggerel by the end of the series.

Some characters I find difficult to classify. Ozma, Polychrome, and the other fairies who show up in Oz from time to time seem unpleasantly dainty to me now, but when I read the Oz books as a child they were among my favorites. Certainly the chorus girls who masquerade as mist fairies, cloud fairies, and flower fairies belong in Class D. They are unfortunate holdovers from the sentimentalism of the nineteenth century, harking back to *The Fairy Egg* and Drake's "The Culprit Fay."

Setting aside Class D—no one can claim that Baum was a consistent writer, no matter how good he is at his best—the remainder of Baum's imaginary host is a noteworthy achievement. Romance writers strained to find some replacement for the countless fairies, goblins, and curious beasts of European folklore. Children's writers of the later nineteenth century either borrowed wholesale from Europe or settled for whimsy. And then there is Baum reworking old motifs with unprecedented conviction and inventing new ones seemingly out of the blue. He not only created an American fairyland where there had been none, but he also filled it with Nomes in the earth, fairies in the air, and an astounding assortment of beings in between.

On the first four point of fantasy Baum rates from good to outstanding. But how about point five: meaning? By this, remember, I mean not some moral lesson but the ethical and philosophical substructure of the fantasy, from which grow world and story and characters. What kind of world view does Baum express through his use of magic?

The answer is a limited one. Baum does adopt Hawthorne's system of symbolization, so that in whatever points a character differs physically from the norm, he is also likely to illustrate a moral issue. Jack Pumpkinhead has something to say about the pumpkin-headedness of us all, and so on for each speaking creature in Oz. But Baum's introduction of characters was haphazard and frequently dictated by his impatience with the progress of the plot. Enduring characters like Jack begin, through simple accretion, to take on some philosophical complexity, but his one-shot, ad hoc creations—the Fuddles of Fuddlecumjig are a good example, being nothing more than literalization of the phrase "to go all to pieces"—can hardly be said to be artistic examinations of the problem of life. Nor are they meant to be. In the often quoted phrase that became the title for the standard biography of Baum, he wrote "to please a child."[22] It is for children, not for critical adults, that he upholds such uncontroversial virtues as kindness, generosity, and self-reliance. Ambivalence and sin, with their meatier dramas, he leaves to Hawthorne.

If there is a grander scheme of philosophy in the workings of Oz, it will show up in the essential rules of magic within which Baum operates, rather than in his piecemeal inventions. The following seem to me to be the fundamental magical operations throughout the series: animation, transformation, illusion, disillusion, transportation, protection, and luck. Now these are not unusual operations; they are found throughout the fairy legend and *Märchen*. But Baum has set them up in a rudimentary system, and that is an important distinction between imitation of folk forms and creative fantasy.

Animation comes in several forms in the Oz books. I have mentioned

22. From an inscription to his sister, quoted by Gardner and Nye, p. 42 n. More of the passage bears quoting here: "... aside from my evident inability to do anything 'great,' I have learned to regard fame as a will-o-the-wisp which, when caught, is not worth the possession; but to please a child 'is a sweet and lovely thing that warms one's heart and brings its own reward. ..."

two: the Scarecrow's unexplained awakening and Jack Pumpkinhead's birth under Mombi's cackling midwifery. The Tin Woodman's case may also be considered as a sort of gradual bringing to life of his new, tin self, though it is also clearly a transformation. Several other characters are brought to life by the alchemical powder that sparks Jack Pumpkinhead: a wooden sawhorse, a flying contraption made of couches and palm leaves, a patchwork girl, a glass cat, a Victrola, a bear rug, and two Munchkins who were accidentally turned to stone. It might be considered animation on the two occasions when people are picked from bushes: a prince of the vegetable Mangaboos and a lovely rose princess. The Woggle-Bug's magnification is really a sort of animation, taking him from insignificant insecthood (the Tin Woodman would disagree with me there) to quasi-humanity, with as much increase in awareness as in size. Glinda the Good is responsible for the life of the Cuttenclips, human-sized paper dolls, and probably for several of the other oddities in her kingdom.

Things always seem to be springing to life in Oz. As I said earlier, it is a remarkably fertile place. But what is the end result of all this magical procreation? It is almost always to the good. By this means Oz has been provided with some of its most valuable and colorful citizens. No one could wish the Scarecrow still hanging lifeless on his stake, or Jack Pumpkinhead rotting on a compost heap. Not everyone is a fan of the talking phonograph, the vain glass cat, or the unpleasantly floppy bear rug, but all three have their uses. The principle here seems to be that it is better to exist than not, no matter what your form or foibles. These animations are part of a general tendency toward increasing richness of life; they represent a universe slanted toward Becoming.

We might note that many of the animations are accidental, without visible agency like the Scarecrow's, or against the intentions of those around. The roses, for instance, did not want their princess plucked into existence. Other characters are created for questionable reasons or by downright wicked characters like Mombi. But in every case, things turn out for the best. It is never wrong, in Baum's view, to create, and, indeed, it is difficult to help it.

Transformation is another matter. There are many people in Oz and its environs capable of transforming objects. Glinda, Ozma, Polychrome, and Dorothy all turn things into other things, and so do Mombi, another witch named Blinkie, Ugu the Shoemaker, Kiki Aru, the First and Foremost of the Phanfasms, Mrs. Yoop the giantess, and the Nome King. The latter group includes the wickedest people in the series; the former group the best. It would seem that transformation is a neutral art, usable for either good or evil ends. But there are two quite different sorts of transformation in Oz. What Mombi and her fellow villains do is to impose a new shape on an unwilling victim, or on themselves for evil purposes. What Dorothy and her friends do is to restore victims to their original form. (I exclude Dorothy's turning Nomes into eggs, which is a matter of self-defense. The Nomes do not have the Western respect for the individual that Oz shares with America, anyway.) The one act is a taking away, the other a giving back of something highly valued in Oz, one's true identity. To alter another's shape is to fail to respect his integrity as a living being. Only a villain like the Nome King could prefer the Scarecrow turned into a golden ornament to his own comical, lovable shape.

In a sense, transformation is the opposite of animation. To desire to change the people and objects around one is to deny their intrinsic importance, to wish them, as it were, unmade. The archetype of all transformations is that fearful operation, threatened by Mombi and performed accidentally by the ambiguous Crooked Magician, petrifaction. Turning someone to stone is the ultimate denial, and of course in Oz it must eventually be undone by the affirmative act of reanimation.

The Crooked Magician is ambiguous, and so is an interesting character named Red Reera. She is a sort of sorceress who specializes in transformations, but she is by no means evil. Roger Sale suggests that she represents Baum himself, for her transformations are harmless, temporary ones, performed for her own amusement, more explorations into the nature of reality than acts of denial or affirmation.[23] She is a fantasist of sorts, an artist, and not subject to the categories of good and evil.

Illusion and disillusion form another couplet like transformation and animation. Once more, the operation that denies reality is evil, and that which restores it is good. The implication is that reality is more wonderful than any obscuring of it, in fairyland or in the real world, a belief which would not seem to lead naturally into fantasy except for the fact that, for Baum, it never hurts to add to the store of existence through imagination. Generally the same people practice illusion as indulge in transformations. But anyone with a little insight can undo an illusion, simply by ignoring it. Several times Baum has his characters pass a seeming obstacle by closing their eyes and walking through, or poking it with a pin, or making friends with what appeared to be an enemy.

One of the shrines of Oz is the Truth Pond, a limpid little body of water that undoes transformations, illusions, and lies. It is a dangerous resort for the enchanted, because, while it can lift transformations that nothing else will touch, it imposes on those it benefits a strict adherence to truth. For those who are too wicked to be converted by the

23. Roger Sale, "L. Frank Baum and Oz," *The Hudson Review* 25 (Winter 1972–1973): 591.

Truth Pond, there is another potent body of water, the Forbidden Fountain, which washes away evil by stripping those who drink of it of their memories, leaving them innocent as babies. Both the Fountain and the Pond carry the message that evil itself is an illusion no more formidable than a film of dirt. How else is it that Dorothy can destroy a witch with a bucket of cleaning water?

Transportation has no particular moral value in Oz, but it does act as a sign that anything in the world is possible and within reach. Dorothy's cyclone, the enchanted road in *The Road to Oz*, Ozma's magic carpet, and so on are simply variations of the traditional seven-league boots, which carry their owner to fame and fortune. Most of the modes of transportation to and within Oz are natural objects, rather than conscious agents. They represent the unpredictability of nature, which to Baum is rarely hostile but always amazing.

Protection and luck are really two views of the same thing. Glinda's spell of invisibility over Oz, the Good Witch's protective kiss, and the Shaggy Man's love magnet are the same as Ojo the Lucky's good fortune in *The Patchwork Girl*. The only difference is that luck is a more mysterious, pervasive thing, not traceable to any knowable cause. Both operations stress, again, the benevolence of the world. It is as if there were watchful parents everywhere, some visible and some invisible.

These basic principles are elaborated in the various individual stories, each of which stresses one or two particular facets of life. They do not make up a very new or rigorous philosophy. It is a child's vision that Baum is presenting, and so he shies away from any more darkness or complexity than he felt a child would be prepared to deal with. Writing for children freed Baum's imagination, . . . but the boon was also a limitation. We have no proof that Baum *could* have written a more mature work of fantasy than Oz, with a more demanding and rewarding reordering of the world's laws, but he certainly could not do so as long as he conceived of fairy tales as the province primarily of children. So we have the Oz books: simple, sunny, utterly delightful, but narrow in their range of emotion and significance.

Yet the barrier had been broken, effortlessly punctured like a wall of illusion. Baum proved, without doubt, that an American writer could write fantasy from American materials, even if those materials were significantly unlike the well-developed tales and legends available to European collectors and storytellers. Other writers could build on his accomplishment, as he built on the efforts of those before him, could gradually bring into their American fairylands those questions he left out. Even with his weaknesses he is our Grimm and our Andersen, the man who introduced Americans to their own dreams.

· Selected Supplemental Reading ·

Baughman, Roland. "L. Frank Baum and the 'Oz Books,'" *Columbia Library Columns*, May 1955, pp. 15–35

Baum, Frank [J.] "Why *The Wizard of Oz* Keeps on Selling," *Writer's Digest*, December 1952, pp. 19, 36–37

Baum, Frank Joslyn, and Russell P. MacFall. *To Please A Child*. Chicago: Reilly & Lee Co., 1961

The Baum Bugle, 1957–current.

Bauska, Barry. "The Land of Oz and the American Dream," *The Markham Review*, Winter 1976

Bradbury, Ray. "Two Balmy Promenades Along the Yellow Brick Road," Los Angeles *Times Book Review*, October 9, 1977, pp. 1, 3

Brotman, Jordan. "A Late Wanderer in Oz," *Chicago Review*, December 1965, pp. 63–73

Buechner, Frederick. "Journey in Search of a Soul," *The Magnificent Defeat*. New York: The Seabury Press, 1966, pp. 51–56

Erisman, Fred. "L. Frank Baum and the Progressive Dilemma," *American Quarterly*, Fall 1968, pp. 616–623

"45 Years of *The Wizard*," *Collier's*, February 9, 1946, p. 86

Gardner, Martin. "A Child's Garden of Bewilderment," *Saturday Review*, July 17, 1965, pp. 18–19

———. "Follow the Yellow Brick Road," New York *Herald-Tribune*, January 2, 1966, p. 14

———. "Librarians in Oz," *Saturday Review*, April 11, 1959, pp. 18–19

———. "Introduction," *The Wonderful Wizard of Oz*. New York: Dover Publications, 1960

———. " We're Off To See the Wizard," *The New York Times Book Review* (Children's Books), May 2, 1971, pp. 1, 41

——— and Russel B. Nye. *The Wizard of Oz And Who He Was*. East Lansing: Michigan State University Press, 1957

Greene, David L., and Martin, Dick. *The Oz Scrapbook*. New York: Random House, 1977

Greene, Douglas G., and Hearn, Michael Patrick. *W. W. Denslow*. Mount Pleasant, Michigan: Clarke Historical Library, Central Michigan University, 1976

Hanley, James M. "L. Frank Baum," *The Congressional Record*, May 15, 1980, p. 3754

Hearn, Michael Patrick. *The Annotated Wizard of Oz*. New York: Clarkson N. Potter, Inc., 1973

Jackson, Shirley. "The Lost Kingdom of Oz," *The Reporter*, December 10, 1959, pp. 42–43

Kopp, Sheldon. "The Wizard Behind the Couch," *Psychology Today*, March 1970, pp. 70–73, 84

Lanes, Selma G. *Down the Rabbit Hole*. New York: Atheneum, 1971

Lurie, Alison. "The Fate of the Munchkins," *The New York Review of Books*, April 18, 1974, pp. 24–25

McCord, David. "L. Frank Baum," *Twentieth Century Children's Writers*, ed. by D. L. Kirkpatrick. New York: St. Martin's Press, 1978, pp. 91–93

Mannix, Daniel P. "The Father of the Wizard of Oz," *American Heritage*, December 1964, pp. 36–47, 108–109

Moore, Raylyn. *Wonderful Wizard, Marvelous Land*. Bowling Green, Ohio: Bowling Green University Popular Press, 1974

Prentice, Ann E. "Have You Been to See the Wizard?," *The Top of the News*, November 1, 1970, pp. 32–44

Reinhold, Robert. "Steinbeck Whimsy Found in Kennedy Files," *New York Times*, January 25, 1974, p. 14

Robb, Stewart. "The Red Wizard of Oz," *New Masses*, October 4, 1938, p. 8

Rogers, Katharine. "Liberation for Little Girls," *Saturday Review*, June 17, 1972, pp. 72, 75

St. John, Tom. "Lyman Frank Baum: Looking Back to the Promised Land," *The Western Humanities Review*, Winter 1982, pp. 349–360

Sale, Roger. *Fairy Tales and After*. Cambridge, Massachusetts: Harvard University Press, 1978

Schuman, Samuel. "Out of the Fryeing Pan into the Pyre: Comedy, Myth and *The Wizard of Oz*," *Journal of Popular Culture*, Fall 1973, pp. 302–304

Seaman, Noah, and Barbara Seaman. "Munchkins, Ozophiles, and Feminists too," *Ms.*, January 1974, p. 93

Starr, Nathan Comfort. "*The Wonderful Wizard of Oz*: A Study in Archetypal Mythic Symbiosis," *Unicorn*, Summer 1973, pp. 13–17

Ulveling, Ralph. "Ralph Ulveling on Freedom of Information," *American Library Association Bulletin*, October 1957, pp. 653–655

Vidal, Gore. "The Wizard of *The Wizard*," *The New York Review of Books*, September 29, 1977, pp. 10–15

Wagenknecht, Edward. "Afterword," *The Wizard of Oz*. Chicago: Reilly & Lee, 1956

Watt, Lois Belfield. "L. Frank Baum: The Widening World of Oz," *The Imprint of the Stanford Libraries Association*, October 1979, pp. 12–18

Wollheim, Daniel A. "Introduction," *The Wizard of Oz*. New York: Airmont Publishing Co., 1965

Zipes, Jack. *Fairy Tales and the Art of Subversion*. London: Heinemann Educational Books Ltd., 1982